PRAISE FOR *ONLINE GRAVITY*

'Extraordinary insight into how the digital revolution is changing our lives forever.'
—**Dr Terry Percival AM, FTSE, co-inventor of Wi-Fi**

'A much needed cosmology of the internet, an articulation of the dynamics currently transforming our social architecture. McCarthy has made a major contribution on this vital topic – a powerful theory about the implications of the most profound transformation humanity has yet experienced.'
—**Daniel Barton, Digital Strategy Director, Creata**

'Timely insight for those navigating a path through digital disruption and looking for new ways to be successful.'
—**Robyn Elliott, media industry CIO**

'If you want to find out what the future holds, read this book.'
—**Ross Taylor AC, Emeritus Professor,
Australian National University**

'The growth of high speed internet connectivity across the globe is changing the game for people and businesses. The gravitational pull of "winning businesses" is staggeringly powerful. Paul's observation of these forces provides a simple framework for how we can understand the maelstrom of disruption that is occurring around most businesses today, no matter where you operate or how big you are.'
—**Rob Wong, CEO, AIMIA**

'A fascinating insight into what makes a success of internet giants; companies and ideas that we would not have imagined even just a few years ago. Novel and thought provoking.'
—**Professor Maurice Pagnucco, Head of Computer Science and** ... les

About the author

Professor Paul X. McCarthy is a leading online-business expert and technology entrepreneur who grew up learning how to pull apart and program home computers that stored their information on regular music cassette tapes as a series of screeching sounds. At university, in between studying sculpture, physics and economics, he enjoyed listening to lots of screeching guitar bands. By this time, computers were screeching down the telephone at one another and the internet revolution had begun in earnest.

After university, McCarthy worked at IBM to help establish an award-winning digital-services unit, and he began to see how all this worldwide screeching was combining to create its own resonance. McCarthy names this new set of unseen economic forces 'Online Gravity', and he explains how we can use it to our advantage.

McCarthy is co-founder and CEO of MBA Analytics, a specialist global talent discovery service, and an adjunct professor at the University of New South Wales, home of Australia's leading school of computer science and engineering. He is an author, speaker and global-strategy consultant.

ONLINE GRAVITY

PAUL X. McCARTHY

**SIMON &
SCHUSTER**

London · New York · Sydney · Toronto · New Delhi

A CBS COMPANY

First published in Great Britain by Simon & Schuster UK Ltd, 2015
A CBS COMPANY

1 3 5 7 9 10 8 6 4 2

Simon & Schuster UK Ltd
1st Floor
222 Gray's Inn Road
London WC1X 8HB

www.simonandschuster.co.uk

Simon & Schuster Australia, Sydney
Simon & Schuster India, New Delhi

The author and publishers have made all reasonable efforts
to contact copyright-holders for permission, and apologise for
any omissions or errors in the form of credits given.
Corrections may be made to future printings.

A CIP catalogue record for this book
is available from the British Library

Trade paperback ISBN: 978-1-47114-085-3
Ebook ISBN: 978-1-47114-087-7

Cover design: Chistabella Designs
Cover image: pixelparticle/Shutterstock
Typeset by Midland Typesetters, Australia
Printed and bound by CPI Group (UK) Ltd, Croydon, CR0 4YY

MIX
Paper from
responsible sources
FSC® C020471
www.fsc.org

Simon & Schuster UK Ltd are committed to sourcing paper
that is made from wood grown in sustainable forests and supports the Forest
Stewardship Council, the leading international forest certification organisation.
Our books displaying the FSC logo are printed on FSC certified paper.

For Nic, Checker and Rennie

CONTENTS

PREFACE

Ka-boom! Scientists believe that our moon is the result of a cataclysmic collision between a prehistoric planet the size of Mars called Theia and a young Planet Earth. This planetary car crash some four billion years ago led to fragments of the Earth and Theia splintering off into space, which later recombined to form today's Moon. If you look at a globe or map of the world, have you ever noticed how there's a huge hole in the middle? The deep Pacific Ocean, lined with its rim of volcanoes on either side, is the Earth trying to 'heal' itself from this ancient punch-up.

But why did the planetary fragments join together? Why does the Moon continue to orbit the Earth without flying off into space? Why does our solar system have one sun and only eight planets, rather than hundreds or even thousands? The answer is the invisible, almost magical, force of gravity.

It is this physical force that gave me the central idea for this book. In 2013, when reading an amazing book by family friend Professor Ross Taylor about how our solar system was formed, I was also juggling questions I'd been pondering for 20 years in my private research about what works online and what doesn't.

Why do some enterprises, such as Google, Facebook and LinkedIn, meet with spectacular success while their once-dominant competitors, such as AltaVista, Myspace and Spoke, struggle for survival?

It is clear to me, and to many other people who work in technology, that the web operates via a set of rules that tends to favour certain outcomes. And then it dawned on me: it's like gravity! Both the physical and the online worlds are shaped by laws that favour the creation of planet-like superstructures with lots of space in between. Just as we have physical gravity, we have Online Gravity.

As traditional industries – such as media, travel, photography and music – are steadily consumed and transformed by what I call 'gravity giants', more and more of the world is coming under the spell of Online Gravity, and new 'planets' are added to the system. Examples include Planet Search (Google), Planet Buy and Sell (eBay), Planet Reference (Wikipedia), Planet Social Media (Facebook), Planet Customer-Relationship Management (Salesforce) and Planet Retail (Amazon).

This book summarises my two decades of research into this phenomenon. It provides distinctive and original insights into the new set of rules that are reshaping the worlds of business, education, health and work. Using clear and simple examples, it explains how you can use these insights to harness the unseen forces of the web, in order to improve your wealth, your health and even your children's education.

Like all writers, I'm indebted to the great theorists who have informed my thinking, and along the way I'll introduce you to their amazing work. But this book draws most heavily upon my own experience as a technology executive, entrepreneur and investor. For nearly a decade in the 1990s, I worked at IBM, where I helped lead the company's early efforts to capitalise on the power of the web and uncover what it was beginning to mean for its clients in banking, entertainment and health.

In 1995, I visited a company in Los Angeles called Digital Domain, in which IBM had made a large investment. Digital Domain is one of the world's leading digital-animation and visual-effects companies for film and TV. I met with its founding CEO, Scott Ross, to create a joint venture in Australia ahead of the soon-to-be launched Fox Studios in Sydney, and I remember being struck by how interested he was in the work we were doing on the web and how uninterested he was in our plans around movies! How right he was.

In the late 1990s, I left IBM to lead a venture-capital-funded tech start-up that I co-founded with a schoolfriend. Our flagship product was EquityCafé – a pioneering social-media service for over 30,000 stock-market investors. The helm of your own start-up is a great place to learn things that you tend not to forget. It's the closest thing to being on stage in a live production, but 24/7. And many of the lessons from EquityCafé have been baked into the concept of Online Gravity. When you build and run a large-scale online service with tens of thousands of individual customers, you get to see behind the scenes of what works and what doesn't, how people behave online and what they really love.

After selling my interest in this start-up, I worked in Sydney as an adviser and consultant to the New South Wales Government. This allowed me to see the widespread changes that the web was effecting in public services such as education, health and the arts. For example, state-owned galleries, libraries and museums were being completely reinvented and transformed in the light of Online Gravity.

As part of my research in the past five years, I have worked in the technology research sector with three of Australia's top science and technology research organisations: the Commonwealth Scientific and Industrial Research Organisation (CSIRO), National Information and Communications Technology Australia (NICTA), and the Securities Industry Research Centre of Asia-Pacific (SIRCA). From these experiences, I've learnt about how some new technologies that will be central to the web over the next decade, such as mobile broadband, machine learning and big data, are contributing to the dynamics of Online Gravity.

I have also studied in detail many of the world's foremost web-borne companies, including Google, Amazon and Atlassian, and how they are using the net in new and fascinating ways, including as a tool to predict and respond to future customer demand, as a platform to create spin-off enterprises and as a low-cost direct-distribution channel to market.

Fortunately for us, I've discovered that Online Gravity follows a series of clear and easily grasped laws that can lead to interesting and sometimes surprising results. By understanding these laws, we can better position ourselves, our businesses and our families to take advantage of the seismic shifts being brought about in employment and education, and tune the awesome power of the web to our advantage.

Many of the smartest people, companies and investors already understand the principles of Online Gravity, and they are putting this understanding into practice. They have front-row seats at the unfolding of a new era of global change. My hope for this book is that it puts you, the reader, in a similarly privileged position.

While the web has been around for over two decades, only in the past few years is it realising its full potential, owing to two main things. First, most people in the Western world are now online. Second, the system that connects us is always on, always with us (via mobile broadband) and operates a hundred times faster than it did a decade ago. Once everyone has a very high-speed internet connection, different things become possible. Online video, which requires a high-speed connection to upload the large files and for smooth replay in real-time, was only available to a few people a decade ago. Now most people have one, YouTube starts to make a lot more sense; and look at its meteoric rise over the past five years – it is absolutely remarkable. So too do video calls through services such as Skype.

And right now a whole army of person-to-person, video-based services is emerging online that would not have worked five years ago, such as a coaching service for Chinese students wanting to get into top-tier international universities (ChaseFuture), apps that enable you to visit your family doctor online (Doctor on Demand), and websites that match start-ups with computer programmers anywhere in the world to work in teams across the internet via video (AirPair).

All these new online services offer incredible benefits, but many of us are concerned that technology and the web are moving too quickly to keep up with. We all worry about change, and the global changes being brought about by the unseen forces of Online Gravity are profound. Do you know someone who has lost his or her job in the last five years working in IT, media, finance or retail? These industries and many others are already feeling the pinch. Online Gravity is unstoppable and its reach continues to grow. Over the next decade, it will dominate the global economy.

What I have written is a guidebook to help you navigate the digital decade ahead. I hope you will find it both useful and entertaining.

Paul X. McCarthy

NB: *All monetary amounts in this book are in US dollars unless otherwise stated.*

INTRODUCTION

WHAT IS ONLINE GRAVITY?

Online Gravity is an invisible force that is driving the development of the economy in the age of the internet. In the way that gravity is the key force that determines how our solar system was formed and appears today, Online Gravity describes the force that is ruling the formation and behaviour of our online world.

While there are other fundamental forces in our universe, such as magnetic force, gravity is the king of them all when it comes to how the stuff in it is organised and behaves. This is because gravity has infinite range, is always attractive and never repulsive, and can't be absorbed, transformed or shielded against.

In both the solar system and the online system, larger bodies exert a gravitational pull on smaller ones within their orbit, until all the smaller ones are swallowed up and the larger ones have become planets. In the online world, the planets are the huge market leaders such as Google, Amazon and Alibaba, and the smaller bodies are would-be competitors and their customers. As online companies start to prosper, they begin to develop their own gravitational field, which attracts more and more customers and subscribers to them. The larger their network of users, the stronger their gravitational pull, so their growth rate starts to accelerate. Conversely, competitors in their sector find it increasingly difficult to compete as the largest online company attracts more and more users. And with more users they become more attractive and again to yet more users. Once online companies become 'giants' like the planets in our solar system, they 'own' the space around them – meaning their industry or sector. They become effectively unassailable in their sector.

We all have an intuitive understanding of how gravity works on Earth. Any of us who enjoy skiing, surfing or snowboarding will have a good grasp of how we can have fun playing with its effects. Roller-coasters at theme parks are thrilling as they temporarily change the experience of Earth's gravity on our bodies by putting us in freefall.

Online Gravity is like this too. And its effects can also be awesome. Even if you don't know what it's called, you probably already have a good understanding of how it works and may even now be using it to your advantage in many ways. As all of us and our world are increasingly connected via the web, none of us can escape Online Gravity's pull. We can, however, through a better understanding of what it is and how it works, do amazing things.

Online Gravity has created a new economic model that is reshaping business and employment at every turn. In many ways, we are at an early stage, where the online galaxy is still being created. And at this foundation stage, it is Online Gravity that is guiding the process of some start-ups growing to become planet-scale businesses. As the world becomes increasingly and inescapably digital, Online Gravity will affect the way we all live, work and play in the next century.

This book demonstrates what Online Gravity does, how it develops, and how you can harness it to improve your working life, wealth and health in an increasingly digitised world. It will help you to:

- distinguish between the next Google and the next AltaVista;
- learn why there are no 'dual-planet' systems like Coca-Cola and Pepsi; Visa and Mastercard or Mercedes-Benz and BMW in cyberspace;
- understand the seven laws of Online Gravity, and why they produce amazing, game-changing companies with huge global impact worth billions of dollars each in less than a decade;
- understand simple ways you can run and grow a small business better, using the smartest tricks from the world's pros of online marketing, such as the amazing custom footwear company Shoes of Prey, run by former Google employees;
- understand the huge opportunities ahead in intangible goods and see the extraordinary things you can now make and trade online from home for fun and profit, like the web designer who has made more than $1 million in sales from a website template;
- learn how global jobs can now appear anywhere but at the same time regional headquarters are dying, so you need to understand where the jobs of tomorrow are likely to arise;
- find out how you can learn new skills online – never before in history has there been a better time to learn new things, with wonderful, often free resources such as the Khan Academy, Coursera and Quora. Everything from how to fix a broken camera yourself to helping your eight-year-old get 100 per cent on every mathematics test is right there waiting for you;
- find answers to nagging health issues for you and your family by being able to better navigate the vast amount of free information available online about health, nutrition, the latest medical research and home remedies – for example, how to find a simple cure for foot warts using banana peel and electrical tape;
- create and execute winning innovation strategies for larger organisations based on the success and lessons of the world's leading innovators, including IBM, General Electric, Google,

Amazon, Sony and, of course, Apple. This includes original insights such as IBM's 'airlock' strategy, as well as reflections from prominent thinkers on innovation such as Professor Clayton Christensen;

- see inside many of today's leading gravity giants to learn about their distinctive 'talent signatures', and the secrets of their surprising and successful hiring strategies. Apple, for example, has seven times the number of liberal-arts graduates on its payroll as does IBM;

- impress your friends with amazing facts and data, such as if you're a German speaker in Montana, you are 30 per cent more likely to drink Pepsi, or if you studied at a Montessori school, you're four times more likely to go on to study computer science at university;

- get a glimpse into the future of health, money and education online, and into how you can better position yourself for success in the decade ahead.

I've divided this book into three parts. The first part looks at the *phenomenon* of Online Gravity, examining its origins, its various characteristics and its implications. As it takes hold in successive online industries, it goes through the same developmental stages, meaning its results (although not necessarily its winners) are predictable. By understanding the phenomenon, we will be much better positioned to take advantage of it.

The second part devotes a chapter to each of the seven fundamental *laws* of Online Gravity, going into what they are and how they work in detail. All of these laws combine to make Online Gravity the unstoppable force that it is, and their operation becomes more pronounced in each market sector the further the phenomenon progresses along its life cycle.

And the third part addresses, from various angles, what all of this means for *the future*. Will Online Gravity bring us a sharing, egalitarian, global society or one characterised by unfairness, segregation and unemployment? How can we and our children find work and prosper in the online era? This part canvasses both the optimistic and pessimistic predictions for the outcomes of the digital economy, and provides practical advice that you can apply to both your private and professional life. I will also take a punt at forecasting the exciting technological developments we are likely to see.

But let's get started by looking at why Online Gravity happens in the first place.

THE
PHENOMENON

WHY DOES ONLINE GRAVITY HAPPEN?

Online Gravity occurs due to three major factors:

- the increasingly democratic and social nature of knowledge;
- the digitisation of that knowledge; and
- the amazing global connectivity of the web.

Good ideas and reliable knowledge are different from many other commodities in our lives. They are not diminished, tarnished or worn out by others using them. And they're not things that any individual or company can own.

The fundamental nature of knowledge is at the heart of Online Gravity, and the web-powered revolution now under way is enabling more of its true character to be revealed.

We all want to know more. I've never heard anyone say 'I wish I knew less'. Knowledge empowers us to be more effective. And to help others too. And most of us naturally want to share the things we've learnt and found useful with others. That's why I've written this book.

Now, a key ingredient in knowledge is information. The two are not the same, of course, but without information – the facts, the data, the good oil about whatever it is you're focused on – you're not going to get very far.

Previously, information used to be very expensive. Today, it's almost free. Let's say you're interested in the Transit of Venus, when the planet Venus passes between the Earth and the Sun. This happens in a pattern that repeats itself every 243 years, with pairs of transits relatively close together, at eight-year intervals, followed by long gaps of over a hundred years at a time.

In 1769, it took Captain Cook and his crew of over 90 people 18 months to record this rare event. They had to sail from the United Kingdom to Tahiti, draw what they saw by hand, then return to London to share the drawings with members of the Royal Society, thereby developing the science of the day.

In 2012 – 243 years later – the Transit of Venus was online. Any scientist, or indeed anyone in the world with an internet connection, could observe it as it happened. NASA streamed the event live from its $2 billion astronomy facility on top of Mauna Kea in Hawaii. Midway through, one of the NASA streams had a total of nearly two million views.

Information today is verging on free. Because computers can now capture, store and distribute it on a global scale automatically without any human intervention, the cost of producing many types of information has dropped to almost zero. And while the cost of information has gone down dramatically, its value has not decreased. If anything, it has skyrocketed. With virtually free information coupled with the capacity of the web to transcend physical boundaries, our potential for learning has never been better.

The last time we saw a change of this scale was with Gutenberg's printing press in the fifteenth century, which underwrote the birth of science, global commerce and the Renaissance.

The web is a realm that more closely resembles the nature of information itself: intangible, replicable and networked. It's the best medium we have ever created for sharing and distributing ideas. And, most importantly, it's our best ever vehicle for learning, whether that is learning from history, learning from our social and natural environments or learning from each other.

INCREASING RETURNS

Once Online Gravity starts to take effect in an industry, the nature of the internet ensures that those effects are major. Things that are social (such as reputations and diseases), global (such as financial markets) and digital (such as computer technology) tend towards snowball-style growth. And since the web is all three, many systems online are subject to its laws. In other words, online growth engenders more growth, at an increasing rate, until the market leader grows so large that it dwarfs and subsumes its competitors, becoming a gravity giant (see also 'Exponential Growth' in the next chapter).

Some industries, such as news, music and travel, are clearly now part of the fabric of the web itself and very much already under the spell of Online Gravity. Others, including mining, steel making and car making, are still largely 'offline' industries and have yet to fall under its spell. For ease and clarity, I'll call the latter 'traditional' industries.

In traditional industries, companies compete against each other for a greater slice of the pie, in terms of the most customers, sales or profits. Many sectors that have been running for more than a hundred years, such as car making or soft drinks, have arrived at a semi-stable state, with a leading company or brand, a number of challengers and a number of niche brands.

Think about any established 'offline' consumer market and there's almost always this same pattern – say, car rental (Hertz, Avis, Alamo), toothpaste (Colgate, Crest, Signal) or German cars (Mercedes-Benz, BMW, VW). In car rental, Avis made a point of the fact that they were the challenger brand with their famous advertising line 'We try harder'.

In the case of carbonated soft drinks, the global leader is Coca-Cola, the challenger is Pepsi, and the niche brands include Dr Pepper, Jolt Cola, and from Scotland, Irn-Bru. Coke and Pepsi have been duking it out in this market for the best part of a century and, despite billions of dollars at stake and many very bright people's greatest efforts, their relative market share hasn't changed that much.

Why is this? These relatively steady states of play are a result of companies acting rationally to maximise their own profits but having a ceiling on how much they can expand in their market. In a world of finite resources, brand preferences and strong competition, there comes a point in most industries where winning that extra customer is more expensive than it is worth, and thus they face what economists call *diminishing returns*.

Could Coke or Pepsi win more market share from each other? Yes, probably a bit, but at what cost? They could double or triple their already impressive global advertising budgets, but if history is any guide, some people aren't going to switch no matter what is spent on trying to make them.

There are also a few 'offline' markets – such as high-tech and knowledge-intensive ones – where a different kind of economics applies: one of *increasing returns*. Professor W. Brian Arthur is a distinguished US economist and researcher who has developed this concept at Stanford University and the Santa Fe Institute. I imagine he may well be a candidate for a future Nobel laureate in Economics.

When I read Professor Arthur's pioneering work in this area written over two decades ago, it resonated with my experiences online. While Arthur's theories were initially conceived to apply to standards-based industries like consumer electronics (VHS vs Beta), I realised that all markets online are subject to the snowball-like effects of increasing returns. His work has helped me to develop one of the key aspects of Online Gravity: that online returns snowball.

Professor Arthur has been examining increasing returns since the early 1980s and has written over 60 articles and two books on the topic, receiving over 20,000 citations from other scholars. In his most famous related paper, Arthur writes:

> by chance gains an early lead in adoption may eventually 'corner the market' of potential adopters, with the other technologies becoming locked out.[1]

According to Arthur, a typical pattern for new markets subject to increasing returns involves:

1. An initial period of jockeying for position among a number of players.
2. One player beginning to assert dominance over its market rivals.
3. Standards being set or de facto standards emerging and gaining market acceptance.
4. Increasing returns starting to kick in, thus further favouring the leader.

Once momentum is established, more and more customers are drawn to the leading player, making that player increasingly difficult for rivals to challenge. Eventually, the leader goes on to dominate or monopolise that category at the expense of all but the smallest of niche rivals. This is due to a number of factors:

- *Network effects.* Many knowledge-based markets enjoy network effects, which means that the more people they can get to join them, the more valuable they become. For example, a telephone network, classifieds market or employment marketplace all grow in value when they grow in participants.

- *High switching costs.* Customers invest time to become familiar with one system, and are hesitant to switch and relearn another system without significant new benefits.
- In earlier work, W. Brian Arthur points to the circular, 12-hour, clockwise clock face as a standard that people learnt. There were many others, including 24-hour and anticlockwise ones, but after the year 1550 the convention was established and other designs were then impossible.
- Another example is the QWERTY keyboard we are all so familiar with, which was originally designed so that frequently used pairs of letters were not next to each other, thus preventing jams in a typewriter's clunky mechanics. Ever since computers replaced typewriters, this has not been an issue, so attempts have been made to reinvent the letter layout to one more optimally designed for speed typing. One such is the Dvorak layout. You can buy these keyboards, but they're still very niche, as nearly the entire world has grown up on QWERTY and relearning is a big job.[2]
- *Technology lock-in effects.* Technology rarely works in isolation, and the integration of specific systems with a broader ecosystem relies on everything being able to connect and work together. This applies to large, complex computer-banking systems but also to home entertainment – where, of course, VHS won out over Beta in the early 1980s and Blu-ray more recently prevailed over HD DVD.

W. Brian Arthur maintains that, in the offline world, increasing returns predominantly occur in 'knowledge-based' industries. My perception is that, in the internet-powered global digital economy, *all* businesses are becoming knowledge-based, as they involve the sharing of rich information in particular formats and standards. Marc Andreessen, co-founder of Netscape, wrote insightfully in *The Wall Street Journal* about software 'eating' traditional industries,[3] and he describes how various online businesses have completely annihilated their incumbent offline rivals, such as Amazon versus Borders and Netflix versus Blockbuster.

Online Gravity loves big winners. And the law of increasing returns boosts the formation of new superstar companies on the one hand while eradicating their foes and traditional-economy rivals on the other.

KEY POINTS

Online Gravity owes its existence to the following factors:

- *The fundamental nature of knowledge.* Knowledge and the information it is based on empowers us and can be shared and used by many people without diminishing the value another derives from it. The web and the computers that power it are enabling us to capture, organise and share valuable information on a vast scale and very low cost – this is at the heart of the amazing economics of Online Gravity.
- *Increasing returns.* In the offline world, knowledge-based industries come under the economic law of increasing returns, because of network effects, high switching costs and technology lock-in effects.
- *The online world is wholly built on knowledge and technology.* So increasing returns apply there like never before, generating Online Gravity.

WHAT ARE THE FEATURES OF ONLINE GRAVITY?

Online Gravity has certain characteristics that manifest themselves in the industries that come under its influence. The formation of planet-sized gravity giants is one of them, of course, but the phenomenon also has other, more subtle features. These include unevenly distributed rewards within a particular sector, the emergence of 'long-tail' companies (as in ones that can sell small amounts of a lot of things), and more concentrated consumption around popular tastes. Let's look at these and other features in more detail.

KINKY REWARDS

The economy of the web has much in common with the economy of the entertainment industry (both offline and online), in that returns are not shared equally.

If you work in movies, books or music, you probably already know this, but you don't have to be an insider to have heard that most actors are lucky to find work and make ends meet, whereas a select few earn more money than the most successful merchant bankers and lawyers.

The same applies to the products of the entertainment industry. Some books, films and albums are blockbusters, but most are not. And it's the blockbusters that keep the business going. Hal Vogel, former investment analyst at Merrill Lynch and author of the bible on entertainment-industry economics,[1] reminds us that a tenth of the films released in the United States each year generate more than half of the total box-office receipts. So while one swallow does not a summer make, in the movie business one *Toy Story* or *Titanic* does make a summer's worth of sales.

David Court, another leading authority in entertainment business and finance, first brought my attention to this many years ago in a talk where he explained that rewards in the movie business are very skewed and 'kurtotic' – a word I'd never heard before. 'Kurtotic' comes from a Greek word meaning 'bulging', and it refers in this context to the 'pointiness' of the industry's spread of incomes and returns.

A normal, familiar pattern of distribution applies to things such as the height of people in a population – so in most communities a small number of people are either very tall or very short, and most are in the average height range, creating a bell curve. In the more kinky, kurtotic space of, say, feature-film box-office receipts, there are a lot more movies in the average space and more movies making either very small or staggeringly high amounts, which creates a steeper, sharper curve with *fatter or heavier tails.*

Normal and kurtotic distribution curves

Normal

Highly Kinky Kurtosis
Peakedness and *heavy-tails.*

As we've mentioned, this applies to the rewards for individuals too. A small group of extraordinarily talented *kurtocrats* runs the mainstream movie business in the United States. 'The kurtocrats are Hollywood's elite, the actors, directors, writers, and producers who are associated with the major movies,' says Arthur De Vany in his book on Hollywood economics.[2]

And the statistics support this claim. The average annual income for an actor working in the US film and TV business is $102,000, according to statistics from the US Government Department of Labor,[3] whereas the top-ten actors earned approximately $460 million in 2012/13, or 14 per cent of the $3.5 billion paid to all 35,000 or so actors working in the US.[4]

Incomes in artistic professions were found to be among the most unequally distributed of all occupations in a comprehensive survey of taxation records in Germany in 2000. The same study revealed that the earnings of doctors, vets and dentists were the most evenly balanced.[5]

There are a few reasons for this high premium on the top artists' incomes. Artists' talents are unique – there's only one Tina Fey (sadly) but there are lots of good individuals with great dentistry skills (thank goodness!) – so there's a much higher risk–reward premium on being an artist, writer or musician. Those who are lucky enough to play roles in large market successes can end up making a motza.

Also with movies, the cast plays a key role in the ultimate success of the product. When people first hear about a new movie, often their first question is *Who is in it*? Because of this cumulative effect we see a small number of actors become 'bankable', meaning their name adds to the financial viability of new films. Similarly, we're seeing talent in online companies being billed as having 'starred in' former iconic companies. Former Google employees are Xooglers and the original foundation team at Paypal are the 'Paypal Mafia'.

To give you a sense of what this kurtosis does, try this thought experiment. Imagine if dentists were paid like actors. Acting is a fickle and risky business, and despite this most film and TV actors still earn less than half as much as dentists. If you lined up all the film and TV actors from highest paid to lowest paid and took the person right in the middle, he or she would earn around $62,000. This is known as the median income. Do the same for dentists and that middle person earns $146,000 – well over twice as much.

Now imagine that Robert Downey, Jr – who, according to *Forbes*, was the highest-paid actor in the world in 2012/13 – was the top dentist, and he was paid the same proportion of the total pool of income for dentists as he is for actors. Instead of his $75 million a year, he would now earn nearly $50 million more a year than he does today, or about $122 million a year. As a group, these top-ten actors turned dentists ('dentors') would take home a tidy three-quarters of a billion dollars a year.

Imagine a dentist who earned over one hundred million dollars per annum! A basic visit to the dentist in Los Angeles for a clean and check-up currently costs $319 on average, and a top-end dentist costs $398.[6] A basic visit to the hypothetical Robert Downey, Jr clinic would set you back $296,047.

Projected earnings of 'dentors' in 2013

Ranking by earnings	Name of actor	Actual income in 2013	Income if paid in 'dentist dollars'
1	Robert Downey, Jr	$75,000,000	$122,413,306
2	Channing Tatum	$60,000,000	$97,930,644
3	Hugh Jackman	$55,000,000	$89,769,757
4	Mark Wahlberg	$52,000,000	$84,873,225
5	Dwayne Johnson (The Rock)	$46,000,000	$75,080,161
6	Leonardo DiCaprio	$39,000,000	$63,654,919
7	Adam Sandler	$37,000,000	$60,390,564
8	Tom Cruise	$35,000,000	$57,126,209
9	Denzel Washington	$33,000,000	$53,861,854
10	Liam Neeson	$32,000,000	$52,229,677

Source: Actual actors' incomes are from *Forbes*, Dorothy Pomerantz; dentist dollars are the author's own calculations using US Department of Labor Dentist Income Data, 2014

So you can see that actors have a kurtotic industry. The dental profession earns more than the acting profession as a whole, but the people at the top of acting's tree get a higher proportion of its rewards than the top dentists get from dentistry.

Due to the global scale of online businesses, you can see this kind of kurtotic behaviour as well. Google, for example, enjoys nearly 70 per cent of market share of online search in many markets. So not only do the top companies clearly attract a disproportionate share of the income for that industry and sector, but these global gravity giants are also able to attract and have the resources to pay for the top people in the world. Unlike dentists, whose impact (and income) is limited by geography and their own time – a computer programmer at Google or Apple can have direct real-time global impact on hundreds of billions of dollars in continuous revenue from billions of global customers.

LONG TAILS

Online companies such as Amazon sell a few things (blockbusters) to a lot of people, as well as a lot of things (a very large catalogue of special-interest items) to a few people.

With economies of scale, Amazon is now able to maintain a catalogue of over 30 million books, including over 20 million different paperbacks. This is a comparable title count to the US Library of Congress. To put this in perspective, compare this with physical bookstores. Barnes & Noble's former flagship store at 105 Fifth Avenue in Manhattan, which the *Guinness Book of Records* clocked as the largest bookstore in the world in the 1970s, carried around 200,000 titles on a massive and impressive 12 miles of shelving. Amazon now offers over a hundred times this number of titles online, via its main global website. This includes more than:

- 22 million paperbacks;
- 8.1 million hardbacks;

- 1.2 million e-books in Kindle format;
- 351,000 audio CDs;
- 138,000 board books;
- 42,000 audio books in Audible format.

Most of these are in English (17 million titles) but there are books in 84 different languages for sale, including large collections in German (two million), French (two million), Spanish (one million), Russian (839,000), Italian (739,000), Chinese (518,000) and even Latin (89,000). The online giant holds more books in Japanese than Barnes and Noble's amazing flagship store held in English!

The 'long tail' is precisely this: being able to sell 'less of more' – as set out in Chris Anderson's landmark book on the subject, *The Long Tail*. Without the limitations of bricks and mortar stores, online companies are perfectly positioned to benefit from long-tail trading. They can stock collections so extensive that even the 'niche' categories outnumber the products available in the largest of high-street stores.

CONCENTRATED CONSUMPTION

Jaron Lanier is a noted futurist, computer scientist, musician and author of the influential book *You Are Not a Gadget*. Lanier writes and speaks engagingly about how the web's fundamental design can tend to support lopsided outcomes.

Inherent in the design of the web is the hyperlink. It's the glue that binds it all together and makes it a web rather than just a series of isolated digital documents on a screen. Hyperlinks are a means of finding your way around, like street signs, but they are also a form of approval. A link is a type of 'like'.

And links, like most things online, are not evenly distributed. A small number of websites are the most linked to and hence become the most visited. Lanier suggests this can lead to banality.

Kevin Kelly, founding editor of *Wired*, and others call this the 'hive mind' – a kind of herd mentality that stems from the grouping together of voices into anonymous votes (links) that remove their context and meaning.

Why does this happen? Well, one reason is that there is so much choice in the online world as to where to spend our time and money that we all suffer from information overload. Research has shown that when we are faced with too many choices, it impairs, not improves, our ability to make a good decision or any decision at all. In one famous study, Professor Sheena Iyengar found that supermarket shoppers presented with a taste test of 24 jams bought less and were less happy with their purchases than those shoppers presented with only six jams.

So people want guidance on where to go, and thus tend to go with the herd in choice. And these paths, once beaten, become easier to find and easier to traverse for others. And while the economics of online has enabled consumers to enjoy choice on a scale previously unimaginable at massive online marketplaces like Amazon, iTunes and Netflix, this hasn't had the impact some had predicted. Many hoped that online would usher in a kind of 'indie' utopia, where everyone could find the exact book, record or movie to suit them and where this increased demand would in turn provide a market for more diverse production.

Instead, as Professor Anita Elberse has noted in her well-researched book *Blockbusters*,[7] the web is having the reverse effect – when the total pie of all books, music and movies is divided up, the slice of total sales of a few titles at the top is growing and the sliver represented by the lowest sellers is going down. So while the long tail benefits of seemingly endless choice are there, Online Gravity is amplifying the head of the long tail – where the hits are becoming even more amplified.

Lanier, who is a composer and performer himself, laments the impact this has had in music. He sees the shrinking participation in free, creative activities such as recording and publishing local independent music as a function of this network effect on consumption. In other words, there is less diversification and more concentrated consumption around popular tastes.

EXPONENTIAL GROWTH

Timing is critical in Online Gravity. Small and sometimes random events can quickly have a snowball effect, with significant impacts, both positive and negative. New products and companies can grow at speeds never before possible, leveraging the enormous platforms of iTunes, Google, Facebook, Alibaba and Amazon, plus the windfalls of increasing returns, lock-in and other network effects.

The key to much of this power is the fact that growth online is exponential. With exponential growth, the output gets put back in at each step, and this has a compounding effect on future growth. It means you get growth on your growth. This is the same as compound interest, where, if you reinvest your money plus the interest it receives, you get interest on your interest and hence a snowball effect. It's also the way contagious diseases spread so rapidly, as the more people who catch them the more they are passed on.

Try this thought experiment to demonstrate the power of exponential growth. If you could receive a rising cash gift for every one of your children's birthdays to put into a trust fund until they turn 21, which of these multipliers would you choose?

a) **$50 for every candle on their birthday cake**
On their first birthday, they're given $50; on their second, $100; on their third, $150; on their tenth, $500; and so on.

b) **Age cubed**
Their age to the power of three in dollars. So, on their first birthday, they get $1 ($1 \times 1 \times 1$); on their second, $8 ($2 \times 2 \times 2$);

on their third, $27 (3 × 3 × 3); on their tenth, $1000 (10 × 10 × 10); and so on.

c) **The two-by-two-athon**

Two dollars to the power of their age. So, on their first birthday, they're given $2; on their second, $4 (2 × 2); on their third, $8 (2 × 2 × 2); on their tenth, $1024 (2 × 2 × 2 × 2 × 2 × 2 × 2 × 2 × 2 × 2); and so on.

While $50 for every candle sounds promising and starts out well, by the time they get to their eighth birthday, worth $400, the aged-cubed option overtakes with $512. The sleeper, however, is the two-by-two-athon, which takes the lead by the tenth birthday and from there continues to surge ahead. This is exponential growth. Below are the results of each on a chart, so you can get the idea.

Comparative chart of birthday cash schemes

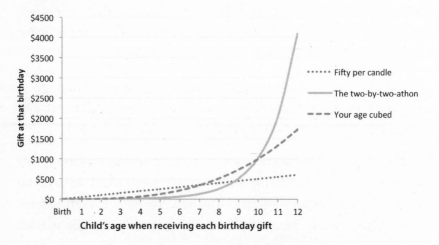

And to give you a sense of the power of exponential growth, let's look at the totals when your son or daughter turns 21:

a) **$50 for every candle on their birthday cake**

At 21, the grand total invested in this fund is $11,550. Not bad.

b) **Age cubed**
   At 21, the grand total invested in this fund is $53,361. Sweet.
c) **The two-by-two-athon**
   At 21, the grand total invested in this fund is $4,194,302. Awesome!

Anything that doubles in size, speed or complexity at regular intervals, like this two-by-two-athon, is growing exponentially. And exponential growth is at the heart of Online Gravity.

You see this growth in areas that involve complex networks of interactions with lots of feedback loops. Hence, as mentioned earlier, many systems that are digital, social and global have a tendency towards it. And the online realm is, of course, all three.

The Way the Snowball Starts Rolling

In order for something to undergo exponential growth, first it has to start rolling. And the web is a great platform for the uptake of new ideas, products and services. For at least the last five decades, the ways in which the public come to embrace innovation have been studied by various interest groups, including:

- people in business looking to bring new products to market;
- people in government looking to effect positive social change;
- people in research looking to have their ideas accepted.

In the 1940s, US researchers analysing how farmers adopted new technology recognised that some people were likely to take on new things and others weren't.[8] The late Professor Everett Rogers, the acknowledged king of this field, famously categorised his findings into three groups:

- a small number of 'early adopters' – people ready to try new things;
- the majority of us, who will come on board but take some convincing (further divided into 'early and late majority'); and

- a group of slow adopters, the 'laggards', who are always last and may never adopt new trends.[9]

You are probably familiar with this idea. I'm sure you know people who are early adopters. They are the ones who love being first to discover new music, go to new holiday destinations or read new books – trendsetters, or 'mavens', as Malcolm Gladwell calls them in his excellent book *The Tipping Point*. We look to them for guidance, information and recommendations. And they are critical to the spread of new ideas and products.

Gladwell explained the way in which trends and ideas can grow exponentially after reaching critical mass – a threshold of activity among mavens that ultimately leads to widespread adoption. This is what he called the tipping point.

Frank Bass was first to recognise how these influential people affect the roll-out of new products in his seminal 1969 paper 'A New Product Growth Model for Consumer Durables'.[10] In it, he looked at the uptake of household appliances, including fridges, washing machines and steam irons, using data from the 1920s to the 1960s. He concluded that products enjoyed exponential growth in initial purchases until a peak and then exponential decay from other new products entering the market.

His idea, which has become known as the Bass Model of Innovation, has its own mathematics to back it up. The Bass Model identifies a number of people he calls 'innovators' (like Gladwell's mavens and Rogers' early adopters) – not people who make new products but those who try new products and services first – and it's from this base that the product is taken up throughout the broader population via 'imitators'.

The Importance of the On-Ramp

Whether we are early adopters or not, we all need a stream to drink from – a source for new ideas, services and solutions to our

The Bass Model of Innovation

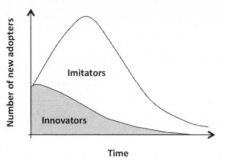

problems. All streams have a fountainhead, all roads a beginning, and all distribution systems a source.

In many cases involving networks, the network itself becomes the source of power. And often the key to that power is the on-ramp, the point at which people gain access to the network. This idea of a magical, perhaps golden, door that can take you into new realms – a bit like the wardrobe in *The Chronicles of Narnia*, or Platform Nine and Three-Quarters in the Harry Potter series – has been with the web since its beginnings, and AOL, Yahoo! and Craigslist are all different forms of portals.

Others, too, have examined the idea that information industries – including those that predate the web – arise from new-technology-enabled, and ultimately *government-endorsed*, on-ramps. In his influential and beautifully written book *The Master Switch*, Professor Timothy Wu describes what he sees as a repeated historic process for all information and communications industries from a sweep of their evolution in the United States. Wu examines the birth and growth of the telephone industry, the film industry, radio, cable TV and ultimately the internet.

He argues that all information industries follow a similar pattern, which he calls 'The Cycle', whereby they start with new, disruptive technology and lots of optimism based on a new open platform for communications. Then there's a period of chaos, confusion and dissatisfaction with the medium due to random competition and incompatible standards. This leads to the third and final stage of regulation and monopoly, where a leading group looks to harmonise the industry and appeals to the government to regulate it and allow them to run it in a more orderly fashion.

This, says Wu, is what happened at AT&T – the US phone company started by the inventor of the telephone, Alexander Graham Bell. Theodore Vail, president of AT&T, believed in the superiority of having a single, national phone system and AT&T adopted the slogan 'One Policy, One System, Universal Service',[11] which it used in its advertising for 70 years.

Tim Wu's book – which is full of great stories from history – recounts how, in 1902, the New York Telephone Company opened the doors on the world's first school for 'telephone girls' – switchboard operators at the first telephone exchanges. There were almost 17,000 applicants for the school's 2000 places, so it was obviously a hot ticket in its day.

It reminds me of Google, which was receiving 75,000 job applications a week for 6000 positions it hoped to fill over one year.[12] Google is without doubt the most desirable company in the world to work for today. In 2014, a fascinating study that ranked companies based on talent movements among LinkedIn's 300 million members found that Google was the number one most desirable company in the United States.

Wu also makes the connection to Google, saying that the company provides a service a bit like the 'telephone girls' of the early 1900s and 'offers a fast, accurate and polite way to reach your party. In other words, Google is the internet's switch. In fact, it's the world's most popular internet switch, and as such, it might even be described as the current custodian of the Master Switch.'[13]

Platform Industries

Some industries naturally lend themselves to exponential growth, and platform industries are a prime example. Their business consists of running a marketplace, which facilitates the exchange of products and services between suppliers and consumers. And most of the effects of Online Gravity are a result of the new, global marketplace businesses that the web has enabled. A clearer understanding of marketplace businesses is key to a better understanding of the dynamics of Online Gravity.

Markets are great money-makers when they work. It is well known to many in commerce that these are among the best businesses there are. All traditional media enterprises, such as film, TV and book-publishing companies, are marketplace businesses that connect people who make media (writers, actors and producers) with those who consume it (audiences). In addition, newspapers, magazines and radio provide a way for advertisers to reach specific target audiences.

Retail is one of the simplest and earliest marketplace industries. Retailers aggregate products from a range of suppliers so that shoppers can conveniently buy them under one roof. Then there's the business of malls – a shop of shops – where a mall operator provides a venue in which multiple retailers can do business.

Real-estate agencies, or realtors, are market businesses too – so, on the one hand, you have people wanting to rent or buy property, and on the other you have vendors looking to lease or sell property.

One of the earliest technology-led market businesses is, of course, the telephone network, where customers look to connect with one another via a common telephone system. This is an industry where size is critical. While you may be quite happy driving an exotic sports car that 99 per cent of the population doesn't, such as the wonderful Aston Martin DB5, how pleased would you be with a boutique telephone system that only you and one other person used?

The web, of course, is a platform industry itself. It's the platform of all platforms. People in the technology sector have known this for some time. In fact, in the early 1980s, the iconic and hugely influential computer company Sun Microsystems used the slogan 'The network is the computer'. So platform businesses and the web are a match made in heaven – like apple pie and ice cream.

It's perhaps no surprise, then, that many of the first businesses to succeed online were trading within platform industries such as retail (Amazon), media (Yahoo!) and stockbroking (E*Trade).

Market businesses, if they reach critical mass, tend to be fairly robust, as there's a range of customers and suppliers interacting whose livelihood depends on the ongoing operation of the platform. Market businesses are also often difficult to compete with, as it is hard to attract participants away from an existing and working marketplace.

In marketplace businesses, as we've seen with telephony, size counts. If you're an advertiser, you're willing to pay a premium for the television network or newspaper with the largest possible audience. If you're in the business of making television programs, then the one with the highest viewing figures will attract the largest share of advertiser revenue and be able to pay for most of your other programs. And if you're running a TV channel, then having the most highly rated programs on it will help bring you the capital needed to keep on outdoing your rivals and being the market leader.

Some market businesses operate in areas where government-owned enterprises, such as national telecommunications companies, used to be, and many also benefit from restrictions placed on prospective competitors. For any new stock exchange, for example, there are both regulatory and capital hurdles to contend with.

There is growing interest in platform industries among academics and economists. David S. Evans, founder of Boston-based Market Platform Dynamics, is one of a handful of world experts in this area, and he has researched and written extensively about it. Evans has studied carefully the emergence of marketplaces that share many of the characteristics of today's online giants but predate the web, such as global credit-card companies.[14]

Marketplace businesses often have multiple sides – meaning different groups of customers coordinated by a central agent. So, for example, in the market for credit cards there are three main groups: the individual cardholders; the merchants, such as restaurants and other shopkeepers who accept payment using the cards; and the issuers, such as Visa, MasterCard, American Express and so on.

Some of these markets are said to be two-sided, such as the business of holiday services (landlords and holiday-makers) and auctions (buyers and sellers). In some markets, participants perform two or more roles – one day on eBay, you might be a buyer and also a seller; mobile-phone customers make and receive calls – whereas in others the participants have more fixed parts to play: many people pay to see movies but few also make them.

The Cost of Connecting

While platform industries prior to the web do favour larger-scale marketplaces, competition between platforms can be strong where the 'cost of connecting' is low. So, for example, most merchants accept payments from multiple credit-card issuers. Taxi-drivers have an increasing number of ways to accept not only payments but also bookings, as well as having to compete, of course, with the emerging Online Gravity giants of ride-sharing, Uber and Lyft.

Unlike merchants, for whom the cost of connecting to multiple networks is low, in many technology- and knowledge-based networks the cost of connecting to multiple platforms is very high. To develop software for two entirely different games consoles, for example, is possible but also very expensive, as it requires a large investment in learning new systems and converting games to them.

This has led to what is known as vertical integration in the console-based video-game industry, whereby some suppliers of games have aligned exclusively with one of the dominant platform providers: Microsoft, Sony and Nintendo. Halo, for example – one of the largest game franchises in history – has been tied primarily to Microsoft's Xbox platform, and its developer, Bungie, is now managed by a Microsoft subsidiary. Mario Bros. is a franchise of games that you can only play on Nintendo's platforms.

While vertical integration intensifies competition between the platforms, it also leads to inefficiencies. Because most people don't buy all three major types of video-games consoles, there are some gamers who would buy the game *Halo 3* but don't own an Xbox, and others who have an Xbox and enjoy playing *Super Mario Bros.* but can't, as it only works on Nintendo gaming systems.

What's more, if you could play any game on any console, the value of buying a console would go up, and more games *and* consoles would be sold – so the total market would grow.

Robin S. Lee, Assistant Professor of Economics at Harvard University, cleverly created an economic model to determine how much extra value would be created in the games-console market-place were it to open up in this way. He found that hardware sales (the consoles and accessories) would increase by seven per cent and the software or games sales would increase by 58 per cent, creating an extra $1.5 billion for the industry as a whole.[15]

So why don't all the console games companies get together and increase their collective lot? This is an interesting question.

Console gaming has its roots and history in the pre-web world and dates back to 'TV games' and the early consoles like the Atari 2600 in the 1970s. While an impressive array of platforms have been established over eight generations of consoles since then, the basic traditional structure of market competition remains. The graphics have improved but essentially the business model is the same.

And in any market where proprietary hardware is part of the platform – like the consoles in video gaming; or in the case of telephony, such as smartphones; or in the case of payments, such as the merchant machine – there is an opportunity for vertical integration. Proprietary hardware adds to the switching cost for the consumer (that is, you need to buy a new device to change platforms) as well as to the supply chain (games makers need to learn new development platforms). And so in these markets, traditional economics are more likely to apply.

Over the past few years, a variety of web-borne gaming platforms are growing in popularity such as the Android-based OUYA and the Linux-based *Steam*. These and others like them will no doubt one day play a role in the ongoing transformation of this lucrative industry. Meanwhile, online games that are PC-based, browser-based and now mobile continue to grow in popularity and market share every year.

The web is, of course, the ultimate and universal platform. Where there are opportunities for web-based solutions to replace proprietary and device-centred, vertically integrated networks, they will – for example, with Stripe and Square in merchant payments and WhatsApp text messaging, which I explore next.

POWER

Another of the features of Online Gravity is its immense power. Consider for a moment the California-based enterprise WhatsApp. The success of this extraordinary start-up company really demonstrates the potential of Online Gravity when it's working in your direction.

WhatsApp was founded in 2009 by Jan Koum and Brian Acton. After working at Yahoo! for nine years, they took a year off and travelled South America together playing Ultimate Frisbee. After failing to get a job at Facebook on their return, they created a company called WhatsApp, and an app of the same name that allows people to communicate with each other freely and elegantly using their phone. Initially, it was based around simple text messaging, but the texts were delivered via the internet rather than the telephone network to offer users a free alternative to SMS.

By 2013, they had over 200 million users worldwide and around 50 staff. In February 2014, Facebook acquired the app for $19 billion. This is an extraordinary amount of money in anyone's terms for what is still a young business.

Let's unpack this and examine it in a bit more detail. What was it that led Facebook to pay such a staggering amount for WhatsApp?

Was it the team?

No. While the team is no doubt brilliant, there were only 55 employees in total at the time of the acquisition, so one would have to say it's not the people that Facebook paid $19 billion for. By way of comparison, an average hairdressing salon has around four staff. Valued on this basis, a typical hairdresser's would be worth over $1 billion.

Was it the sales at the company?

No. There were no sales until 2013 as the app was initially free. In 2013, they switched to a paid model of 99 cents per year after an initial year of using the service for free. So, at 400 million users, that's nearly $400 million per annum, but *Forbes* estimated their 2013 sales to be $20 million.[16] At $19 billion, the amount Facebook paid for the company was over 900 times the previous year's sales.

By way of comparison, the average local auto-repair business in the United States employs four staff and has annual sales of $322,114.[17] If you were to sell one of those businesses on the same basis, it would be worth $300 million. Next time you visit your garage, ask yourself whether you would pay $300 million for that business.

Was it the profits?

No. While profit margins will no doubt be very high for this business as the costs were largely fixed at the time of the sale, no massive profits had yet accumulated.

The answer lies in Online Gravity and the number of people using the service – a staggering 450 million users worldwide and growing at over a million users a day.

Was it a bargain?

Perhaps. On a per-user basis, this works out to $42 per person actively using the service. As the chart below from *MIT Technology Review* illustrates, Facebook may have got a bargain in WhatsApp. Mike Orcutt, research editor at *MIT Tech Review*, calculated the value of each user on a variety of different social networks by dividing the value of the network or company by the total number of active users. On this basis, the amount Facebook paid for WhatsApp on a per-user basis was very similar to that it paid for Instagram (about $45 per active user), and still much less than the market has valued each user of Snapchat ($60), Twitter ($130), or Pinterest ($195). And still less than a third of the value of Facebook users itself. Now with over a billion active users, each Facebook user is valued at around $150.

The value of a social media user

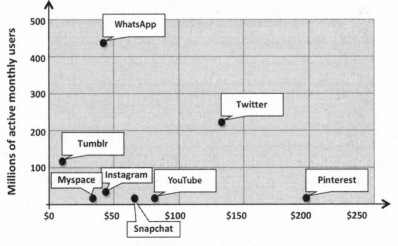

Note market value refers to market capitalisation as at Feb 2014, or valuations in private investment rounds or at time of acquisition. Chart data source: *MIT Technology Review*[18]

But even more important than the number of users is the fact that WhatsApp is likely to become the gravity giant of this new form of mobile social communication, which already spans the world and has a huge footprint in Asia. Online Gravity ensures that being the leading global player delivers massive rewards, as the difference between first place and second place is monumental – like the difference between the Earth and the Moon.

MEASURABILITY

Finally, Online Gravity can be detected through the presence of the gravity giants it creates, and gravity giants are not particularly hard to spot. They all have the following characteristics:

- *Significant market share.* Typically more than 50 per cent of the total global market for their segment.
- *Global footprint.* A geographically diverse set of users from around the world.
- *Large share of mind.* Degree of perceived ownership of a category resulting in unprompted recall (for example, Google has become the verb *to search*), and habitual use (Airbnb is the go-to site for third-party holiday lettings).
- *Highly active communities.* In terms of frequency and time of engagement.
- *Developed ecosystems.* Sophisticated network of other third-party enterprises that have invested in building upon the platform.
- *Large herd.* Habitual visitors who have invested in skills to learn how to use the platform.

Each of these characteristics can be quantified, allowing the emergence of new Online Gravity giants to be observed via a set of measures, as follows.

How to spot a gravity giant
There are many online tools for the analysis of emerging and

established Online Gravity giants. Here are a few popular useful ones.

Online Gravity measures	Unit measured	Data sources
Online users and usage	Market share Growth of usage Users Time spent	Alexa Hitwise Quantcast Nielsen
Talent Metrics	Employees	LinkedIn Recruiter
Company Metrics	Investment	Crunchbase
Social Metrics	Tweets	Twitonomy
	Facebook likes Instagram	RivalIQ
Search data	Search frequency Search terms	Google Trends Spyfu
Technology used	Types of online technology	Builtwith

Discovering the next Google or WhatsApp before it has hit prime-time is often difficult, as they are often small private companies. Fortunately, there are a number of organisations who make it their mission to hunt down the giants of tomorrow and produce interesting lists of companies in contention for such honours, including the MomentumIndex from Akkadian Ventures Private, which lists private tech companies according to a range of signals; and Mattermark, who offer an online commercial research service in this area. Angelist.com is a marketplace for early stage and funding for companies like WhatsApp; and SharesPost is a market for shares in private companies that employees and investors want to sell to others. Each of these provides valuable insights into this world, too.

KEY POINTS

Online Gravity has the following features:

- *Kinky rewards.* Returns are not shared equally between companies who operate within the same segment of the web. Instead, once mature, each segment such as search, transport or accommodation arrives at the equilibrium state of a planet-sized leader and a number of moon-scale niche businesses.

- *Long tails.* This is the fostering of large-scale marketplace companies that are able to sell 'less of more' – an enormous variety of products and services enabled by the global scale, flexibility and efficiency of the web.
- *Concentrated consumption.* As the catalogue and choice grows, paradoxically diversity in demand for the products and services being consumed is shrinking. A growing range of goods and services are now the subject of blockbuster economics as more local and national markets migrate toward readily addressable global markets.
- *Exponential growth.* The snowball effect, which means the rate of growth of new services and products and the potential for future faster growth continue to accelerate and compound.
- *Power.* The ability to deliver massive rewards to the winners and have global impact from a small team that leverages the web and its global reach.
- *Measurability.* Its effects and dynamics can be measured through data.

HOW DOES ONLINE
GRAVITY FUNCTION?

Online Gravity operates by digitising knowledge and making it increasingly democratic, social and global. The right knowledge at the right time can and does change people's lives. The best health outcomes, investment decisions and education choices are all a function of having the best information at hand. Fortunately, Online Gravity is giving us access to low-cost or free information like never before.

Online services such as Google, Wikipedia, Quora, and others you may not have heard of that I'll outline throughout the book, are incredible new sources of information that didn't exist a generation ago. And the thing that makes these services work so well is they are based on many of the successful principles, mechanisms and social systems used to power our traditional great sources of knowledge – universities, colleges and research laboratories – for hundreds of years. What Online Gravity is doing is taking elements of these systems and scaling them in altogether new and amazing ways.

The central idea for Google, for example, is based on the principle of academic citation. Wikipedia's open-contributor policy and need for verifiable sources is akin to academic scholar-ship. And the way that Quora cleverly organises articles, authors and topics mirrors how academic journals have for centuries focused the minds of scholars and researchers with common interests and themes.

There are a few key reasons why these traditional systems have worked so well. Ask yourself how scientists and engineers figure out which ideas are better. Yes, they test them with experiments if they can, but to a large degree they rely on the wisdom of their colleagues, who, over the course of a lifetime, carefully read, digest and refer to others whom they find interesting.

This is how it works. Scholars fashion their ideas into short essays known as papers or articles and try to get them into special-ist academic magazines called journals, run by experts in their field. If the team who run the journal like the article, they may send it to other experts for their views, and then they come to a decision as to whether to publish it.

When experts find something valuable or interesting in another person's work, they refer to it in their papers. These mentions or citations are very carefully counted up, as they represent the currency of knowledge in the academic world. And the more cita-tions a paper receives, the more credibility and significance it has among other scholars. Citations have become the stock and trade of academic credibility, a kind of knowledge currency, especially in scientific domains.

And this is precisely the way Google works. Instead of citations, though, it counts links. The more that other parts of the web link to a particular website, the higher that website appears in people's search results, as the backlinks (in-bound hyperlinks) reflect the popularity of that site. So, if you search for a recipe for gluten-free blueberry muffins, you will get a list ranked on a number of factors – a key one being how many other websites have linked to that recipe.

Google's ranking actually improves on the model borrowed from academia. With academic-citation ranking, all citations are equal, independent of the quality of the sources, whereas with Google's ranking system, links from more credible or authoritative sources are given more weight.

And how are those sources judged to be more credible? Through the number of backlinks *they* have accrued. A website that has been linked to by lots of websites that have themselves been frequently linked to will be propelled up the rankings, which will in turn attract more visitors to that website and the opportunity for more backlinks. This is where things start to snowball, leading to the creation of gravity giants.

CUMULATIVE ADVANTAGE

Every endeavour has its superstars, and in the field of science there are a number of 'laws' that describe how they rise to prominence. One such is the 'Matthew effect', or superstar effect, which says that in each field of research a small number of scholars produce the majority of the papers, attract the lion's share of citations and also go on to hold the prestigious academic positions.

But what are all the other scholars doing? In the main they're working very hard, but just not getting the limelight.

There's also a thing known as Stigler's law, whereby 'No scientific discovery is named after its original discoverer'. Instead, naming rights and kudos are almost always awarded to the most senior researcher involved in a project, even if all the work has been done by a graduate student.

In the 1960s, Yale professor Derek de Solla Price showed that one-quarter of all scientific authors are credited for three-quarters of all published papers. This became known as Price's Law. Price also showed that a few elite scientists in each field enjoy what he called 'cumulative advantage',[1] where the credit is distributed among a number of individuals according to how much they already have.

Sometimes credit is delayed, too. In Hollywood, there's a saying that people often win Oscars for their previous movie, not the one they were nominated for. So, for example, Russell Crowe won the Academy Award for his role in *Gladiator*, but many in the business feel it was really a belated award for his performance in *The Insider*.

So, through cumulative advantage, a relatively small number of people tend to attract the majority of the citations, kudos and fame in their fields. This is also the way that physical gravity functions and, indeed, Online Gravity too. Now turn your mind back to the online world, and ask yourself how you work out which services and products are best suited to your needs.

Our first impulse these days is to use Google. Say you want to buy a book online. You may type its title or the author's name into Google and, lo and behold, there it is. Almost magically, almost instantly, Google produces a ranked list of sources most likely to deliver what you need – from all over the world.

Google does this, of course, by matching what you type with its giant catalogue of what is available on the web. And Google knows a lot about what is available on the web. Its computers are diligently and tirelessly trawling the entire public web day and night to keep the index up to date with new things being published.

But not only is it large and up to date. What makes Google's catalogue of web information so valuable is that it is also *ordered*. The first things to appear in the results of any Google search are the advertisements, and underneath them, in rank order, are the 'organic' search results, meaning unpaid.

The details of Google's famous ranking formulae are a closely guarded secret, but it is known that at the heart of the system is a combination of relevance determined by counting links from other websites related to that search phrase, and the trustworthiness, or authority, of each source hosting the links. It's this second part – the authority part – that is the most interesting, as authority begets more authority.

Most people know that being ranked first on Google is good news. If you're a business and you're in the 'first page club' – meaning you appear in the first page of search results for your category – that's likely to be very good news for you, as it will mean you get an enormous amount of extra visitors.

A new global industry known as 'Search Engine Optimisation', or SEO, has sprung up around crafting and tweaking your online presence to be favourably considered in this process. There's over 20,000 full time professionals in this space worldwide now and over 50,000 freelancers on Freelancer.com and oDesk offering SEO services.

If you type 'surfing holiday in Sydney' into Google, you will see over 20 pages of results. Most people most of the time don't go beyond page one. And, in fact, most people don't scroll down to see results below the bottom of the screen – known as 'below the fold'. Over half of all the clicks from Google Search are in the first ten results.

What happens online is there is a natural feedback loop that tends to make some products and services tremendously success-ful and others invisible. Online Gravity is the reason why new web services have the potential to become huge very rapidly. With more users and more usage comes more visibility, and with more visibility comes more users and usage. In the creation of planets, size counts.

The above mechanism is very much like the formation of the Earth and the other planets in our solar system, where rocks were attracted to each other because of the laws of gravity. The more rocks that joined the party, the greater the mass and hence the greater the gravitational pull. In the end, just about all the nearby rocks and gas clouds were vacuumed up by their larger neighbours to form the eight planets we know, which explains why there is a lot of empty space between the planets. And we now have the relatively stable state of play where those eight massive balls are orbiting one even more massive Sun.

Online Gravity works in a similar way. As new categories of online services and products emerge, players providing these services compete for attention via global discovery platforms such as Google, Facebook and the iTunes Store. The more popular these services become, the more kudos they receive from these discovery platforms and the bigger they become again.

And so, wherever there is a possibility that one planet-sized service could emerge in a particular online sector, it will.

Consequences

One of the fundamental consequences of gravity-giant formation is the way in which it is influencing the shape of products, companies and ultimately the whole economy online.

Online Gravity and its seven laws explain why we see the configuration of global companies that we do, and it continues to influence the development of the online realm as new planets are formed and existing planets continue to expand.

In the online sphere, the network itself plays the role of the Sun, and the giant enterprises are like the planets around it – large and autonomous, each occupying their own space.

The Online Solar System

If we were to draw a map of the online solar system, it might look something like this, with Apple, Google and Amazon being the Jupiter, Saturn and Uranus of this world.

Planets of the online solar system

The chart following shows each gravity giant as a planet whose company value is reflected in its size. Each gravity giant holds sway in its sector: online investments, SoftBank; Chinese search, Baidu;

retail, Amazon; Chinese social media, Tencent; mobile devices and apps, Apple; search engines, Google; social media, Facebook; and wholesale, Alibaba.

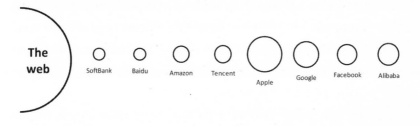

Some companies who are titans in their own right, such as Microsoft, Samsung and IBM, are omitted as, while they are dominant in some online areas (Microsoft with Skype, for example), the majority of their income is still from offline sources. Microsoft earns most of its revenue from Windows and XBox, Samsung from televisions and LCD panels, and IBM from computer software and services for enterprises.

Smaller in scale than these eight giants are a further fifteen dwarf planets, each of which is the largest but not the only such body in its particular orbit, as follows: auctions, eBay; African online media, Naspers; travel, Priceline; universal web portals, Yahoo!; transport, Uber; customer-relationship management, Salesforce; résumés, LinkedIn; microblogging, Twitter; films and TV shows, Netflix; Japanese retail, Rakuten; human resources and payroll, Workday; online storage, Dropbox; ephemeral social, Snapchat; holiday accommodation, Airbnb; Indian online shopping, Flipkart.

Dwarf planets of the online solar system

eBay   Naspers   Priceline   Yahoo!   Uber   Salesforce   LinkedIn   Twitter   Netflix   Rakuten   Workday   Dropbox   Snapchat   Airbnb   Flipkart

Planets sized by relative market valuation. Data source: Public company valuations January 2015 or for private companies valuation at most recent capital raising.

The likely fate of these is that they grow into planets of their own accord, or they combine with or are subsumed by other dwarf planets and satellites to become truly planetary in scale.

Now let's take a closer look at the structure of Online Gravity planets. If we were to draw a picture of Amazon, the online-retail giant, and its nearest competitors to scale, it would look like a planet with a series of moons. Below is such a diagram, with the online-retail sales of each company represented by the size of the circle.[2] With over $60 billion in global sales, Amazon is the clear king of online retail, more than tripling the online sales of its nearest competitor, Apple.[3] This is the same in many online industries – there is often only room for one planet surrounded by a number of moons.

The online-retail gravity giant and its satellites

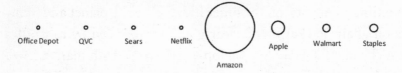

But when we draw the same picture for offline industry segments, it looks very different. Take, for example, the global business of soft drinks. We know there are clearly two planets in this orbit: a leader, Coke, and a strong challenger, Pepsi. As well, there are a number of smaller but still significant bodies, such as Dr Pepper and Snapple. In the offline realm, clearly, different laws apply; otherwise, these two largest bodies would have merged or collided and absorbed everything else, leaving room only for some small satellites.

Offline soft-drink planets and dwarfs

In payments, the difference between offline and online is even clearer. In the offline world, there are a number of planets in the credit-card and debit-card arena: Visa, MasterCard, UnionPay, American Express, Japan Credit Bureau (JCB) and Diners Club International. Here are the top-four players by market share and how they line up:[4]

Offline payment planets

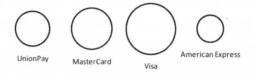

Planets sized by relative worlwide market share of credit card payment revenue.
Data source: Nilson Report, March 2014.

In online payments, on the other hand, it's a one planet and many moon affair. PayPal is the clear giant, surrounded by a handful of niche players. Here are the top-four players, with market share represented by the size of the circles.[5] You can see the difference Online Gravity makes.

Online payment planets

Planets sized by global market share of websites using payment technology.
Data source: Builtwith.com: Payments, Market Share, January 2015.

WHERE IS ONLINE GRAVITY FELT STRONGEST?

The industries already under the influence of Online Gravity are those characterised by:

- online services – where things happen or are initiated and managed online, such as online shopping, online trading and online banking;
- self-service – where customers can help themselves to advice, information and purchases, such as Instagram, which provides its users with tools to share and apply special effects to digital photos;
- platforms – where the business is in providing a marketplace, whether it is for audiences and advertisers (Yahoo!, Craigslist), suppliers and customers (Alibaba, eBay), or groups of suppliers and groups of customers, such as iOS developers and the iTunes App Store;
- knowledge and information conveyance – such as advertising, entertainment and communication. These industries are where Online Gravity's influence is most obvious, as they lend themselves to remote, automated, digitally mediated delivery.

And the segments already clearly under the influence of Online Gravity include:

- search, with Google;
- encyclopaedia, with Wikipedia;
- social media, with Facebook;
- payments, with PayPal;
- microblogging, with Twitter;
- content management, with WordPress;
- video, with YouTube;
- telephony, with Skype;
- transport, with Uber;
- instant messaging, with WhatsApp;
- surveys, with SurveyMonkey;
- travel, with Priceline.

Currently, Online Gravity's effects are felt more strongly by some individuals, companies and industries than others, but its influence is expanding rapidly. As industries become increasingly digitised and connected online, they are all turning into information industries. In an age where self-driving cars are not far away, we can see how industries such as automotive are also now opening up to the same forces, meaning the effects of Online Gravity on the online economy will one day be universal. Even industries as far from consumer technology such as mining are coming online with real-time low-cost online satellite-imaging, which is set to revolutionise minerals exploration as well as mine operations.

KEY POINTS

Online Gravity functions in the following ways:

- *By building on traditional knowledge systems.* Not only is online information digital and therefore more easily shared, it is also ranked in terms of credibility and relevance, in a way that improves on the academic citation system.
- *By fostering cumulative advantage.* Whereby rewards are distributed among a number of online enterprises according to how many they already have, in a feedback loop.
- *By creating an online solar system.* Whereby planets are formed that swallow up everything in their orbit leaving space only for smaller bodies to coexist as satellites.
- *By expanding into new space.* The realm of Online Gravity is growing in strength and reach until ultimately it will come to affect every industry, and all our endeavours.

THE LIFE STAGES OF
ONLINE GRAVITY

As with the formation of planets, there are three distinct phases in the development of an industry that comes under the influence of Online Gravity:

- *Infancy.* This is an initial market-discovery and definition phase characterised by a number of competitors, usually start-ups, and whoever was the original online market innovator.
- *Adolescence.* A period of competition and rivalry where the players are clear and the market is established. Here, the focus shifts onto market share – or, as Timothy Wu puts it eloquently in *The Master Switch*, 'from somebody's hobby to somebody's industry'[1] – and the original technology innovator often exits at this point.
- *Maturity.* One clear victor emerges, surrounded by an array of niche providers. At this point, any direct challenges to the leader are likely to be unsuccessful.

Below is a table of the leading companies in markets that are at different stages of the Online Gravity life cycle. Some markets, such as peer-to-peer lending and the 'internet of things' (objects that are not computers, smartphones or tablets but nevertheless have in-built internet connectivity), are still in their infancy; some, such as online real estate, online shopping-cart services and mobile payments, are in their adolescence; and others, such as online search, social media and payments, are mature.

Life stages of Online Gravity

Stage	Market Category	Pioneers (infancy) Contestants (adolescence) Victors (maturity)
Infancy	Big data storage	MongoDB
	Digital currencies	Bitcoin, et al.
	Internet of things	Nest Labs (thermostats and smoke detectors), The Climate Corporation (weather data and insurance for farmers)
	Peer-to-peer lending	Moneytree, Lending Club
Adolescence	Accounting	Xero vs FreshBooks, NetSuite, Intuit, Wave
	E-commerce	Shopify vs Bigcommerce
	Legals	LegalZoom vs Rocket Lawyer
	Mobile payments	Square vs Stripe, Dwolla, Google Wallet
	Outsourcing	Freelancer.com vs oDesk
	Real estate	Zillow vs Trulia (*Zillow acquired Trulia in 2014*)
	Rich mail	Campaign Monitor vs MailChimp
	Wagering	Bet365 vs Betfair marketplace
Maturity	Auctions	eBay
	Blogging	WordPress
	Customer-relationship management	Salesforce
	Encyclopaedia	Wikipedia
	Microblogging	Twitter
	Payments	PayPal
	Search	Google
	Social media	Facebook
	Surveys	Survey Monkey
	Video	YouTube

INFANCY

The infancy stage is when a new segment of the economy first falls under the spell of Online Gravity. What we see is a pre-competitive phase of partnering and experimentation with new ideas.

It's a bit like dating. Initially, there are lots of folks experimenting with new ideas, not sure whether or not there is a match. But there's love in the air and a high degree of hope and anticipation. A lot of this behaviour involves young university students, either on campuses or recently left. After a while, some of the folk in the scene get serious, and before long there's a clutch of newborn enterprises on the block.

Finding Stuff Online

Think about how you find stuff on the web. In the early 1990s, as the web grew and more and more people were publishing information and services online, finding what you needed became increasingly difficult.

As with the first television programs, which drew heavily on radio shows and live theatre for their ideas and formats, the first business model for organising information was something we were already familiar with – an index like a yellow-pages phone directory.

After the British computer scientist Sir Tim Berners-Lee established the World Wide Web in Switzerland, he set up the first one of these directories, called the Virtual Library, in 1991. When Yahoo! came along in 1994, it was king of this early world of the web, but there were many others prior and following, including:

- Best of the Web Directory – established in 1995 at the University at Buffalo in New York State;
- LookSmart – Australia's shining star of the early web, established by Evan Thornley and Tracy Ellery in 1995 with funding from Reader's Digest;

- Open Directory Project – started as Gnuhoo in 1998 by Rich Skrenta and Bob Truel, engineers at Sun Microsystems, and now called DMOZ.

Most of these directories were catalogued by an army of editors – which soon became a big job and quite expensive to build and keep up to date. Then a new batch of would-be daters entered the scene, exploring a new theme called web search.

Search-Engine Baby Boom

In 1994, Brian Pinkerton at the University of Washington gave birth to WebCrawler, the first of the full-text online search services. But, as is the way of Online Gravity, soon after there were many other babies in the web-search nursery too. The next three years saw the creation of more than 15 others, over half of which sprang from the research labs of universities and corporate research facilities around the world. Eventually, a service called Submit It! emerged for notifying all the different search engines of newly launched websites. Then MetaCrawler and Dogpile came into being, which enabled you to search all the other search engines!

In 1998, Google launched its search service based on a new technology developed as part of a research project at Stanford University, which delivered more accurate results than ever before. And we all know the outcome from there.

While the search-engine baby boom has continued ever since, with around five major new search engines launching every year, no one has been able to put the slightest dent in Google's supreme position in the English-speaking world. (Baidu holds a similarly dominant position in China, and Yandex in Russia.)

Something Funny Happened on the Way to the Stadium

There's a youthful interim stage for new segments of the economy that fall under the spell of Online Gravity: post-infancy but still pre-adolescence. At this point, it's now clear that there is in fact a market, but the gloves-off stadium death match has yet to begin. Rather, it's about to be decided who gets to compete in the final play-offs. I have a very keen interest in this stage, and I believe many other people in the technology sector do too.

Why would this be of interest? Some are paying attention because they are in a start-up themselves, or aspire to be; others are interested from an investment point of view; and others still – as a function of being in the technology industry – are acutely aware of the value of choosing and using the standards and systems that end up being dominant.

The folklore of technology start-ups is now well established, through movies such as *The Social Network*, about the formation and growth of Facebook. And many people understand the idea of the maverick genius company founder or co-founder – such as Mark Zuckerberg or Bill Gates – with a passion for computer science and changing the world. Along the way, there are some investors and venture capitalists to help fund the growth of the business, and then there's the spectacular stock-market listing.

If you know the likely endgame – say, for example, for Google, Facebook or PayPal – it's interesting to wind back the clock to identify the 'tipping point', as Malcolm Gladwell would say. And I'm interested not in the point where it looks like they have won the Grand Final – or, in Facebook's case, its battle with Myspace – but in the point where it became clear there was going to be a tournament at all.

Below, I share with you some characteristics that I've observed, and that others have shared with me, of this early filtering process and how it plays out.

Being Fashionably Late Has its Benefits

In the world of Online Gravity, being first is overrated. This may seem odd or counterintuitive, but it is rare that the first product or company operating in an Online Gravity-affected market makes it to adolescence, and even rarer that it becomes the ultimate victor. Some examples of this are as follows:

- *Smartphones.* Palm was a leader in the personal-digital-assistant (PDA) market and ahead in the smartphone race when Apple launched the iPhone in 2007, and yet Palm lost out to Apple.
- *Search engines.* WebCrawler was perhaps the first in 1994, a year ahead of the tournament-stage leader, AltaVista, and four years ahead of the segment's ultimate victor, Google, in 1998.
- *Tablets.* Apple's ill-fated Newton tablet, which in hindsight looks like an iPad ahead of its time (as it was pre wi-fi), demonstrates clearly the power of market timing.

The latecomers' advantage is due to the nature of network economics rather than a function of technology. As David S. Evans, Chairman of Global Economics Group, has also observed astutely, Diners Club was first in cards and yet has not gone on to lead in that market.[2] Conversely Google was very late to the search business – there were already seventeen other major search engines available when they launched. When online marketplaces are still in their infancy like this it is like the early stages of a big university party. New entrants with something different to offer are still very welcome and greeted with enthusiasm by the already assembled guests. Companies too are experimenting with the products and services they offer and the prices they charge. This experimentation and open door policy continues until the market enters the adolescence phase, described on page 57.

Universities Play a Starring Role

The full role that universities have played in establishing tournament-grade new companies and products is not that well understood.

As well as being great places to meet co-founders, universities have a quiet but very powerful function in providing much of the long-term, often publicly funded research and intellectual capital that makes new products and services possible. Google was founded by graduate students at Stanford University, and the work that informed the famous Google search technology – originally called BackRub – was funded by a governmental National Science Foundation Grant for a Digital Library Initiative.[3]

Apple's multi-touch technology, which made the iPhone what it is today and set the smartphone bonfire alight, came from a company it acquired in 2005 called FingerWorks, which was based on the research of Professor John Elias and his doctoral student Wayne Westerman at the University of Delaware. They were investigating low-impact ways of interacting with computers using touch for people suffering from repetitive strain injury. Their early work was again supported by National Science Foundation funding.[4]

Pay Attention to Kingmaker Venture Capitalists

Venture capital, aside from providing growth capital for early-stage companies, plays a more subtle role in the creation of authority and approval. Attracting the attention and funding of a small group of elite, US-based venture-capital companies such as Accel, Union Square, Kleiner Perkins and Sequoia has become a badge of honour and a cue for others looking to partner with you, buy services from you or be employed by you.

For some very hot emerging companies, such as WhatsApp and Atlassian, the venture capitalists Sequoia and Accel had to court the companies, not the other way around. Increasingly, a small band of influential angel investors are playing this role too.

You can follow the moves of various venture capitalists, their investments and investee companies on CrunchBase, the authoritative source of data on deals, companies and investors in the tech world. AngelList has also become a journal of record for start-ups and angel funding.

There are many other signals that may or may not be predictors of success, including the alma mater of the founders, participation in one of the elite start-up training schools known as accelerators such as Y Combinator, the company's choice of technologies, and even the company's address, such as San Francisco's South of Market Area, Surry Hills in Sydney and Shoreditch in London.

And now there are momentum-discovery enterprises, such as Mattermark, that follow the signals emitted by these early-stage companies very closely and report on them as a service.

ADOLESCENCE

The adolescence life stage of Online Gravity can also be described as the contest stage. As we have seen, it is when the market becomes established and the biggest teenagers on the block duke it out for the rewards. Let's take microblogging as a sample arena in which this tournament has taken place.

When Twitter Roared

In 2007, the concept of microblogging – or communicating with friends and followers online via a stream of short text messages – was beginning to find traction.

At one point, there were a number of microblogging services around the world – perhaps over a hundred in total. Plurk, Jaiku, Pownce, Brightkite and FriendFeed were all early rivals to Twitter in this new arena.

Jaiku.com – a Finnish microblogging site – was acquired by Google in October 2007 in its attempts to enter the rapidly growing social-media segment. At the time, Jaiku was a credible rival to Twitter, as was Pownce, a company founded by Digg founder Kevin Rose.

Twitter's popularity was radically accelerated at the 2007 Texas-based South by Southwest Interactive conference. Twitter's co-founder Evan Williams had this to say about the event: 'We launched it nine months before – to a whimper. By the time SXSW 2007 rolled around, we were starting to grow finally and it seemed like all of our users which were probably in the thousands were going to Austin that year.

'. . . I don't know what was the most important factor, but networks are all about critical mass, so doubling down on the momentum seemed like a good idea. And something clicked.'

The young company splashed out and spent up big on large-screen TV displays in the main hall of the conference which the founders installed themselves. These displayed live tweets from conference-goers and generated buzz aplenty and thousands of new sign-ups.

By 2008, despite both Jaiku and Pownce continuing to enjoy good growth, interest in Twitter had skyrocketed. And going into 2009, the victory was complete and clear.

In April 2008, the Jaiku page on Wikipedia was still getting around ten per cent of the traffic of the page about Twitter, but by April 2009 Jaiku's page attracted less than one per cent that of Twitter. Interest in Twitter had grown over 1000 per cent in the 12 months to 2009, decimating all its rivals in the process.

The adolescent phase can be very brief – and the tournament over in less than year as in the case of Twitter vs Jaiku; Google vs Altavista and Facebook vs Myspace. The contest also has the potential to be more drawn out over a number of years depending on the degree the product and services are integrated with the network.

More recent tournaments such as Uber vs Lyft; Freelancer.com vs. oDesk; Xero vs. Freshbooks which combine online services and with large scale offline systems have the potential to be a longer-term battles.

Other adolescent contests may have been deferred due to language, government and geography still playing a role in markets like China where domestic gravity giants have arisen in search (Baidu); wholesale and retail (Alibaba) and social media (Tencent) flourish and thrive in parallel with their Western counterparts Google, Amazon and Facebook.

MATURITY

Once the tournament has a winner, the gap continues to widen until the dominant player settles into its position and becomes a planet in its own right.

Ten years ago, the marketplace for content-management systems, which enable people to publish simple websites, was crowded. In the latter part of the last decade, the market began consolidating, and three clear contenders for the crown emerged: Joomla, WordPress and Drupal.

We can see what happened from the Google Trends chart following, which shows the relative keyword search frequency over the last decade. During the jousting, Joomla surged ahead for some time in 2007, but the tipping point occurred around June 2009 when WordPress, with continued market momentum, and gathering more and more steam, took the lead. From then on, WordPress has continued to consolidate its lead and is now used by over half of the top one million most popular sites on the web. And today this gap continues to widen ever steadily, as WordPress settles into its role as the world's leading web content-management system.

There is a fourth stage beyond maturity that for simplicity I've omitted here and that is obsolescence. While I think it is nearly impossible to steal Google's march as the world's leading search engine (Microsoft and many others have tried their best with all their might and failed), what will happen one day is that search will no longer be such a big thing itself. Perhaps new ways

Google searches on 'Joomla', 'WordPress' and 'Drupal' from 2005 to 2014

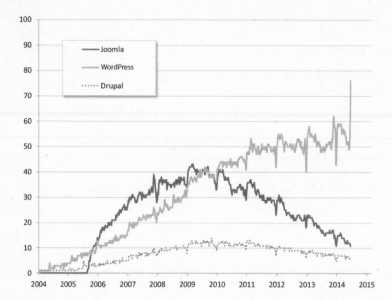

Chart represents relative share of global web searches for those terms over the decade to 2015. Data source: Google Insights, January 2015.

of discovering information will emerge that involve using our gestures and thoughts rather than keywords.

Gravity giants, rather than be usurped by contenders for the same crown will ultimately suffer a fate of irrelevance as the world's technology and business models move in a different direction altogether. Consider for example the personal computer. Microsoft Windows was the key platform enabler of that era and enjoyed incredible market dominance. Even today the overwhelming majority of the world's desktop computers run Windows – but what has happened in the meantime is the world has moved into a new era of mobile computing and smart web-connected devices where a new giant rules the waves: Apple.

KEY POINTS

The life stages of Online Gravity are as follows:

- *Infancy.* A pre-competitive phase of collaboration and experimentation, before a clear market is established. This period has a secondary stage as the market moves towards adolescence, when the future competitors start to emerge.
- *Adolescence.* An all-out battle for dominance among the major players.
- *Maturity.* The winner becomes a gravity giant.

COUNTEREXAMPLES AND EXCEPTIONS

There are a number of industries that are conspicuously not currently affected by Online Gravity and continue to behave in a more traditional fashion. Offline economics, with its tendency towards open competition and a number of leaders who compete on cost, quality and geography still applies to the following markets, even though they have gone online:

- Markets with substitutable products – such as online stockbroking – where there is intense competition on price and service.
- Markets with different local business practices – such as online real estate, where in some countries the agents pay for advertising the sale of a house and in others the vendor pays for advertising directly, and which supports listing with multiple realtors in some countries but not in others, where it is against the law.
- Markets closely related to local law – such as online banking and online accounting, as both industries are heavily regulated in most countries and therefore tend to produce local companies.

Other exceptions are highly regulated service industries that have not yet been fully globalised, such as telecommunications and airlines, and industries that have clearly been global for some time, such as automotive and soft drinks, whose revenues from the products they sell are still largely offline.

It is also worth noting that some countries where languages other than English are dominant have produced their own domestic gravity giants – for example in search, domestic Google-like gravity giants exist in Russia (Yandex), China (Baidu) and Korea (Naver).

CURRENTLY OFF-GRID INDUSTRIES SOON TO BE ON-GRID

Almost every industry where the activity is still mostly offline is ruled by more traditional economics, featuring a leader, a small number of major challengers and many niche rivals.

Car making has been a competitive business from the beginning. In the late 1800s, there were hundreds of car manufacturers. Over the past century, there has been considerable consolidation, with a smaller number of global groups emerging that own the various brands we are familiar with.

Volkswagen Group owns VW but also Audi, Bentley, Lamborghini, Porsche, SEAT and Škoda. Toyota Motor owns Toyota but also Lexus and Daihatsu. General Motors now makes cars in 37 countries under ten brands, including Chevrolet, Buick, GMC, Cadillac and Holden. BMW makes BMWs but now also owns Rolls-Royce and Mini. Iconic British car brands Jaguar and Land Rover are now manufactured by Indian car maker Tata. Swedish car-safety pioneer Volvo is now owned by Chinese car maker Geely. And iconic Italian sports-car makers Alfa Romeo, Ferrari and Maserati are now all part of Fiat.

Despite this frenzied buying of brands and putting them under one roof to lower global costs, there still remains strong competition among the eight leading parent companies, each with more than $100 billion in sales.

Car making has not one but eight global giants

Company	Country	Sales ($ billion)
Volkswagen Group	Germany	$261.50
Toyota Motor	Japan	$255.60
Daimler	Germany	$156.60
General Motors	United States	$155.40
Ford Motor	United States	$146.90
Honda Motor	Japan	$117.70
Nissan Motor	Japan	$104.00
BMW Group	Germany	$101.00

Source: *Forbes*, 2014

What remains to be seen is how this industry evolves as it becomes increasingly data-intensive and connected online.

Google has made no secret of its interest in self-driving cars, and its research program in this area has already demonstrated success. Recently, it has acquired more than ten companies in the robotics space or that could be applied to the field of self-driving vehicles and personal robotics. Google's recent purchases include:

- Skybox Imaging – satellite imaging;
- Titan Aerospace – aerial robots;
- Nest Labs – smart home sensors;
- Boston Dynamics – robotics;
- Autofuss – advertising, design and robotics;
- Bot & Dolly – robotic cameras;
- Holomni – robotic wheels;
- Meka Robotics – humanoid robots;
- Redwood Robotics – robotic arms;
- Industrial Perception – computer vision and robotic arms;
- Schaft – humanoid robots;
- Flutter – gesture-recognition technology.

There has been speculation, too, about Apple or Google acquiring the technology-rich electric-car manufacturer Tesla. Or a more likely outcome is partnering around advancing battery technology, which they both have a huge interest in.

Tesla, along with other advanced-car companies, is now collecting data from the cars it sells after they leave the showroom. The fact that it does so in a connected, central fashion makes it very much in the vein of many of the Online Gravity giants. With this information, the company will be uniquely positioned to better understand both its cars and its customers. Here is an excerpt from the Tesla subscription-service agreement:

> Vehicle Telematics Subscription. Your car includes an activated subscription service that records and sends diagnostic and system data to Tesla to ensure that your car is operating properly, to guide future improvements and to allow us to locate your car under certain limited circumstances. There is no charge for this service.[1]

There is also a new generation of third-party data-services companies emerging to log, record and aggregate car-movement data for insurers. These insurance telematics providers include Octo Telematics (Italy), The Floow (UK) and Wunelli (UK).

REGULATED SERVICES INDUSTRIES

Banking, Insurance and Finance

Outside of payments, banking and finance has been staunchly resistant to the pull of Online Gravity. In traditional banking, there are many 'planets', both within a particular country but also globally: Wells Fargo, JPMorgan Chase & Co., Industrial and Commercial Bank of China, HSBC, Bank of America. Following is a picture of how these banking giants stack up in relative size.[2]

Offline global banking planets

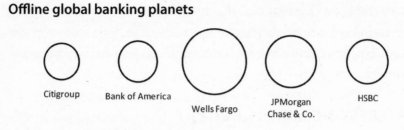

Citigroup Bank of America Wells Fargo JPMorgan Chase & Co. HSBC

Planets sized by relative market value of the world's leading retail banks.
Data source: Public company valuations, January 2015.

It remains to be seen how this most regulated of industries will evolve as a whole in the light of Online Gravity, but we are already seeing the following developments in some of its segments:

- In retail banking, in the area of personal lending, peer-to-peer online-lending clubs such as Zopa in the United Kingdom, SocietyOne in Australia and Lending Club in the United States are innovating in this arena, though cross-border players have yet to emerge.
- In 'new concept to product' financing, the crowdfunding website Kickstarter has created a speculative-finance market-place from early users and customers willing to experiment and risk investing in pre-orders for promising new services and products.
- In personal travel insurance, WorldNomads has carved out a global segment online.
- In money transfer and foreign exchange, traditional players such as Western Union and MoneyGram now offer online services for transferring funds to family and friends internationally. Small businesses who need foreign-exchange services have a number of new, global, non-bank companies that can deliver their requirements online, including Currencies Direct, World First and OzForex.

And while it is commonplace now to go online to buy a dress or some shoes from overseas, or even shares in a company listed on an overseas stock exchange, much less common would be having a bread-and-butter mortgage or savings account with an overseas bank. Nor have cross-border mortgages yet become a mainstream product.

INTERESTING MIDDLE GROUND

Halfway between companies that live offline and those that live online are businesses such as Nike and Tesco, which are doing a great job of straddling both worlds.

Nike's share of sales from e-commerce, while still small (estimated at only around two per cent of total sales),[3] is growing rapidly, and the company's pioneering web-connected products such as the Nike+ Sensor and the now discontinued Nike+ FuelBand demonstrate its willingness to venture into the online world.

Nike's idea of putting sensors into sneakers that enable you to record your run and then share it with your friends online is a very interesting way of using the web to enhance a product. The Nike+ digital ecosystem now has more than 18 million people using it all over the world.[4]

The United Kingdom's largest retailer, Tesco, is another offline giant with a reputation for being a leader in online strategy. In 2014, its online sales grew 14 per cent on the previous year, with online grocery orders up 11 per cent and non-food orders growing at 25 per cent.[5] Due to its online success, Tesco is now the United Kingdom's largest CD retailer – ahead of Amazon and high-street retailers.

Tesco also launched a direct-banking arm called Tesco Bank in 1997, in response to a similar move by its main national competitor, Sainsbury's.

COMETS NOT GIANTS

The competitors in some markets, such as online stockbroking, are all selling an end product that is the same or very similar. And these markets are more resistant to having one global player who can dominate the entire segment.

So, for example, when Google and Bing offer different services that compete to do the same job – web search – *the results you get when searching with them are different.* However, when you buy stocks in companies online – say in Nike or General Electric – *the results are the same* whether you get them via Ameritrade or via E*Trade. It's the same end product you're buying, so the competition becomes about the quality of the experience and price of commission they charge, not the product.

Other markets have partially developed the dynamics of Online Gravity. Domain-name registration, for example, does have a clear and dominant leader in Go Daddy, but not with the commanding position of, say, Google in search or Facebook in social media, both of which have more than 60 per cent of the total market share.

In these hybrid markets, there is still no clear market challenger, as the number-two player has less than a third of the leader's market share. Instead, there is a 'long tail' of smaller, niche competitors that collectively have more market share than the leader but individually are all relative minnows. I refer to leaders in these types of markets as 'comets', which have a long tail of much smaller competitors trailing them.

KEY POINTS

Offline economics still apply – in differing degrees – to the following markets, although many of them are starting to feel the pull of Online Gravity:

- *Online stockbroking.* Because the competitors are offering essentially the same product.
- *Online real estate.* Because of country-specific business practices.
- *Online banking, tax and accounting.* Because they are heavily regulated by their home nations.

- *Car making and soft drinks.* Because their products, and the revenue from their products, remains largely offline.
- *Groceries/general merchandise and athletics wear.* Because the leaders of these industries are still in two camps, trading mainly offline but expanding into the online sphere.
- *Domain-name registration.* Because this market, like online stockbroking, has only one main substitutable and ultimately identical product to offer, so the companies that succeed tend to be comets, not giants.

THE LAWS

LAW 1

ONLINE GRAVITY IS NATURALLY GLOBAL

The first of the seven fundamental laws of Online Gravity is that, by its very nature, Online Gravity is a global force. The web is not limited by geographical boundaries and can tap into international markets with ease. A global customer base means a global income base, and this has profound implications for individuals, companies and governments alike.

WHAT THIS MEANS FOR INDIVIDUALS

For individuals, it means you can buy and sell goods and services from anyone, anywhere.

If you work in an office in a metropolitan city, you'll no doubt be familiar with the phenomenon of employees bringing parcels into work for posting to eBay customers around the globe, plus the more frequent phenomenon of having small parcels arrive at the office from Amazon and thousands of other online retailers globally.

This happens because online retailers can sell to anyone and consumers can buy from anyone. And, like the globalisation of the telephone system over a hundred years ago, the open global marketplace has created huge opportunities for consumers and retailers, as well as a rising tide of small packages crisscrossing the planet. Thanks to Online Gravity, cross-border e-commerce has grown to represent more than ten per cent of all trade in global goods in less than a decade.

And, naturally, this trade is subject to the ups and downs of global currency movements in ways that consumers have never had direct exposure to before. In the last five years, for example, Australia's economy has been strengthened by the success of its large mining industry and an increasing demand for the iron ore it exports to China. As a result, Australians have enjoyed surges in the value of their dollar against the US dollar and UK pound. Australian shoppers, realising the growing value of buying online from US and UK retailers, have taken to it in droves. Once the Australian dollar climbed beyond its long-term average of around US$0.85 in 2009, it reached a tipping point and triggered a tidal wave of overseas shopping. Though the Australian dollar is currently below its average, many UK and US online stores have reported far-flung Australia as their second- or third-biggest market.

Since shoe-sizing systems in Australia are different to those in the United States and United Kingdom, my research shows a direct link between the number of people typing 'shoe conversion' into Google in Australia and the number of searches in Australia on how many US dollars one Australian dollar buys. Never before has shopping for shoes been such a global experience!

Online shopping is huge. Just ask Sarah Jessica Parker, of *Sex and the City* fame, who has recently agreed to 'curate' pieces carefully selected for the online jewellery retailer WeTheAdorned.

Some goods are more amenable to selling online than others. Owing to their global nature, shipability and known quality, it's perhaps no surprise that music, books and movies are ahead of fresh food in terms of coming under the spell of Online Gravity. Endorsed, curated and branded goods also naturally do well online, as buyers feel it reduces the risk of not being able to inspect the quality of the merchandise in person. And two of the United Kingdom's largest, most successful online companies are the global fashion retailers ASOS and Net-a-Porter, who have leveraged this feature of the web by stocking the best and most wanted brands in the online fashion world.

The US Census Bureau has been carefully recording and releasing e-commerce statistics for online retail in the United States since 1999. Some online sales categories have advanced faster than others, with books, music and electronics having the most traction, while fresh food still remains largely the domain of in-store.

Online share of US retail sales by category

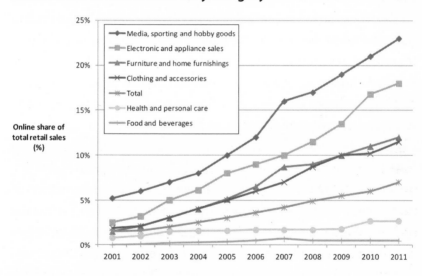

Note: Media includes books, music and video.
Data source: U.S. Census Bureau and Jeff Jordan http://jeff.a16z.com/

Many of the principles of online retail also apply to catalogue marketing, for which certain types of shippable items, such as books, recorded music and jewellery, have always been staples.

Another feature of mail-order marketers that has translated into online success is a money-back guarantee. The pioneering nineteenth-century US catalogue retailer Sears, Roebuck & Company, which in 1907 was the first retailer to successfully list on a public stock exchange, advertised proudly on its letterhead of the day, 'We sell everything by mail order only. Your money will be promptly returned for any goods not perfectly satisfactory and we will pay freight or express charges both ways.'

It's not surprising, then, that some of the world's leading catalogue marketers have transitioned very easily into highly successful online retailers. Mail-order veterans Sears, L.L. Bean and the billion-dollar queen of online lingerie Victoria's Secret are all businesses that have benefited rapidly from their experience of catalogue retailing. The difference online is that their customer base and field of competition are now very much global.

While online retailers such as Victoria's Secret have dominated in their category, their online sales still represent a small part of their total sales. There is, of course, one retailer for whom online is not a secondary business but instead its reason for being: Amazon. Like the amazing river it is named after, which is the largest in the world by volume discharged, Amazon.com is a force of nature and without doubt one of the most impressive companies of our era.

It is hard to believe that Amazon is just over 20 years old. After its launch in 1994, it quickly grew to become the goliath of online books, and today it stocks over 30 million titles. Soon after opening, it quickly diversified to sell music, videos and electronics. Today, it sells almost everything you can ship – a staggering total of over 200 million different products.

And Amazon is so far ahead of its nearest US rivals it is amazing. While Walmart retains the crown as the world's largest retailer, Amazon's online-retail revenues rule and are larger than its four next-largest US competitors combined. That includes Walmart, Apple, Staples and QVC.

Amazon now has around ten massive fulfilment centres in the US and Europe, including a one-million-square-foot fulfilment centre in Scotland, serving the United Kingdom. That is around half the floor space of the entire Empire State Building.

Global online retailers such as Amazon well know the value of exports. In 2013, 40 per cent ($29 billion) of Amazon's total revenue was from sales outside the United States. And the gravity giant has developed a famously efficient global e-commerce enterprise that ships to 66 countries around the world from bases in only six, where it has significant on-the-ground operations: United States, United Kingdom, India, Ireland, China and Canada.

There is, of course, another online retailer I have yet to mention here, one that has more sales than both Amazon and eBay combined: Alibaba. Alibaba began as a business-to-business marketplace for small companies to buy from each other, and it became the go-to site for Western companies looking to source products from mainland China. In 2003, Alibaba launched Taobao (meaning 'digging for treasure'), its consumer portal. The move was designed to compete with a push into China by eBay, which at the time dominated consumer shopping.

With both contestants understanding that they were locked into a death match, the competition became fierce. The market leader, eBay, invested over $100 million in the Chinese expansion of its global platform, locking in advertising on all the major online portals. Alibaba fought back with major advertising campaigns on television, and optimised its services for an increasingly mobile-phone-based audience that it knew and loved.

Jack Ma, the charismatic and funny founder of Alibaba, used his home-ground advantage to the maximum, describing the battle famously in an updated version of a traditional Chinese parable: 'eBay is a shark in the ocean. We are a crocodile in the Yangtze River. If we fight in the ocean, we will lose. But if we fight in the river, we will win.'

One of the key success factors for this tournament was the integration of real-time communications into the platform, so buyers and sellers could communicate with each other at the time of the sale, and this could be done via mobile phone.[1]

By December 2006, it was all over. Alibaba had won, and eBay shut down its site and merged its operations with a Chinese mobile operator. In 2007, Alibaba's Taobao enjoyed an 84 per cent market share. In addition to its original businesses, the Alibaba Group has consolidated its lead and now enjoys leadership positions in many key areas online, including:

- Online payments, which is dominated in many countries outside China by eBay's PayPal but in China is led by Alibaba's Alipay.
- Group buying and time-limited online 'flash sales', pioneered in the US by Groupon but in China led by Alibaba's Juhuasuan.
- An online-mall platform for third-party retailers, which outside China is dominated by eBay and Amazon but in China by Alibaba's Tmall.

Alibaba Group is now an Online Gravity giant of planetary scale. Its listing on the New York Stock Exchange in 2014 has confirmed this and seen the value of the company rise to over $220 billion – larger than two other iconic global Asian consumer-technology companies, Samsung and Sony, combined.

Despite the amazing journey so far, the unfolding global story of online retail still has a long runway ahead of it. In many ways, we are yet to leave the departure lounge. Online retail has been over 20 years in the making and yet still only represents less than ten per cent of all retail sales. This percentage, however, continues to grow, and, unlike the catalogue boom of a century ago, which catered especially for people in rural areas within their own country, this time around it's clearly a global phenomenon. Despite rising fuel prices, Airbus predicts worldwide air-cargo demand to continue to grow at almost five per cent every year for the next 20 years.

Online retail has flourished and continues to expand in a global manner because it reflects the broader nature of Online Gravity, which is independent of geography.

The Future and Past of E-Commerce

While the future of commerce in the online sphere will increasingly revolve around Asia, its origins are in the United States and Europe. The underlying connectivity of the internet itself was developed in the United States as part of university and defence research in the 1970s at the University of California, Los Angeles (UCLA) and Stanford, whereas the World Wide Web was a European invention. Both of these things came together to create the powerful platform for e-commerce that we have today.

Being the avant-garde people that they are, the French actually had their own, advanced, web-like communications service ahead of everyone else: *sacré bleu*! French people enjoyed the benefits of a prototype web in the 1980s and 1990s via a national system called Minitel. This technology, also known as the French Wide Web, pioneered many of today's online services, such as banking and financial services, directory services, social media, and e-commerce for travel and retail. Minitel deployment flourished in the 1980s and into the 1990s. In exchange for not receiving a printed 'white pages' telephone directory the national telecommunications company France Télécom would lend terminals for free to subscribers, which offered an electronic white pages alternative. At its peak, it was a significant channel for online commerce, accounting for almost 15 per cent of sales at La Redoute and 3 Suisses, France's biggest mail-order companies.

At the same time, in neighbouring Geneva, a global revolution was just beginning at CERN – the scientific research lab that in 2012 was home to the discovery of the subatomic particle known as the Higgs boson, first predicted by English and Belgian physicists Peter Higgs and François Englert (for which they received the Nobel Prize in 2013). But before this discovery, back in 1990 at CERN, another British–Belgian scientific duo – Sir Tim Berners-Lee and Robert Cailliau – were about to change the world by blending two existing technologies: hypertext (or documents connected by clickable links) and the internet. The result was the World Wide Web. Until then, the internet had primarily been used for email and file transfer, but their pioneering work transformed it into a new, global, networked medium for publishing and, later, commerce.

The Future of Online Services Beyond E-commerce

Online services where there are no physical products to be mailed – such as travel, finance and e-ticket sales – are also huge global consumer businesses but are often not included in online-retail statistics. These too have their gravity giants, such as Uber, TripAdvisor and Airbnb, and PayPal, E*Trade, Charles Schwab, Ticketmaster and StubHub.

Also not included are online classifieds for real estate such as Zillow, Zoopla and Realestate.com.au, and jobs such as Monster, Reed and Seek; and dating portals such as eHarmony, Match.com and Zoosk.

Many of the online-travel and online-dating category leaders are clearly already global businesses. In online travel, Airbnb, for example, lets you choose other people's houses to rent from over 500,000 listings in 33,000 cities and 192 countries. And there are only 195 countries in the world! And Uber can now get you from A to B in the cities of over 45 countries worldwide, including Paris, London and Sydney. Similarly, in online dating, eHarmony already has members in 150 countries, Zoosk in 80 countries and Match.com in 25 countries.

Other categories of online services, however – such as real-estate advertising – remain more focused (at the moment) on the individual countries in which they operate. Zillow, for example, leads the market in the US, Zoopla in the UK and Realestate.com.

au in Australia. In the highly regulated industry of house sales and rentals, where local law, taxes and banking play more of a role, it is understandable why this might be the case. In the world of Online Gravity, these national, siloed businesses will not last forever, and the clues for this are already here.

To a large extent, we can predict the future of our society by simply looking at what the rich are doing now. Just think about it. From the use of mobile phones and air travel to the latest health trends, it's often the wealthy who are at the vanguard. Many new consumer trends start with the rich and, over time, with increased production efficiencies and rising standards of living, become available to all.

Think about mobile phones. Gordon Gekko, the powerful stockbroker played by Michael Douglas in the 1987 Hollywood film *Wall Street*, was named by *Forbes* magazine as one of the top-five wealthiest fictional characters ever to appear on screen. Gekko is also the first on-screen character to own a mobile phone – one of the first-generation brick-sized phones, which he uses during a memorable early-morning scene on the beach in his dressing-gown. In 1987, such phones were the preserve of the super-rich. Back then, less than one in every thousand people in the world had one, but now almost every adult on the planet has one, with over six billion subscribers worldwide.

Another version of this idea, expressed by the father of cyber-punk, William Gibson, is 'The future is already here – it's just not very evenly distributed'.

So what are the rich doing now online? Buying and selling houses around the world – that's what. While millions are using Zillow in the US, Zoopla in the UK and Realestate.com.au to buy houses in their own country, there is also a growing number of people buying investment properties in other countries.

Simon Baker, the founder and former CEO of Realestate.com. au, is now running ListGlobally – a service that enables premium properties to be listed with real-estate portals around the world. In 2014, ListGlobally merged with Swiss-based Edenhome to create the world's largest portal for global house listings.

Already, one million residential properties in Spain and around 200,000 in France are owned by Britons, who use them as holiday homes and investments. So popular are Spanish houses with the British, the UK Government has posted a special online reference page containing information on the subject for its citizens as part of its UK Government portal.

With a more buoyant economy, UK buyers are now getting more adventurous, expanding their acquisitions into Turkey, South Africa, Thailand and even Brazil. And while cross-border mortgage finance is still in its infancy (watch this space!), other online services such as World First, OzForex and Currencies Direct are providing the foreign-exchange currency-transfer services needed to buy houses overseas.

The Chinese, however, are the real leaders in this cross-border real-estate investment wave. Juwai.com is one example, providing details of international investment opportunities to investors in mainland China on a Mandarin-language website.

This is only the beginning of a global wave of online cross-border property investment by individuals looking to marshal the power of Online Gravity to their advantage.

WHAT THIS MEANS FOR COMPANIES

For most companies, the inherently global nature of Online Gravity can be used to great advantage. More detailed advice and suggestions are outlined later in the book, but here are a few general suggestions to get you started.

In the technology venture-capital community, potential investee company founders are often advised 'we don't want you spending our money on *undifferentiated heavy lifting*'. What the prospective backers mean is they don't want you spending the money they invest in your company on servers and database software unless you *are* a server company or a database software company. Another way of putting this is 'If you can buy it, don't build it; if you can rent it, don't buy it'. (See the 'Seven Ways to Turbo-Charge Your Small Business Online' near the end of this book for more on this subject.)

Many industries that are project-based by nature – such as film, TV and construction – are also familiar with this line of reasoning and would never think of owning scaffolding or movie props themselves when a myriad of specialist support companies have sprung up to provide them with these services.

Most technology start-up companies routinely employ swag loads of other people's online global services, which can provide them with significant competitive advantages, cost savings and improvements in quality. Why not use the same services and tools that the smartest companies in the tech-start-up world, such as Google and Amazon, are using for your business?

One example of this is A/B testing, which enables you to run lots of mini-experiments on your new product offers to optimise your marketing.

In the online world, access to tens of millions of curious users means demand even for niche products can be explored in ways never before possible. LIFX Labs, an innovative San-Francisco-based electronics company, invented a new LED light bulb and pre-sold $10 million of product globally via Kickstarter – the web service that aggregates demand from individuals interested in new products and services. And over half of the initial orders were from outside the United States. The money LIFX raised from pre-orders enabled the inventors to finish the design of the new product, and manufacture and distribute it to a global audience of foundation customers.

One of the key lessons for most businesses is to understand the essential nature of Online Gravity and figure out how it can provide the most value for current and future customers. This should also make business owners aware – or more aware – of any meteors that are coming to disrupt their industry in the way they have for, say, photography and music.

Stateless Income

Many small goods purchased online from overseas avoid local taxes and duties, and have caused some upset among local retailers. However, there's perhaps a more vexing question in relation to taxation for online services generally.

Companies such as Google, Facebook and LinkedIn collect and choose to recognise revenue from services delivered in many different countries via one office – based, for example, in Ireland – in an effort to minimise their global taxation footprint. This modern-day version of a practice known as transfer pricing – where companies arbitrarily set prices of goods and services and assets traded between various subsidiary companies to manage cashflow, minimise tax and maximise group revenue. This is legal but means many governments can lose taxation income from industry revenues that are effectively 'offshored'.

Ever since the world's first global company, the Dutch East India Company, was founded in 1602, commercial enterprises have been using transfer pricing on a product level to reduce tax and maximise corporate returns across their own respective empires. In the 1960s and 1970s, the use of transfer pricing accelerated, as the scale and might of global companies began superseding that of many individual countries. As the fictional media chairman Arthur Jensen puts it in the satirical film *Network* (1976), there are no nations of the world, and no democracy, only massive companies like IBM and AT&T.

But in the last two decades, according to leading global taxation scholar Professor Kimberly Clausing, there has been a profound increase in the number of global businesses using not just transfer pricing on their internal product accounting but also creative venture structuring from the get-go, with the principal aim of minimising tax. The shifting of profits by multinational companies is costing Europe and the United States at least $100 billion per year in lost tax revenue, according to Clausing. And digitisation and the web mean that more and more firms are global, and even simple products are global.

Many of the new accounting practices would be possible on paper but are made more efficient and workable online – as millions of small credit card payments for example for online advertising or other services can be booked as revenue directly to an offshore entity. In the consumer products and service marketplace, this is often easy to see. For example, Google's UK and Australia subsidiaries, each of which attract billions of dollars in global revenue, yet pay substantially less company tax than their local traditional media rivals.

In the typical tax-minimisation structure, used by Google, Apple, LinkedIn and others there are two offshore Irish subsidiaries involved – one based in Ireland and another somewhere else, referred to by tax attorneys as the 'Double Irish' and 'Dutch Sandwich'. Foreign profits are moved via Ireland and the Netherlands to Bermuda. In Google's case this enabled them to avoid about $2 billion in income taxes a year, according to a Bloomberg analysis in 2013 of Google's company filings.[2]

In the United States, a clear distinction is emerging between two different types of firms in relation to this global tax game: *players* and *non-players*. The *non-players* are companies that have mainly domestic operations with not a lot of research and development or intangibles, such as Walmart and CBS Pharmacy. The *players* include all the technology companies, such as Google, Facebook, Amazon and Apple, as well as General Electric, Pfizer and even Starbucks. Players and non-players have different policy objectives and hence lobby for different things in government. Non-players simply want a lower statutory tax rate. Players are less concerned about this and instead favour better tax treatment of foreign income and a move towards the territorial systems of countries such as Ireland.

WHAT THIS MEANS FOR GOVERNMENTS

The impact of globalisation on governments again comes down to a question of tax. Their problem lies in keeping it onshore, and there are two main ways of addressing it: internally and internationally.

International Solutions

Liaising with other nations to create a common tax base would require sufficient political will on all sides, but it is possible. The tax could be levied on things you can measure, such as assets, payroll, sales, customers, or it could take a formulaic approach, as favoured by the OECD and many tax experts, such as Professor Kimberly Clausing.

Internal Solutions

Japan has effective tax-base-erosion protection for its own multi-national corporations. So, for example, income earned in Bermuda is taxed at home. But there is still tension around the issue, and inter-country competition for foreign investment too. So, on the one hand, national governments want to offer lower tax as an incentive to attract global businesses and foreign investors, but, on the other, they need a solid tax base to fund their home nation's growing health, education and public infrastructure needs.

Sweden and Denmark have a higher consumption tax, so that helps to lower the base. Also in these relatively high-tax countries, there are clearer benefits for everyone, such as universal health and education, which leads to more community support for a higher tax base. Some argue that Sweden's lack of migrants has helped to maintain a sense of community and support a higher tax base too.

The United States, conversely, has one of the lowest set of taxes relative to GDP of all rich countries. So, at a community level, the benefits of further tax payments are not so visible, meaning it is harder politically to make any increases in tax.

The web was born global – it is in its very nature. But only in the last few years is it beginning to live up to its worldwide potential. In recent years reliable global payments, efficient global postage, and the growing adoption of mobile and broadband are the building blocks from which the web's global nature continues to bloom and flourish.

KEY POINTS

Online Gravity's fundamentally global nature has the following important implications for individuals, companies and governments:

- *Individuals*. You can buy goods and services from anywhere in the world and also sell them to anyone in the world. Increasingly, these goods and services will include a broader range of things than just books, music and clothes. The global nature of online services means finding a perfect match, landing a job and buying properties in foreign countries will soon become commonplace.
- *Companies*. Companies can benefit from a range of specialist global online services which can help with a range of business services such as online product testing to optimise the design and marketing of new products and services.
- *Governments*. Global income means stateless income, allowing gravity giants to channel their revenues, and their tax liabilities, through nations with favourable tax regimes. Concurrently, governments are losing tax revenue through these practices, and must look at internal and multinational ways of addressing the problem.

LAW 2

ONLINE GRAVITY LOVES BIG WINNERS

In most traditional industries today, global competition thrives. And typically, in each market within each industry, there are leaders, challengers and multiple niche players who can coexist and compete yet still make a good living. For example, in the business of carbonated non-alcoholic beverages, the two market leaders Coca-Cola and Pepsi have competed vigorously for over a century. Despite this, both continue to be very profitable and viable global enterprises, each with a market value of over $100 billion.

However, in online markets, the picture is quite different. For example, in the market for social media, one company, Myspace, was established in 2003 and became the clear global leader in 2006. The young company was so hot it was snapped up by global media giant News Corporation for $580 million in July 2005, and by 2007 it was riding high as the most visited social-networking web service in the world. At its peak, when News Corp attempted to merge it with Yahoo! in 2007, Myspace was valued at $12 billion.

But Facebook, which was established in 2004, was gaining on its rival, and in April 2008 it overtook Myspace in terms of traffic and users, decimating its audience and its advertising-derived revenue. By August 2008 Facebook had rocketed past 100 million users (MySpace peaked at about 80 million users). Once ahead, Facebook went on to continue to grow and vanquish its rival and command almost complete control of the entire category, creating the first and only $100 billion player in social media. News Corp then sold Myspace in June 2011 to a private company called Specific Media Group and Justin Timberlake for approximately $35 million.

Myspace was the clear leader and pioneer in its category, yet today it has been relegated to a niche player. As the market had yet to mature, users were still in a mood to shop around and the door was still open for Facebook to overtake and dominate the market for social media. By 2012 their network had grown to be used by over 1 billion active users worldwide.

Online Gravity loves big winners because businesses online share three fundamental characteristics: they are digital, connected in a network and increasingly global. These three characteristics create this effect for the following reasons:

- Switching costs due to digitisation can be high – the digital part means there's a tendency towards standardisation to support interconnection with other systems and its users. Technology standards, once adopted, have a tendency towards 'lock-in', so it becomes hard or very expensive to switch. This applies to people ('Do I really want to learn how to use a new word-processing program even if it is better?') as well as the systems themselves ('I've got an Xbox so I'll keep buying Xbox games – if I bought a PlayStation, I couldn't play my old Xbox games on it').

- Bigger networks are more valuable for new customers and so become larger and larger. For many businesses, choosing to be part of a bigger network makes sense, whether it's choosing a ride-share system such as Uber, a professional social network such as LinkedIn or a holiday-house rental marketplace such as Airbnb.

- Any business that can serve everyone around the world online will do so and will defeat businesses confined to one country or locality. This is because they can spread their fixed costs across a global revenue base and in turn attract and pay top dollars for the best talent on the planet to do the job better than anyone else.

This law explains why, once mature, markets online tend towards a stable state of equilibrium involving one planet-sized gravity giant like Facebook with no direct competitors, surrounded by smaller niche satellite players like Twitter, Instagram and WhatsApp.

What we don't find online is the more familiar pattern 'offline' of a leader like Coca-Cola *and* a major rival like Pepsi Cola. Were it not for the influence of Online Gravity – the MySpace vs Facebook dual could have ended differently and MySpace today would be a highly profitable and credible global rival also worth over $100 billion like Pepsi is to Coke, BMW is to Mercedes or Tiffany is to Cartier. Instead MySpace is a now a specialist online music company less than 100th the size of the Dr Pepper Snapple Group.

This led me to the shorthand expression for the result of this law that explains 'Why there is no Pepsi in cyberspace' – meaning why there is no Pepsi-like businesses that are global, profitable and challengers to the category leader.

THE DIGITAL ECONOMY RELIES ON PATIENT RISK CAPITAL

Investing in the global digital economy requires lots of patience and a large appetite for risk. Most of today's leaders were unprofitable and incurred substantial costs before becoming the stars they are today:

- Amazon was unprofitable for its first five years.
- Google and Facebook each began without clear business models.
- YouTube was a massive loss leader.

This is something the high-technology venture-capital business is very used to, and why many of the early leaders of the digital economy – such as Amazon, Netflix and eBay – have sprung from roots in the Silicon Valley technology investment community.

Online Gravity means that the returns from global digital-economy investments will mostly come from a few large successes. This is very similar to those in the preceding PC-era, which witnessed the birth of many of today's leading global technology companies, such as Dell, Microsoft and Cisco.

In a review of 1720 technology companies listed on the stock exchange between 1980 and 2002, investment bank Morgan Stanley concluded that about two per cent, or less than 50 companies, accounted for almost 100 per cent of net wealth creation.[1]

Y Combinator is the most famous and successful start-up accelerator (a kind of boot camp for early-stage technology operators) in the world. Twice a year, a batch of founders and new start-up companies are admitted to the California-based three-month intensive program. In exchange for seven per cent of the company, Y Combinator offers participants a small investment of $120,000, its own expert mentoring and the opportunity to pitch to many of the world's top technology investors at the end. Over 600 companies since 2005 have been through the prestigious program and there have been many successes. In financial terms, though, the Y Combinator founder Paul Graham has noted that the program's overall prosperity stems from two or three *very* successful companies:

> The two most important things to understand about start-up investing, as a business, are 1 that effectively all the returns are concentrated in a few big winners, and 2 that the best ideas look initially like bad ideas.[2]

In 2014, the total value of the 600-plus companies that have passed through the Y Combinator program is estimated at $26 billion, but only three companies account for over 80 per cent of this value: Airbnb, $10 billion; Dropbox, $10 billion; and Stripe, $1.75 billion.

The health of the digital economy as a whole is a bit like that of the Monte Carlo Casino in Monaco, where the well-being of the house relies on the patient application of lots of wagers from high-stakes players over considerable periods of time. Most of these individual wagers will fail, but some stellar wins keep the high rollers playing and the house lights on.

Online Gravity also means that early backing of an asteroid that goes on to become a planet brings with it stellar and incomparable returns.

AMERICA IS THE UNSPOKEN HOME OF GLOBAL ONLINE

Online Gravity loves big winners, and you'd have to count the United States as a whole as the biggest. To date, the overwhelming majority of the world's gravity giants are US companies, and Google is the king of these in pure play online – meaning 100 per cent of its revenues are from online services – noting that Apple and Microsoft are larger still but derive a lot of their sales offline. Similarly, most of the world's technology billionaires in the last decade have made their fortunes by founding US online enterprises that have become gravity giants, with the exception of Jack Ma and Alibaba.[3]

Internet billionaires

Name	Net wealth $ billion	Age	Company
Mark Zuckerberg	$34	30	Facebook
Sergey Brin	$31	41	Google
Larry Page	$31	41	Google
Jeff Bezos	$30	50	Amazon.com
Jack Ma	$19	50	Alibaba
Pierre Omidyar	$8.2	47	eBay

A large part of the success of the US-originated global gravity giants is access to capital – the availability of deep pools of founder-friendly, risk-tolerant, patient venture capital. Facebook, YouTube and Google would not be where they are today were it not for people willing to make large, high-risk investments in them when they were unproven businesses.

Investment in digital-economy companies is not for the faint-hearted. Online Gravity means that investment outcomes are increasingly unforgiving, and often there are no second prizes at all.

It also clearly requires a portfolio approach, which in turn requires a critical mass of companies, investments over long invest-ment horizons and increasingly over a large global geographic footprint. This is a particular risk for industry incumbents looking to 'self-insure' against future digital disruptors by making their own investments in digital, like Kodak did by acquiring Ofoto, an online photo service, in 2001.

If, for example, Kodak had made many more bold and stra-tegic investments and acquisitions of future digital giants like YouTube they might have arrested their decline. YouTube, which was acquired by Google in 2006 for $1.6 billion, is now a business estimated to be worth over $40 billion

But to do this successfully, Kodak would have also needed to invest in hundreds of other companies which weren't as successful as YouTube – many of which would have failed. And executives would have had an almost impossible task getting this type of strategy through their board. For venture capitalists, however, investing in hundreds of companies that fail is business as usual. For Google – who came from and understand this culture too – this is doable. Google have acquired over 170 other technology businesses – a handful of which have resulted in their spectacu-lar successes outside of search in video (YouTube), maps (Where2) and advertising (DoubleClick).

Another risk for online media and services companies (and those that invest in them) is a focus on only one or a few domestic markets. In Australia, for example, three companies dominate online employment, led by Seek, which is now facing a wave of competition from the number-one global player, LinkedIn. Seek, however, is countering this attack by investing in its own global strategy, and now has international interests in Asia, Africa and Latin America. Combined, these now produce more revenue than its Australian and New Zealand business, and as a result have exposure to much higher growth.

Whether you're at the helm of a company in the midst of an Online Gravity force field or an investor in companies, the message is the same: it's not for the faint-hearted and you need to 'go big or go home', as is often the mantra in the tech sector.

EMPLOYMENT IMPACTS OF ONLINE GRAVITY

Much has been made of the disappearance of jobs due to the digitisation, automation and networking of many traditional industries – most notably in traditional media – but careful global economic analysis has shown that the internet has in fact added more jobs than it has destroyed.

According to McKinsey & Company, the internet has created 2.6 new jobs for every one deleted. What's becoming increasingly apparent, however, is that these new jobs are appearing in new locations and settings.

The Death of the Regional HQ

Like Caesar's Rome, the online economy is characterised by centralisation of employment around company headquarters. This has potentially profound consequences that have yet to be understood or fully felt.

Employment patterns at selected global companies

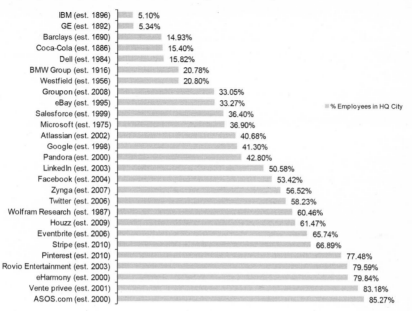

Data source: LinkedIn, January 2015.

Before the rise of the web in 2000, leading global companies such as Dell, the personal-computer manufacturer based in Round Rock, Texas, or Westfield, the retail-property group in Sydney, Australia, typically employed up to one in five, or 20 per cent, of their total global employees in their hometown headquarters. This is great for the workers fortunate enough to share a home town with these companies, as company-headquarter jobs are generally higher paid, more global in scope and typically include roles in global marketing, global finance, research and product development that are not often found outside of HQ.

In the past, there was a natural limit to the concentration of companies around their HQs. As global companies grew, regional headquarters necessarily emerged. Previously, companies typically became more decentralised as their geographic expansion unfolded, driven by the twin incentives of:

- increasing the sales of the company by selling in every territory possible; and
- decreasing the cost by making things wherever it was cheapest.

Increasing the sales in every territory had an unintended consequence that I refer to as the 'Jaguar effect'. In the enterprise-software business, and many others where what you are selling is expensive, complex, and requires a high degree of trust and confidence in the vendor, you need a talented, on-the-ground and socially connected team in every market to sell the products face-to-face. From the point of view of aspiring global companies, this traditional expansion route required a fleet of prestige cars, or 'Jaguars', in every major market you intended to serve, and a talented team of local managers and sales executives to drive them. But now, in an age of Online Gravity, the days of these Jaguar jobs are numbered.

Previously, global expansion needed highly networked sales staff in each local territory, resulting in an abundance of 'Jaguar jobs'. Now, in the PC software giant Microsoft, for example, around 40 per cent of its total global workforce of 95,000 is concentrated in or around its headquarters in Seattle. In online media and services, this figure climbs significantly to between 40 and 80 per cent of the total team. Younger and early-stage companies such as Facebook, LinkedIn, Atlassian and the social-gaming developer Zynga have well over half their employees in their city of initial establishment.

In its early days, Atlassian famously had no sales or marketing staff at all, as its enterprise-software products were so simple and popular they sold themselves online directly from HQ. Company executives around the world bought the software online them-selves with their corporate credit cards, downloaded it themselves, installed it themselves – and that was it. All the support they needed was also offered online.

Similarly Amazon has developed a famously efficient central-ised global e-commerce enterprise that ships to and trades in 66 countries around the world, yet without the need for local operations, sales or distribution staff in most of these locations. Research for this book based on LinkedIn data indicates that over 91 per cent of Amazon's 88,000 staff are located in only six of the countries where it has significant on-the-ground operations: the US, the UK, India, Ireland, China and Canada.

In the same way, Google, Facebook and most other online global ventures trade with and derive revenue from customers in most countries around the world yet have staff and on-the-ground operations in only a select few of these.

As a new generation of companies such as Sydney-based Atlassian, Wellington-based Xero and San Francisco based Box have clearly demonstrated, without the expense of field sales staff you can sell and support not only consumer services online but also enterprise solutions, globally from one or two well-resourced hubs.

This is increasingly important for policymakers as it means that, unless your city, region or country is home to and fosters the creation of global digital-economy enterprises, the number of high-value jobs available in your area is likely to shrink dramatically over the next decade.

And it's not just 'traditional' industries where jobs are at risk. The *Harvard Business Review* of November 2013 chronicles the long-term decline in employment within America's information industries. After manufacturing, the information sector, which includes media, IT and telecommunications, has had the greatest employment contraction of any sector in the US in the past decade.

This tidal wave of change is just beginning and we will no doubt continue to see large-scale transformation of the jobs market in the United States and most other Western countries over the coming decade and increasingly in sectors previously untouched by large-scale technology disruption such as health, finance and agriculture.

While Online Gravity is leading to many Jaguar jobs disappearing in Western countries through the centralisation and automation of many online services, it is not all bad news for the developing world. The World Bank has made the point in its 2013 report 'Connecting to Work' that the rise of open, global, online labour marketplaces such as Freelancer.com, oDesk and Elance means that, once connected to the internet, many people in developing countries can now have direct access to employment opportunities that were previously impossible.

Gazelles and Rocketships

IT economist David L. Birch showed in the 1970s that the majority of national job growth and losses in the US came from enterprises with fewer than a hundred employees. Nearly 20 years on, Birch refined his thesis to show that not all small businesses are equal, with only four per cent of these companies – a high-growth cohort he terms 'gazelles' – accounting for around 70 per cent of the jobs created.

Gazelles are companies that demonstrate consecutive, double-digit annual growth, and they are now seen by many as the engine room of future economic development. Follow-on research by Zoltan J. Acs and Pamela Mueller has identified gazelles as 'only start-ups with greater than 20 and less than 500 employees' and 'only in large diversified metropolitan regions'.[4]

Many of these gazelles – such as Google, eBay and Freelancer.com – are fuelled by the power of Online Gravity and also classify as 'rocketships'. Rocketships are a new generation of online global enterprises that grow from start-up to $50 million in revenue in their first five years. Atlassian, Facebook and Google all fit this definition.

In his excellent 2009 article and interactive graphic for *The Wall Street Journal*, 'How Long Does it Take to Build a Technology Empire?', Scott Austin showed that a previous generation of global technology companies such as Microsoft, Oracle and SPSS don't make it into the rocketship club, having taken between eight, ten and 14 years respectively to reach sales of $50 million.

The rocketships that go on to become companies valued at over $100 million are now referred to in venture-capital circles as centurions, while those that reach a value of over $1 billion are known as unicorns – because of their rarity, beauty and potential. This latter term, coined by Aileen Lee, founder of Cowboy Ventures, has gained traction, and now there's a concept of a club for unicorn companies.

There has been discussion for years in venture-capital circles about the annual number of new tech companies that ultimately reach a valuation of $1 billion or more, says Fred Wilson, prominent East Coast venture capitalist and co-founder of Union Square Ventures. Some feel that only one of these unicorns is born worldwide each year. From the data she's analysed, Aileen suggests it's more like four, whereas Fred Wilson believes it's more like ten per year. Whatever it is, it's a small number, and you don't get to find out for as much as a decade later.

A very small number of these unicorns go on further to become gravity giants, worth $10 billion or more, and a mere handful end up being worth more than $100 billion – Jupiter-scale gravity giants, or gas giants.

Lessons and Opportunities for Local Industries

Employment is being reinvented, and the jobs that are being disrupted are reappearing in different settings and enterprises around the world. Policymakers, politicians and parents worldwide should be mindful of these changes to best position their approach for employment in a new era of Online Gravity.

Immigration is a key part of this story too, as there are talented people everywhere, not just in the tech hot spots where tomorrow's gravity giants are emerging, such as Shoreditch, Brooklyn and Surry Hills. Countries, regions and cities with a strong culture of support for creative, diverse, multicultural communities are better positioned to do well, as Richard Florida has demonstrated in his work on the rise of the creative classes.

But if you're looking to land a job at one of tomorrow's gravity giants, there's no need to pack your bags for San Francisco or Shanghai just yet. While it is true that most of today's Jupiter-scale gravity giants are from either the US or China, companies are increasingly emerging from outside the major markets, such as Xero – the amazing global online-accounting-software company that comes from Wellington, New Zealand, a city with a population of around 200,000 people. And Rovio, which is responsible for the *Angry Birds* phenomenon – the most successful mobile app ever created – is from Espoo, Finland, a city of similar size. Or CCP Games, makers of the breathtakingly large multiplayer online space adventure game *Eve Online* with over 500,000 players worldwide which is built and run from Reykjavík, Iceland, with a population of around 100,000 people.

KEY POINTS

The fact that Online Gravity loves big winners has the following outcomes and implications:

- Big winners also means big losers, so investing in tech start-ups is a risky business and requires a portfolio approach with acceptance of many failures.
- The United States is currently the world's gravity-giant power-house because of its access to high-risk, patient venture capital and a deep technology talent pool.

- Employment in many new companies is becoming more centralised with the web's potential to serve customers anywhere from one location.
- Unless your region can foster the creation of high-growth globally competitive companies – online gazelles – the number of high-value jobs available in your area looks set to shrink in the near future.
- Signs of a new wave of global companies emerging in unlikely places such as New Zealand and Iceland augur well for well-educated, creative and connected communities everywhere.

LAW 3

ONLINE GRAVITY APPLIES TO INTANGIBLE GOODS

Many say that the key differentiator of economics online as opposed to economics offline is that, online, many of the goods are intangible. Or, to quote MC Hammer, 'U Can't Touch This'.

With offline economics, even when the goods themselves were intangible, as in the case of music, there was a physical packaging that you could touch, collect and look at. In music, this packaging moved through a number of technology-led phases, from vinyl to cassettes to compact discs. All three were physical, packaged things that had some artwork on the front, stored the music and allowed you to replay it on your turntable, tape deck or CD player.

So what actually happens when you buy a song in digital format online? Say, for example, you buy Blondie's album *Parallel Lines* from the Apple iTunes Store. Apple sends some numbers that represent the music and song titles, artwork and so on down the telephone line from their computers to your smartphone, tablet or computer. And in this process there is no physical packaging. And so there is no transport or warehousing, and the product itself is weightless.

If you listen to this album on a music-streaming service such as Pandora or Spotify, then the numbers representing the music are simply streamed to you and turned into sound on the fly. They are not stored at all on your phone or computer.

There are a lot of different types of intangible goods and services that are part of the online economy. Digital media such as songs, movies and books are clearly one type, but there are lots of others too, resembling the five good-fortune charms of a new bride:

- *Something old* – second-hand digital goods.
- *Something new* – online video games.
- *Something borrowed* – the sharing economy.
- *Something blue* – blueprints for computers to follow.
- *A sixpence in her shoe* – online cash.

Something Old – Second-Hand Digital Goods

Old books, CDs and DVDs remain the lifeblood of every good flea market. The trade in second-hand books has been a serious business for over two hundred years, with famous second-hand booksellers lining the banks of the River Seine in Paris. Books were the most popular type of second-hand traded goods before the Second World War and today are only beaten by clothes because of the renewed interest in vintage clothes since 1980.

And while online markets for second-hand goods, such as eBay, and handmade goods, such as Etsy, have flourished online, the market for second-hand digital goods such as ebooks, digital art and digital music has yet to flourish. Digital goods are ideal for resale as, unlike their real-world counterparts, they don't degrade with time and use. Ebooks don't get dog-eared, digital movies don't get scratches in them and digital artwork doesn't fade with time.

Why isn't there an eBay for second-hand digital goods, then? In part, this can be attributed to the natural cautiousness of artists and publishers, who, at the moment, mostly don't benefit from their resale and are wary of the risks of piracy due to fear of people keeping their own copies as well as reselling to others.

In some countries, though, such as France and Australia, there is a law that enables visual artists to receive a royalty payment on future resale of their works. Under this type of approach, the artist receives the proceeds of the initial sale of the work, and, if that owner resells the work, the artist gets a smaller royalty on that sale too, and so on. This is known as a resale royalty or in French *Droit de suite* (meaning 'right to follow').

Also, some technologies have been developed to reduce some of the risks of resellers keeping copies themselves by keeping an online registry of who owns what, as is done with company shares or computer software. Other technologies have been developed to provide a mechanism for easy distribution of royalty commission for publishers and authors each time a digital work is resold. Amazon was awarded a US patent in 2013 for just such a system, called 'Secondary market for digital objects', and Apple have applied for a patent in this arena too, under 'Managing access to digital content items'.

If successful, these markets for used digital goods have huge potential to change the nature of media creation and consumption. Imagine if, like the borrowing-slips inside old-style library books, you could optionally store a record of your ownership and use of a book, movie, music album and so on, and this could potentially be passed on with the title. So, in a hundred years' time, you could buy a second-hand ebook version of *Online Gravity* and find out where it was originally purchased, who else had owned it over the years, who had read it, how long they'd spent reading it, and so on.

You could potentially also have, say, your music collection made publicly visible – so others could see online what titles you'd bought lately, what you'd been listening to and perhaps what you'd be willing to sell or trade with others.

An early entrant in this space is a Massachusetts-based company called ReDigi, which aims to be the premier market-place for pre-owned goods. It has begun by allowing users to resell digital music based on US copyright law's 'first sale' doctrine, which lets people resell physical content. This is still being tested in the courts, and EMI have sued ReDigi as they have concerns about ensuring the seller deletes his or her copy of the file.

Despite the slowness to date, there are some areas where markets for tradeable pre-owned and homemade digital goods are starting to take off. You can, for example, buy and sell the following:

Virtual Goods

These include vorpal swords, potions and virtual spaceships in online games. A virtual space station in the game *Entropia Universe* sold for $330,000 of real money. In another fascinating online multiplayer game known as *Eve Online*, over 4000 players engaged in a huge battle, destroying in the process spaceships paid for with over $300,000 of real money. Created by Crowd Control Productions in Iceland, it's the world's largest online game and has over 500,000 players worldwide all interacting in the one virtual universe.

Perhaps the most well-known space for virtual goods, though, is *Second Life*. This online virtual world has markets for most things, including land, buildings, vehicles, clothes, works of art, and a whole range of animals such as horses, turtles and its own breedable, tradeable pets known as Meeroos (which look a bit like meerkats but are immortal).

Designer Goods

Do you like Monopoly? Scrabble? Ever fancy designing your own board game? Now you can. The capability for individuals to design physical products such as specialty board games and have them made at low cost and marketed online is a new feature stemming from the power of Online Gravity. The Game Crafter in Madison, Wisconsin, enables you to have your designer board game manufactured in small quantities for you and your friends to play. It also offers a marketplace for you to sell the games you design to other indie board-game enthusiasts. Their bestselling product *[d0x3d]* is a contemporary spy game about hacking into a computer network.

Some games that started out as independent titles on The Game Crafter store, such as *Flash Point: Fire Rescue, Jupiter Rescue* and the brilliant dice and card game *Roll for It!*, have been picked up by mainstream games publishers around the world and gone on to sell tens of thousands of copies.

As 3D printing takes off, we're likely to see much more of this, where you can design your own clothes, furniture and home wares, and resell them online.

Domain Names

A potentially lucrative online industry exists in buying up domain names that are likely to be valuable to someone or something else and selling them on. Privatejet.com is a good example of this, which sold for $30 million in 2012. And rising Chinese consumer electronics company Xiaomi paid $3.6 million for Mi.com in 2014.

Website Design Templates

One designer, Christian Budschedl, has made more than $1 million in sales of his website design templates, one of which, priced at $55, has been resold over 25,000 times at Envato's ThemeForest.

Global markets for second-hand and homemade digital goods

Types of goods	Marketplaces
3D-printed objects	Ponoko, Shapeways
Art and designs for T-shirts	Design By Humans, Threadless
Board-game designs	The Game Crafter
Designs and merchandise	CafePress, deviantART, Redbubble, Zazzle
Fabric design	Spoonflower
Handmade goods	Bonanza, DaWanda, Etsy
Music	CD Baby, CreateSpace (Amazon), TuneCore
Photo books	Blurb, Lulu
Photographs	500px, Fotolia, PhotoShelter, Shutterstock
Pre-owned music and videos	ReDigi
Study resources	Flashnotes, NoteUtopia, Stuvia
Web templates	ThemeForest, Mojo Themes, Mooz Themes
Websites, domain names	Afternic, Flippa, Sedo

Something New – Online Video Games

Online video games are a huge, new, shiny segment of the global digital economy worth over $100 billion – about the same size as the movie business. This new industry's core products are all digital, intangible goods, and they are increasingly distributed and played online through a variety of platforms from smartphones and consoles to PCs.

Online-games production is among the most competitive fields of the digital economy. It is a highly speculative, hit-driven business. Akin to feature films, a small number of blockbuster titles enjoy the majority of revenue and the industry is very fragmented, with hundreds of small game-making companies known as studios.

Many of today's most successful and bestselling games were created by small, independent producers, including: Mojang, in Sweden, which made *Minecraft*; ZeptoLab, in Russia, which made *Cut the Rope*; Halfbrick Studios, in Australia, which made

Fruit Ninja; Playdead, in Denmark, which made *Limbo*; and, of course, Rovio Entertainment, in Finland, which made *Angry Birds*.

The creative originators of such titles are not the largest companies in the industry – instead, it's the publishers (such as Electronic Arts and Activision Blizzard), console makers (Microsoft, Sony and Nintendo), and online and mobile platform companies (Facebook, Apple).

While there are no games-creation giants, new games are vital to many platform empires and have a symbiotic relationship with their larger hosts. Social games on Facebook such as *FarmVille* by Zynga and *Candy Crush Saga* by King Digital Entertainment are thought by some to be key drivers in extending Facebook's reach beyond the United States. Hanna Halaburda and Felix Oberholzer-Gee expressed this persuasively in the *Harvard Business Review* of April 2014:

> Most Norwegians, for example, don't care that Facebook is the leading social network in the United States, because they do not have many American friends. So why did Facebook displace domestic competitors such as Blink and Playahead?
>
> The answer was social games like Zynga's *FarmVille*. These games, which used Facebook as a platform, allowed users to interact with strangers in an engaging manner, bridging the differences between Norwegians and Americans. Moreover, when Zynga developed its next game, it was able to spread the fixed cost of game development over millions of users, increasing development budgets and, it hoped, the quality of the games.[1]

Something Borrowed – The Sharing Economy

Accessing other people's physical assets – such as renting a stranger's apartment in Paris via Airbnb while you relet yours to other holidaymakers – is one of the most phenomenal shifts in value enabled by Online Gravity.

Smartphones and social media have meant that sharing assets is now relatively easy, which has given rise to new business models involving peer-to-peer sharing. Trust is a key aspect of this new economy. 'People are normally trustworthy and generous, and the internet brings the good out far more than the bad,' said Craig Newmark, founder of Craigslist, commenting on Rachel Botsman's and Roo Rogers' definitive guide to the sharing economy, *What's Mine is Yours: The Rise of Collaborative Consumption.*

Online communities have been created to support the sharing of holiday apartments and houses (Airbnb), cars (Zipcar), bicycles (Spinlister). There's even services to share tools (Sharehammer); musical equipment (Gearlode) and luxury boats (Boatsetter).

There's even a growing number of services that lend money in the form of peer-to-peer loans including the Lending Club in the US, which listed on NASDAQ in 2014, Zopa in the UK and SocietyOne in Australia.

There are a range of automated online systems, tools and services that make the sharing of these things practical and efficient in ways that would not have previously – without any paperwork and on the go, so for example you can book shared cars online either via a computer or smartphone and the cars themselves have a GPS system that enables the share car company to easily keep track of them too. And central to many of these peer lending clubs is an eBay-like buyers' and sellers' ratings system that means participants' reputations are a matter of public record and can be used as a way to reward good behaviour, build trust and loyalty. These systems too naturally are 'sticky', as to switch from one community to a competitor's sharing platform means you need to rebuild your reputation and good name from scratch, thus encouraging participants to stay with one company, and thus further reinforcing the second law that Online Gravity loves big winners.

Something Blue – Blueprints for Computers to Follow

Another really valuable form of intangible goods online is recipes. Not the kind of recipe for making oatmeal cookies but the kind of recipe that computers can follow. That's not to say that the other type of recipe – for example, Jessica Seinfeld's 'Oatmeal Raisin Cookies' in her *Deceptively Delicious* cookbook – are not *also* really valuable!

The way that Google ranks its search results or Facebook matches the faces of its users in uploaded photos is expressed as a formula, a set of step-by-step mathematical instructions, known as algorithms. These algorithms, or blueprints, are a hugely valuable and intangible part of today's leading online businesses.

Consider Google. The world-famous search engine is powered by software, and the 'secret code' behind this software is the central part of its business. While, famously (and possibly, mythically), Google allows its staff to work on a project of their own choosing one day a week – known as 20 per cent time – Google computers don't get such breaks and instead work nonstop for the company 24/7, 365 days a year. These diligent robots scour the web according to an algorithm known as PageRank, devised by Google's founders Larry Page and Sergey Brin. This creates the massive ranked index that you and I search nearly every day to find what we are looking for online. Part of the magic of Googling something is how accurately the results match what we are looking for.

The fact that Online Gravity works with intangible, immaterial goods is extraordinarily important as it means these enterprises can expand enormously – in the case of Google's web index, to cover all the websites in the world – without needing an entire world of warehouses to contain them. And, because they are digital, they can also refresh or update their entire global inventory at breathtaking speed.

While massive warehouses filled with computers are vital to the intangible empires of Google, Facebook and Netflix, they're still tiny compared with the warehousing required by the tangible goods giants Walmart, Tesco and Aldi.

Global Open Recipe Bake-Off

Computer software, such as the *Angry Birds* game on your smartphone, starts life as a series of instructions that a software engineer or computer programmer types into a computer to get it to do certain things, such as animating a bird flying from a catapult. These programs are written in a series of computer languages that look a bit like English, and in this form it's easy for people with training in computer programming to read the code and modify it, in the way a chef can read and understand a recipe, a trained musician can read sheet music or an architect can read a set of drawings. Once the software is designed and ready to work, the English-language-like code, known as source code, is often converted into a format that computers are more comfortable with, known as executable code.

Open-source software is computer code where the recipe and list of ingredients are published freely, along with the software itself. The *open* part means it can be passed on to others and often modified or built upon freely, and the *source* part means it's the recipes in their original human-readable format that are shared, not the final computer-executable versions.

In other words, it's like sharing the recipe itself, not just the cake. By having the recipe, you can easily experiment, build on it and improve it by saying, 'What if I added two eggs instead of one?', 'What if I baked for another 20 minutes?' and so on. Whereas, if you just have the cake and no recipe, and you don't know how it was made, it's not so helpful.

Traditionally, most commercial software companies only share the finished 'baked products' with their customers. This is often referred to as 'proprietary' software, in which the owners keep their recipes secret – under lock and key from both their competitors and their customers.

In contrast to the commercial software industry, over the last two decades a worldwide online community of computer programmers who believe in the idea of sharing code has emerged. They are known as the open-source movement, and the result of their efforts has been nothing short of a revolution in technology. Much of this movement works on volunteer labour, which is organised and coordinated via the web. The products of the open-source projects are most often but not always free of cost and distributed via the web.

The power of the web to support global collaboration makes open source possible. The web makes organising the labours of groups of ad hoc volunteers from around the world viable, workable and, most importantly, cumulative. It also reduces the cost of distribution to close to zero, which means it is feasible to develop products, such as Mozilla Firefox, that everyone in the world can use for free.

What has resulted is truly remarkable. Most of the internet itself now runs on open-source software, and certainly most of the hottest online technology companies in the world choose to use open source for much of their core building blocks. Why? Because it's mostly free or lower cost than its baked-goods alternatives. Yes, that's part of the reason, but it is also because it can be lower risk, higher quality and more flexible.

Having one company with the responsibility for developing and finding errors in a critical piece of software can be a big risk, but if people are sharing a common platform and others are continually developing on that platform, the risk is spread across a much larger user and developer base – it is, in effect, a form of technology insurance.

And most of today's Online Gravity giants – including Google, Facebook, Apple and Amazon – rely on open-source software that has been developed in a cooperative fashion by a tireless global army of volunteer programmers over many years.

Similarly to Wikipedia – the free global encyclopaedia that anyone can edit and contribute to – open-source software seems at first glance to be highly unlikely and a somewhat incredible idea, but its results are astonishing. The intangible nature of software, like knowledge itself, means that it has the potential to be used and continually improved on by many authors around the world, without detriment to any.

Thomas Jefferson, third president of the United States, expressed similar sentiments over two hundred years ago in a letter to a colleague about the nature of invention: 'He who receives an idea from me, receives instruction himself without lessening mine; as he who lights his taper at mine, receives light without darkening me.'[2]

Apple and Google Share a Cookbook – For a While

Apple wanted to create its own web browser way back in 2001, explains software developer and writer John Siracusa[3] and rather than start from scratch, it decided to build on an existing open-source community-software project known as WebKit. Later, in 2008, when Google had the same wish, it too decided to join the WebKit party. So, for about five years, from 2008 to 2013, underneath both Apple's Safari and Google's Chrome was the same engine, and they both contributed to ongoing development and maintenance of this engine, along with private individuals and many other companies, such as Nokia, Research in Motion, Samsung and Adobe.

But in 2013 the party was over. Google announced – like the Church of England in the sixteenth century – that it was time to take its own direction – still open-source, but as a 'fork'. In other words, it would pursue a new stream of development and a new project with its own community, known as Blink.

Forking is a common phenomenon in open-source software – since it is an intangible good anyone can copy the complete project and take it in a new direction. This has parallels to the way in which animals and plants mutate in new directions from a common genetic base – some more successfully than others.

Like ecological adaptation, online technology also continually evolves. Its recipes are continually evolving and updating. As a result, the ongoing success of projects like these relies less on the recipes as they exist today but more on the potential of the software professionals involved in leading these projects and taking them forward. This illustrates why people's talents are perhaps the ultimate intangible good in the online age. And Google's decision to take its own direction with Blink was a signal it has confidence in the capability of its team to take leadership on this project.

Encyclopaedia Forking

Forking is not only limited to software projects. Community media projects, such as Wikipedia, have the potential to be forked too. And, indeed, that's just what happened to create Citizendium.

Wikipedia's lesser known co-founder Larry Sanger disagreed with some of the principles of the online encyclopaedia's editorial policy, so he decided to launch an experimental rival 'forked' from Wikipedia with different contributor rules. He called it Citizendium, and at its launch in 2007 he implemented his new, stricter editorial policy, which he hoped would lead to higher quality articles.

Influential technology author Clay Shirky argues in an essay published in 2006 that the success of Wikipedia was in part due to its democratic focus on the information in each article rather than the qualifications of the contributors.[4] He goes on to predict that Citizendium's greater focus on establishing the identity and authority of its contributors would hamper not help its growth. Nearly eight years on, while Citizendium continues to add articles to its collection, its growth rate over recent years has slowed, and many observers have concluded it has failed to meet the high expectations and hopes of its founders.

By the time Citizendium launched, its editorial policy was probably an irrelevant factor in its aims to improve on Wikipedia, as it was already too late. Wikipedia had been running for six years and had reached a critical mass of authors and readers – making it a gravity giant, free from competition from all but the most radical of innovators in this category.

Open Solutions to Specific Problems

While the open-source software movement is a kind of global cooperative workshop, social network and grand bazaar for creating, improving and distributing computer software, there are also emerging specialist marketplaces for solutions to address specific company and industry challenges. This phenomenon has been termed open innovation – as it is a way of looking to source potentially novel solutions from outside the walls of large companies.

In the 1970s, many large industrial companies such as Xerox had their own in-house, blue-sky research and development labs in which to cultivate and incubate products of the future. Today, this is less common, and companies are looking for external ideas and talent to drive the innovation they all now recognise is vital for their ongoing success.

Because great ideas can come from anywhere and the web can be used to hold quests or challenges, companies are putting their problems to the market, and individual professionals, small companies or even students can tender their responses in an open competition. Kaggle is one such global talent marketplace. It runs open, public challenges to solve difficult and complex problems – often involving quantitative prediction and large data collections. Each problem is sponsored by an industry partner, which contributes a substantial cash prize to the best solution offered within a set time.

One such prize was a $3 million award sponsored by Heritage, a US health-care firm. Kaggle awarded it to the team who did the best job out of the 35,000 entrants of working out which patients in a group were most likely to require a visit to hospital within the next year. Such advanced predictions enable early interventions and can even prevent costly hospitalisations. The competition ran for two years and was won by a global team that included a quantitative analyst from a Florida-based hedge fund, a vice president of a health-care company, a business-intelligence expert from the Netherlands and a data-mining-software expert from Australia.

In another competition, the Government Freeway Authority in Sydney, Australia, published its historic transit times and asked the Kaggle community for a better way of predicting commute times to help improve traffic planning for the whole city.

Patents

In the wonderful 1950s Hanna-Barbera cartoon series *Tom and Jerry*, there's often a 'blueprint scene', where Tom plans to create the perfect mousetrap to catch Jerry the mouse. Another great cartoon series from that era, *The Road Runner*, by Warner Bros., also features blueprints, in which a hapless Coyote, sourcing his parts from the Acme Corporation, draws up elaborate plans to capture the Road Runner.

And it's not just cartoon characters who are interested in these special 'recipes'. We need only look at the blueprints being registered at the patent office to see that real people are creating new ones all the time.

Simon Dewulf is a renowned global industrial innovation expert and CEO of Aulive, a global online innovation tools company who use the power of the web to enable customers to access and analyse the patent collections of many countries, including the US, Europe and Australia. Increasingly, these collections are being published online in large, freely searchable databases. And Dewulf and his colleagues do something very interesting with them. Using clever software that he and his team in Belgium and Australia have devised, he extracts all the words used in all the patents and then groups them together.

In this way, he is able to explore all the different things, actions and processes described in these patents. So, for example, a piece of glass may be able to be washed, agitated, scored, rotated, heated and so on in order to achieve desired changes to it such as cleaning it, strengthening it, masking it or melting it. This is great for ideas generation, as people working in one area can learn from those in other fields. A sunglasses manufacturer may, for example, learn innovative manufacturing techniques already patented and now being used by people in car manufacturing to form curved glass for, say, car windscreens.

All patents, generally speaking, aim to solve a problem by inventing or improving on a product – like a mousetrap. One major fascinating conclusion that Dewulf arrived at by analysing the treasure trove of patent data he amassed is that *often the best 'mousetrap' is no mousetrap at all*. Or, in other words, the ideal solution to many problems is to remove the problem altogether.

So, for example, the best lawnmower is no lawnmower – or a self-mowing lawn. And this exists! Someone has cultivated a grass that stops growing at a certain height.

Self-Service and Automation

The web's ability to present services that are tailored to your individual needs is an important part of the intangible magic of the web. There are two keys to this online magic – providing ways you can help yourself (Who better understands your needs and preferences?) and using computers to anticipate what your needs may be and attempting to fulfil them —automatically, or *automagically* as is often said in computer circles.

We can reflect on this and see that self-service and auto-mation have brought about revolutions in many industries – not just online. From his analysis of the archive of all the patents, if the problems can't be removed altogether, then often the next best thing, says Dewulf, is either an automatic or a self-service solution. In the car industry, for example, we now have self-service petrol pumps instead of full-service garages, and electronic tags for automatic toll payments instead of paying cash at a booth. Also, we've seen waves of automation within the car itself, from automatic transmission to automatic air-conditioning and safety features such as airbags. Newer cars can now park themselves, and self-driving cars are on the horizon.

Much of the beauty of doing things online is simply the fact that a lot of it is self-service. You can do your banking, shopping and travel booking whenever it suits you. And now, with growing mobile connectivity, you can do many of these things wherever you are too.

The web also has its share of automation. When you search for things online, it's usually a two-step process. You type what you're looking for into a search engine, then you click on the best result. With the addition of a service called Instant Predictions, Google attempts to anticipate what it is you are looking for by automati-cally making suggestions based on other search phrases that are popular with other people like you. So if you type 'San Diego' it presents a list including San Diego Zoo and so on. Google's fabulous 'I'm Feeling Lucky' button saves you a click by taking you automatically and directly to the closest match. Behind the scenes, Google also has a huge amount of automation in its continual refreshing of its global web index, in how it chooses which adver-tisements to show to which users, and in the management of its online services such as Gmail.

Facebook automatically reminds you of your friends' birth-days, automatically suggests other people on Facebook you're not connected with but may know, and can even automatically recognise people in the photos you upload.

Choosing which videos to watch used to be a chore. Now, Amazon, Apple and Netflix automatically make lots of excellent suggestions about which other books, songs and movies you may enjoy based on your previous habits and those of many other people.

A wise person once said, 'If you don't know jewellery, know your jeweller.' And this approach of taking advice from an expert applies to any areas in which we don't have the required knowledge or cannot practically acquire it ourselves. It also comes down to taste. It's not just the expertise of a jeweller you're looking for but also how well their tastes fit with yours. One person's idea of heaven is another's idea of hell.

Many of us have a favourite radio station for discovering new music and emerging artists that are likely to appeal to us. 'If you don't know music, know your radio station.' And we rely on the programming of a radio station and the DJ to play us music we already know and like. The radio station doesn't know us, though, so while the model works reasonably well, it has its limits.

Imagine, however, that you had an automatic radio station. One that *knew you* and automatically played music it knew was good based on its music knowledge but also tailored to your specific tastes – like your own private celebrity DJ. There are, of course, services like this today. Pandora uses computers to automatically 'listen' to music and analyse it for hundreds of different characteristics: rhythm syncopation, key tonality, vocal harmonies and many other things. It then categorises all the music according to this information – as great radio stations and DJs carefully organise and index their collection. It also automatically 'listens' to you. The choices you make tell it what you like and what you don't like, and what many others similar to you listen to and like. In this way, it combines expertise with personalisation.

Automated personal advice such as this is emerging in many online areas – not only in media but also in other spheres where good advice is at a premium, such as education and health.

The top 20 gravity giants are well aware of the public's appetite for self-service and automation, and there has been a growth in the patents they've taken out in the last year that incorporate these features. Not only that, but those patents have been the most valuable to their respective companies.[5]

A Sixpence in Her Shoe – Online Cash

The intangible nature of digital media and the networked nature of the web means that new types of digital money, such as Bitcoin, are now possible and emerging online. These work without the need for a central authority to support them. You can send Bitcoins and receive them from others using your computer or smartphone via the web, without having to use a bank account or clearing house.

You can buy Bitcoins using your own, real money at one of many online exchanges or you can buy them from individuals directly. So Bitcoin is like a casino currency, you can take your money, convert it into 'chips' for as long as you want to hold them, buy things with them, save them and so on. You can also convert them back into traditional govermnent-backed currencies at any time using an exchange like Coinbase, Circle or Trucoin.

Bitcoin and many others like it are known as crypto-currencies, meaning the money itself is simply stored and shared as a series of secret codes. (The word 'crypto' derives from a Greek word meaning 'secret'.) The codes resemble credit-card numbers but are much longer. Transactions are shared on a public ledger that says how much everyone has. 'Bitcoin isn't the 194th National currency, it's the first transnational currency,' says Andreas Antonopoulos,[6] author of the O'Reilly book *Mastering Bitcoin*.

And while Bitcoin is the best known, it is still early days in this game and there are now over a hundred different types of crypto-currencies and the space remains one to watch. Some watchers feel that Bitcoin will continue as the leader as the market matures, while others are more cautious. Bitcoin certainly is the current clear leader.

There is about $8 billion of Bitcoin in circulation world-wide – which is actually quite small compared with most national currencies. The World Bank estimates that migrants transferred $436 billion in funds back to family and friends in their developing home countries in 2014.[7] This process is known as remittance – and globally, using traditional methods, this is expensive. On average, remittance using traditional means costs ten to 20 per cent of the funds transferred. So about $70 billion of this money is currently taken by banks and wire-transfer companies in commissions and fees.[8]

Antonopoulos suggests this is a role where Bitcoin can add value – as each Bitcoin transfer costs less than a dollar, versus, say, $20–$30 for a transfer of $200 using current major wire-transfer services.

About $23 million in Bitcoin changed hands every day in 2014, making it by far the largest and most active of all the crypto-currencies – about five times its nearest rival. Other leading types include Litecoin, VeriCoin and Darkcoin. These early currencies have not been without their challenges and controversies, including charges of money laundering and their use as currencies of pref-erence for illegal activities such as the drug trade, because of the difficulty or impossibility of tracing transactions back to individuals.

The largest Bitcoin exchange, Mt. Gox, declared bankruptcy in February 2014, announcing at the same time that $473 million of customers' funds was missing – most likely due to theft. Five other leading Bitcoin companies (Coinbase, Kraken, Bitstamp, Circle and BTC China) issued a joint statement distancing themselves from Mt. Gox and reassuring the public they remained committed to supporting this new form of currency.

In March 2014, the United States Internal Revenue Service ruled that Bitcoin was to be treated as an asset not a currency for tax purposes – confirming many people's views that its main use to date has been as a form of speculative investment as opposed to a practical alternative currency.

Online Stock Exchanges

It's not just currency marketplaces that are getting a shake-up in the pull of Online Gravity but also stock markets. In 2013, a brand new type of online stock exchange called the Investor's Exchange (IEX) was established by Brad Katsuyama, a former senior executive of Royal Bank of Canada responsible for online trading.

Stock markets around the world have sped up over the past ten years. A lot. As computers become more and more powerful, and computer networks become faster and faster, markets can run at speeds previously impossible. What has happened at the same time is that a segment within finance has emerged called high-frequency trading, to take this to the max. It's the Formula 1 end of trading, where, with enough tweaking and lots of money spent on technology and even technology research, you can get a performance edge on your competitors: the other traders.

Most of the time, this is a good thing, which results in more efficiency in the market, but it has been argued by some that it can also be used simply as a way of fleecing money from others who don't have the latest trading systems.

This fascinating story is explored in Michael Lewis's bestselling book *Flash Boys*, in which he says 'the market is rigged' and then focuses on Brad Katsuyama and his innovative solution to many of these systemic issues, through his IEX stock exchange. His principle is a bit like dodgem cars at a fairground – level the playing field to ensure everyone can compete on the same terms

and remake the focus of the market to be about investment decisions, not technology prowess. A fairground dodgem set-up with
five fast cars and 45 slow cars would be a very different game to
one in which they are all more or less the same. At IEX, orders
are deliberately delayed for at least 320 microseconds in an
effort to reduce the impact of automated high-frequency trading
robots designed to take advantage of the slower traders in the
market.

Shadow Banking

Some online marketplaces are so large and powerful it is possible
for them to become their own banks and issue their own credit
instruments directly to their customer base. Alibaba, which
started as China's answer to eBay and Amazon, has now branched
into finance.

This has been talked about for some time, and indeed the orig-
inator of the term 'lateral thinking', Edward de Bono, put forward
an idea of company-issued currency in 1993 to a London-based
think tank for innovation in financial services called the Centre
for Study in Financial Innovation. *Wired* magazine ran an explanation of this interesting idea in their 'future of money' feature
in 1996:

> Edward de Bono argued that companies could raise money
> just as governments now do – by printing it. He put forward
> the idea of private currency as a claim on products or services
> produced by the issuer.
>
> So IBM might issue 'IBM Dollars' – theoretically redeemable
> for IBM equipment, but also practically tradeable for other
> vouchers or cash.
>
> To make such a scheme work, IBM would have to learn to
> manage the supply of money to ensure that – with too many
> vouchers chasing too few goods – inflation does not destroy

the value of their creations. But companies should be able to manage that trick at least as easily as governments do, particularly as they don't have voters to cope with.[9]

In China, Alibaba is now on its way to realising this vision, to the extent where it has generated considerable attention and discussion from the Chinese government and Chinese media as to whether it constitutes a 'shadow' bank. It already has a PayPal-like payment platform called Alipay and has now begun selling investment products, including one called Yu'e Bao, which means Leftover Treasure – a new high-interest product created to attract investment from its customers' online payment accounts. Through the Yu'e Bao platform, writes Judith Evans in the *Financial Times* of 15 June 2014, Alibaba now has more than '541 billion Yuan ($87 billion) in assets under management, making it one of the world's top four money market funds'.[10]

In a June 2013 article in the Communist Party's official newspaper, *The People's Daily*, Jack Ma wrote, 'The finance industry needs a disrupter, it needs an outsider to come in and carry out a transformation.' And it appears in Alibaba they now have one.

Gaming World Currencies

Second Life is the world's first global-scale alternative-reality gaming world. Started just over a decade ago, it now has about a million regular users. Its virtual currency is Linden dollars (L$), which function on the inside of the world and are exchanged for real dollars. Unlike Bitcoin, Linden dollars have enjoyed a relatively stable exchange rate from 2008 to 2014, of between L$250–L$270 per US$. The total size of the *Second Life* 'resident' economy grew to around $567 million in 2009, representing 65 per cent of the entire US market for virtual goods. Gross resident earnings were $55 million in the same year.

Second Life also produced the world's first 'virtual million-aire' – a virtual property developer and entrepreneur called Ailin Graef. In 2006, Ailin announced to the world that her *Second Life* avatar, known as Anshe Chung, was 'the first online personality to achieve a net worth exceeding one million US dollars from profits entirely earned inside a virtual world'.

She started by developing custom animations and objects and selling these to other residents in the game. Then she used that money to buy land within *Second Life* – of which there is a finite amount – and started trading it with others. In her own press statement, Anshe said:

> The fortune Anshe Chung commands in *Second Life* includes virtual real estate that is equivalent to 36 square kilometres of land – this property is supported by 550 servers or land 'simu-lators'. In addition to her virtual real-estate holdings, Anshe has 'cash' holdings of several million Linden Dollars, several virtual shopping malls, virtual store chains, and she has established several virtual brands in *Second Life*. She also has significant virtual stock market investments in *Second Life* companies.
>
> Anshe Chung's achievement is all the more remarkable because the fortune was developed over a period of two and a half years from an initial investment of $9.95 for a *Second Life* account by Anshe's creator, Ailin Graef. Anshe/Ailin achieved her fortune by beginning with small scale purchases of virtual real estate which she then subdivided and developed with land-scaping and themed architectural builds for rental and resale.
>
> Her operations have since grown to include the development and sale of properties for large-scale, real-world corporations, and have led to a real life 'spin off' corporation called Anshe Chung Studios, which develops immersive 3D environments for applications ranging from education to business conferenc-ing and product prototyping.[11]

While Ailin's efforts and capabilities were developed in the intangible online space, they've now had tangible, real-world impacts too. Her company Anshe Chung Studios employs a team of ten to develop immersive online environments for real-world corporations. This kind of 'off-ramping', where capabilities, skills or even assets developed in a virtual world find real-world application, is a growing and interesting phenomenon.

THE WEB IS A HIGH-GRAVITY AND LOW-FRICTION ENVIRONMENT

While there are significant gravitational forces at play among the online platforms for intangible objects, there is also very much less friction within these environments. Naturally, there is a literal lack of friction, due to these goods and services being formless and weightless, but also the transaction costs associated with them can be very low or almost non-existent, as they can be shared across a massive customer base. This often means there are huge productivity improvements, due to some new, technology-enabled ways of doing business.

Examples of this include:

- 'Megalisters' such as Thriftbooks, who buy second-hand books by the ton, scan their barcodes, catalogue them using robots and resell them online at the cost of postage plus a small margin. Megalisters also sometimes relist other booksellers' books and on-sell these too.
- Google AdWords advertising services, and similar self-service advertising services on Facebook and LinkedIn, which enable very low-cost, very targeted, effective advertising to be delivered to customers around the world at extraordinarily low prices.
- 'Hands-free' marketplaces, such as eBay, Taobao and Trade Me, which provide third parties with a really efficient way to

trade but don't get involved in the real-world logistics involving freight, inventory and so on. This enables eBay, for example, to achieve incredible gross margins of up to 70 per cent.

- Commission-free markets. As the variable cost of individual online transactions at scale approaches zero, there are some innovative companies taking advantage of this. Robinhood offers the ability to trade shares for free and, instead of making money from commissions which are typically $10 per trade, look to instead make money from interest on customers' deposits and margin lending.

SERVICES

In addition to facilitating transactions with goods, most of the trade online relates to the original form of intangible goods: services. Prior to the web, services such as hairdressing or running a hotel have always been 'untouchable' or intangible. One way of thinking about traditional services is that they perform one or more of the following functions:

- *Give advice.* They provide you with reviews, recommendations or advice.
- *Enable access.* They allow you access to people or things.
- *Perform tasks.* They perform tasks on your behalf.

Pretty much all services fall into one of these three categories or a combination of them – so, for example, an architect may provide design advice but also help you secure government approvals for building and thus enable access. And these three categories apply equally online. The contemporary web enables you to get advice, get access and get stuff done.

Three Generations of Online Services

Early online services were focused on giving advice. These included investment discussion forums (Motley Fool, since 1997),

restaurant reviews (Yelp, since 2004), and attractions and entertainment listings (Time Out, since 1996).

Later, as the e-commerce capabilities of the web were enhanced,
new online services started focusing on providing access to
markets and DIY purchasing, such as booking flights (Expedia,
since 1996), booking hotel rooms (Wotif, since 2000), and, more
recently, planning complex around-the-world trips (Rome2Rio,
since 2010).

Increasingly, however, radically new types of online services
are emerging that provide markets for getting things done in
innovative ways through the power of online community, often
combined with the new-found capacities of the web to support
mobile, real-time and big data interactions.

I call this third generation of services 'online alchemy', as it
has much in common with the influential proto-science of yore.
Although the alchemists never managed to turn base metal into
gold, we have a lot to be thankful to them for. In particular, their
sleeves-up approach to experimentation – mixing, processing and
testing materials to explore their properties and interactions – gave
rise to the science of chemistry, which informed and developed
major industries of the seventeenth century, such as distillation,
leather tanning, metalworking and the production of inks, paints
and gunpowder.

Individuals and companies are now practising alchemy online,
mixing and matching the web's capabilities as an organising
platform with its networking power and the needs of the public.
And the effects on the online industries that come under its influence are amazing.

Airbnb, for example, allows you to easily find and temporarily rent someone else's apartment, villa or castle – yes, there are
castles available! You can arrange this directly with the owner,
anywhere in the world. It has transformed the idea of accommodation and created a billion-dollar business in the process.

Zopa lets you borrow money online directly from other individuals – which is transforming the idea of personal lending. You can, of course, also play the role of banker and invest in lending money to others on Zopa.

Kickstarter enables you to pitch ideas for new products or projects to others to raise the money needed to make them happen. This new way for entrepreneurs, artists and business people to attract investment from people online everywhere is known as crowdfunding. You may have used it already to fund a project of your own.

Have some ideas for share-market investment? Motif Investing allows you to create your own fund based on your own personal preferences – like, for example, solar power or ethical soy products – and you can create a hybrid investment product that is a mix of many types of shares that fit with this idea or 'motif'. Others, too, can invest in your motif or simply follow its progress and compare it with others.

Twitch, which was acquired by Amazon for $970 million in 2014, is a platform and community that provides a real-time global video environment for gamers. It's like a global cable sports network for video gaming but with all the content coming from the fans playing video games.

Examples of how online services have developed in particular industries

Industry	First generation: advice	Second generation: access	Third generation: alchemy
Business	Yelp	Go Daddy	Kickstarter
Entertainment	Time Out	Ticketmaster	Twitch
Finance	Motley Fool	eTrade/TD Ameritrade	Motif/Vested Interest/Zopa
Tourism	TripAdvisor	Expedia/Rome2Rio/Wotif	Airbnb
Work	Glassdoor/Skillsroad/Wetfeet	CareerOne/LinkedIn/Monster/Seek	Airtasker/Freelancer.com/oDesk/TaskRabbit

KEY POINTS

The advantage of intangible goods over tangible, physical ones is that the former are 'friction free' and have very low transaction costs, lending themselves to the forces of Online Gravity.

The economy of the web is very much based on intangible goods, and these come in many varieties, including:

- *Second-hand digital goods.* There is currently no eBay (or equivalent) for this market, but there will be. Its products include digital things such as: 3D-printable designs, pre-owned digital books and music, online study resources, web templates and domain names.
- *Online video games.* This is one of the most competitive fields of the digital economy and is a speculative, hit-driven business (*Angry Birds, FarmVille, Candy Crush Saga,* etc.).
- *Shared goods.* These include holiday apartments, houses (and even backyards for camping), cars, bicycles and money (in the form of peer-to-peer loans).
- *Algorithms.* A well-known example is PageRank, which powers the Google search engine and is a central part of its business.
- *Online cash.* Crypto-currencies such as Bitcoin.
- *Services.* Online services have developed in three waves, from advice to assets to alchemy.

LAW 4

ONLINE GRAVITY ACCELERATES EVERYTHING

The world is getting richer, smarter – if not wiser – and faster than ever before. And this is largely due to technology, and in particular the web.

The online revolution is acting on the flow of information like never before. It is changing its direction and speeding it up. And with acceleration of the global flow of information comes acceleration of the global flow of goods, wealth and knowledge.

It took 150 years to double the wealth of the nine million citizens of the United Kingdom from before the Industrial Revolution in 1700 to after it in 1850. In our web-enabled world, the emerging economies of China and India have doubled the average wealth of their citizens in just the past two decades. As each country has more than a billion people, compared with the UK's 9 million in the late 1700s, this is a remarkable job that is over 100 times as big, and yet it has been done in a tenth of the time. The chart following, using data from the management consulting company McKinsey & Company illustrates this amazing trend.[1]

Years to double per capita GDP

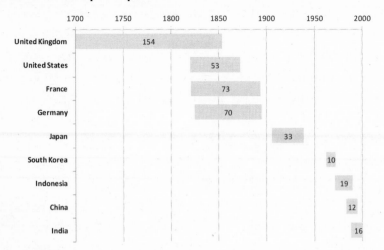

Economic growth accelerating with globalisation. The years to double GDP per capita from USD$1300 to USD$1600 has shrunk dramatically since the 18th and 19th Centuries even across huge billion people emerging market economies such as China and India.
Data source: James Manyika, Jacques Bughin, Susan Lund, Olivia Nottebohm, David Poulter, Sebastian Jauch, Sree Ramaswamy, Global flows in a digital age, McKinsey & Co, April 2014.
Angus Maddison, The world economy: Historical statistics, OECD, 2003.

And while Online Gravity is accelerating the growth of emerging economies – by opening the doors to cross-border trade, online education and global markets – it is now the central driver of value in established economies too.

Noted Harvard Business School scholar Professor Thomas Eisenmann estimates that most of the revenue from 60 out of 100 of the world's largest corporations now comes from platform markets[2] – or, in other words, ones that are governed by Online Gravity. That's most of the sales from most of the largest companies in the world.

Thanks to the growth of the web, huge tidal waves of information are now crisscrossing the planet every second, from city to city and country to country. Internet traffic across national borders has grown eighteen-fold in just seven years.[3] And a lot of this information is financial. Already, over two million transactions per second are taking place on the world's stock exchanges and other types of financial markets, yet this continues to grow and accelerate every year.

Online Gravity is not only accelerating trade, industry and the world of commerce but it is also speeding up the growth of what we know and understand about the world. In the realms of science and academic knowledge, things are continuing to heat up. The volume of scientific and academic literature being published each year has exploded since Sir Isaac Newton published his scholarly papers on gravity in the late 1600s.

When Newton died, there was about one new scientific paper being published every day – around 350 per annum. Today, there are about 5000 new scholarly works published daily around the world. And while Newton carefully read and digested nearly all the scientific literature published in the past thousand years, today that task would not be possible. By one estimate, over 50 million scientific and academic articles have now been published.[4] So if you read and digested 100 papers a day, it would take you over a thousand years to read all the literature.

At the current growth rates, the total number of articles is set to double again, exceeding 100 million over the next two decades. And by the end of this century, we could have as many as a billion scholarly articles.

The total amount of scientific knowledge in the world has more than doubled since the introduction of the web. Specifically, in the two and a half centuries from 1726 to 1989, the world's scientists and scholars produced 27 million papers, compared with 33 million papers in the brief 26 years between 2015 and the introduction of the web in 1989. Now that's a productivity improvement! It's like making a sum of money more than all the money you've ever made in your entire life in only a tenth of your working life. So, if you've worked for ten years, say, it's like in the eleventh year you earn more than in all the previous years put together.

It's not just the flow of information, money and knowledge that is speeding up. The flow of global goods around our world has grown tenfold in the past three decades.[5] This is in large part due to the explosion of e-commerce, with its attendant grand network of retailers and consumers globally. But it's not only retail goods that the web is putting a rocket under. The global buying and selling of assets such as real estate and stocks is growing at an accelerating rate too.

While Online Gravity is continuing to rev things up on the web, the impact of this is most clear when we consider it in contrast to many of the traditional industries and business models that it is disrupting.

Gravity boots are ankle supports designed to allow a person to hang upside down for apparent medical benefits. Online Gravity is like gravity boots for traditional industries. It's no secret that traditional industries are being turned upside down by online rivals. It has been going on for more than a decade. First, it happened within information businesses such as encyclopaedias and directory listings, then it spread to transaction services such as travel booking, and then it expanded to media businesses and, of course, retail.

But the speed of people accepting and buying new technology in each successive wave is increasing. It took over three years for Apple to sell ten million iPods, but by the release of the iPhone it took the company only two years, and by the release of the iPad ten million devices were sold in just over six months.

Technology platforms build on each other and enable further waves to be dispersed more quickly each time. And many of the fastest growing businesses in history have explicitly leveraged these platforms, such as WhatsApp, which launched on the iTunes Store, and Zynga, which launched its games through Facebook.

It's not only the platforms but also upgrades to the web's underlying plumbing that are contributing to the acceleration. The world's telecommunications infrastructure has undergone radical transformation over the last decade, with roughly half of the planet's seven billion inhabitants now online and over a billion now using a very high-speed connection, capable of high-bandwidth, real-time applications such as streaming video and hi-resolution maps, telemedicine and gaming.

ONLINE GRAVITY INFORMS AND ACCELERATES CHANGE

Acceleration is not just about speeding up along a straight line; it also applies to changes of direction. Online Gravity is powering change and transformation too, largely by allowing online companies to learn from their environments.

You've probably heard the story of the frog being boiled alive. It stems from a rather cruel experiment from over a hundred years ago where a live frog is put into a pot of water and the pot is heated very, very slowly. The story goes that, because the water temperature increases very slowly, the frog is unable to detect it and so stays in the pot and is boiled alive. This is contrasted to the fact that, if you put a frog into a pot of hot water, it knows it is hot and jumps out immediately. While many frog experts have since disputed the accuracy of this story, it still serves as a useful metaphor for the dangers of not being aware of small but important changes in your environment.

The brilliant historian and sociologist Jared Diamond points out in his book *Collapse*, which is a detailed study of societies in decline, that the downfall of Easter Island was due to a similar problem. While many people on the island could see the need to change the practice of gradually cutting down all its trees, the ruling elite of Easter Island were unable to perceive or appreciate the effects of deforestation as they continued to live the high life in what was very much a two-speed economy. So the tree felling continued.

Trees were vital to the islanders' prosperity as much of their food was harvested on seagoing canoes. In addition, removing the trees drove away birds and encouraged erosion, meaning other sources of food and crops were unable to be sustained.

The Easter Island decision-making elite couldn't feel the temperature of their water rising as they were insulated from feeling the consequences of their decisions. A civil war emerged and, in what sounds like a Dr Seuss story gone wrong, the islanders continued chopping until no trees were left and they all perished.

The Easter islanders' failure was a failure to adapt. Adaptation requires changing course, speeding up or slowing down based on new information, or new analysis of old information, and in this sense it can be seen as a form of accelerated learning.

Conversely a community that has done very well at adaptation is the company General Electric (GE), which was founded by Thomas Edison over a hundred years ago. In 1896, it was one of the first 12 companies in the Dow Jones Industrial Average Index and is the only original one to continue to be in that index today. There have been many years in which GE has been the largest and most successful company in the world, and its management style has been studied by numerous people hoping to emulate its success.

What is it that has made GE so successful for so long? How is it that the company has been able to adapt in the face of huge waves of technological change over the last century? I asked this question of one of its senior executives, Steve Sargent, who is president and CEO of GE Mining, its global mining technology and services business, and he said it's a form of paranoia.[6]

Paranoia is a mistaken belief that everyone is out to get you however being 'paranoid' in business means constructing an imaginary enemy who is constantly trying to defeat you. This means you keep having to do things better, both internally and externally, and this can be a great motivator – especially when there is no visible or obvious external competition. It keeps everyone on high alert and focuses the minds of the people running the business on the external environment. Successful organisations whose principal focus is internal are in great peril.

GE operates many different businesses in many different industries, but one common goal for all, says Sargent, is to evolve and change faster than the industry in which each business operates.

Online Gravity supports many new forms of adaptation for individuals, companies and even nations. By bringing together large amounts of detailed, real-time information about social and environmental changes in our world, it gives us better opportunities than ever to see the temperature rising and – unlike the frogs or the Easter Island chiefs – act before it's too late.

GROWTH HACKING

Growth is front of mind for all small businesses. They all need to develop new products, find new customers and keep in touch with existing ones. Traditionally, this is known as 'marketing', and it includes research and development, sales and customer support.

Online, there are services to help with all these things. And it is increasingly being referred to not as marketing but as 'growth hacking', especially in the world of tech start-ups. The term was invented by Sean Ellis after his experiences at the file-sharing start-up Dropbox.

Hacking is an interesting word but can sometimes cause confusion, owing to its different meanings. It can refer both to breaking and entering using a computer and, in current slang, to creative problem-solving, often using innovative short cuts.

Hacking as Breaking and Entering

Hacking originally meant gaining illegal entry into someone else's telephone system and has been around since the 1960s.[7] As computers became connected to each other via the telephone network, a new form of hacking became possible: computer hacking – cracking the passwords or bypassing other security to gain unauthorised access to someone else's computer system and files. About a decade ago, as mobile phones became digital and popular, phone hacking again hit the headlines, especially in the UK, as newspaper reporters used very simple but illegal techniques to gain access to private voicemails.

And the motivations for this kind of hacking vary widely. Some hackers are individuals with the simple criminal motivation of theft, others are organised criminals involved in sophisticated commercial espionage, and yet others have turned to hacking for political motives, such as contributors to WikiLeaks, who believe that publishing secret government documents will lead to greater transparency.

And for some people, especially back in the early days of computing, hacking was simply a thrill-seeking hobby, all about the challenge of breaking into official computer systems.

For Chris McKinlay, a Los Angeles-based University of California PhD student, hacking the database of the online-dating website OkCupid in June 2012 was part of his quest to find the perfect date. OkCupid works by offering its members thousands of multiple-choice personal questions to provide answers to. Each member selects and answers 350 questions but also rates how important each question is to them and how they would like their potential dates to answer them. It then runs an algorithm across all the mutually answered questions to find potential matches and recommend dates. But some questions get more responses than others and so you get a lot more dates by selecting some questions rather than others.

McKinlay found his initial random selection of 350 questions yielded very few good matches but he figured if he could work out the right questions to answer – and answer them honestly for the kind of women he was interested in – he'd be able to match with all the relevant girls in LA who were right for him.

Because you can only see others' answers to questions you've chosen to answer yourself, McKinley created twelve fake OkCupid accounts who answered questions at random using computer programs to drive the accounts and was able to gather 6 million answers to questions from over 20,000 women all across the United States. Then, using all this data, he categorised the women into seven distinct clusters – each automatically grouped using statistical analysis of their profiles and responses. Then he worked out which of these seven 'types' of girls most suited him – two were too young, one too old, one he deemed too Christian. One group he decided was just right for him – mid-twenties bohemian musicians and artists. And another similar group he also liked was slightly older and more professional, who worked in publishing, music and the arts.

Equipped with this data on what mattered to the type of girls he wanted to date most, he set about creating the best view of himself he could. He created two genuine profiles: one with a photo of him rock climbing, another with him playing guitar in a band. He then looked at the questions most popular with these women and selected these as the questions to answer and provided his answers to these honestly. McKinley's elaborate plan paid off. Requests for dates started to flood in.

According to the fascinating account of this tale by Kevin Poulsen in *Wired* magazine, it ended well for Chris, as 88 dates later he found his match and confided in her about his unusual approach. At the time of writing, they'd both suspended their OkCupid accounts, with plans to marry.[8]

The Other Type of Hacking – Cunning Problem-Solving

Unstructured computer programming on the fly that requires little preparation, documentation or planning is said to be hacking. It's like the stand-up-comedy end of computer programming: ad hoc, unconventional and capable of delivering welcome surprises.

This positive association of hacking is connected to the do-it-yourself spirit of the pioneers of the computer movement in the 1960s who designed the internet, and the hobbyists in the 1970s who went on to build the personal-computer and software industries. Included among them are Clive Sinclair, founder of Sinclair Research, Bill Gates, co-founder of Microsoft, and Steve Jobs, co-founder of Apple.

More recently, Finnish-American software pioneer Linus Torvalds – the principal force behind the free, open-source computer-operating system Linux – has become the poster child of this movement. Linux, while not that well known outside the technology community, is very important to the web as it powers many gravity giants' web servers, including those of Google, Amazon and Facebook.

And it is this adventure-seeking, puzzle-solving aspect of hacking that has led to its positive uses.

Many governments and large companies, once fearful of an army of bad-guy bedroom hackers, now hold 'Hackathons', or open days, where independent students and computer programmers are invited in to create new products and experiment with new ideas for prizes and glory.

Recently, hacking has moved beyond computer programming to apply to any efficiency-boosting short cut. There are now work-hacks, first-date hacks and life-hacks. And there are over a thousand people on LinkedIn who now list 'hacker' as part of their current job title. 'Hacker' has become one of a trinity of catchy new job titles used by start-ups, alongside 'hipster' (design and domain expertise) and 'hustler' (general management, operations and sales).

SEVEN GROWTH HACKS FOR BUSINESSES

One of the most popular new uses for the word 'hacking' is in the concept of 'growth hacking', which describes a range of clever online-marketing and product-development experiments that have been used to attract and maintain customers – especially in high-growth tech start-ups such as Facebook, Twitter and Freelancer.com.

Large-scale web businesses with tens of millions of daily users are in a position to learn a lot about their users' behaviour and nudge them in directions that are beneficial for both them and the platform. Many of these large companies are known to routinely experiment with their user design and product offerings to see what works and what doesn't.

Below are seven growth-hacking tips from the pros that are easy to implement in your own company.

1. Use a Distribution Fire Hose

Matt Barrie, CEO of Freelancer.com – which has grown from one million to over ten million users in less than five years – explains how online growth hacks can deliver results that are impossible to achieve through conventional advertising and marketing:

> If I buy billboards on a freeway somewhere, the number of users that might sign up to my service or buy something from my website will just be a bump, depending how many billboards I buy, where they are, how long they show and what the creative looks like. But if I figure out a trick to get you to refer all your friends and your friends to tell their friends, you can see the growth is rapidly exponential. These techniques get even more powerful the more users you have and grow exponentially without a corresponding increase in cost.[9]

Many of the most successful growth-hacking strategies involve working with what Barrie calls the 'distribution fire hoses' of Google, Facebook and, of course, the Apple iTunes Store:

> Virtually all the massive consumer internet companies you hear about today tapped into a distribution fire hose to get ridiculous

growth and become big so fast; there's simply no other way it can be done so quickly.

And he is right. Google AdWords was central to the early growth of the now multibillion-dollar online-enterprise-software company Atlassian, and we already know about Zynga leveraging Facebook, and WhatsApp harnessing the power of the iTunes Store to rapidly grow to over 500 million users.

Matt Barrie also points out that there's a growing number of online distribution fire hoses and these are only getting better – with more and more users around the world connecting online and becoming part of these global networks, including:

- Twitter followers;
- Reddit readers;
- Amazon buyers;
- Kickstarter financiers;
- YouTube watchers;
- Freelancer workers.

The fire hoses you use will depend on your sector, but a simple start would be to create a Twitter, Facebook and YouTube account for your business.

2. Offer Targeted Giveaways and Freebies

In an interview with *The Wall Street Journal*, Steven Blustein, co-founder of PrideBites, a maker of washable dog toys (and now also customised pet products) in Austin, Texas, explains how his company has been experimenting for the past six months with what he considers to be:

> a productive growth-hacking strategy: sending free toy samples to users of Instagram, Facebook and Twitter who post mainly photos of dogs in hopes of encouraging them to share images of their pets using the product.[10]

After testing, the company found the online photo-sharing service Instagram was where most of its sales were coming from, so it focused its energy there:

> The two-year-old company, on track to have $1 million in sales this year, gained more than 11,000 new customers and increased its monthly sales nearly tenfold to $9000 during the past six months. 'We found a sweet spot,' Mr. Blustein says.

Instagram is a favourite platform with many growth hackers as its hundreds of millions of users are all smartphone users – which instantly qualifies them as more likely to come from higher-income households.

3. Put Out the Welcome Mat for First-Time Visitors

We all know first impressions count, so many of the most sophisticated online companies pay special attention to first-time visitors. While these visitors are often not ready to buy on the spot, their experiences and first impressions do correlate to future sales.

Over half the first-time visitors to the innovative global custom shoe company Shoes of Prey are there out of curiosity. The company enables customers to design their own custom shoes using easy-to-use tools on the website. As you progress, it saves the design, and if you only get halfway through the process and have to go for some reason, it helps complete the design and emails you two hours later. This helpful follow-up feature resulted in a 25 per cent increase in sales from these customers.

When customers are expressing interest in your products or services for the first time, it's great to be responsive, but for many small businesses it may not be possible to have someone respond to queries 24/7. So many use clever autoresponder services, such as AWeber, that allow you to respond immediately to new contacts – even if it's at 3 am. And you can automatically send a sequence of personalised follow-up emails to visitors who register with your website.

It's also good, wherever possible, to respond in real-time and learn from them while they are 'in-store', and there are a number of online services to make this easy. Olark provides you with the ability to chat with your customers live on your website to provide them with better customer support for their first and subsequent visits.

4. Don't Second-Guess Your Customers' Desires, Measure Them

Imagine if you could work out exactly what your customers wanted before you went and built it or bought it? The famously successful online clothing retailer Zappos did just this. Zappos is so good at understanding customer service it was acquired by Amazon ten years after it was started for over a billion dollars.

Zappos founder Nick Swinmurn decided to test the customer demand for buying shoes online. And, rather than having a huge range of shoes in stock, negotiating with suppliers, running warehouses and finding money to finance the inventory to get started, he simply asked local retailers whether he could photograph shoes that were already on sale in their stores and then, as orders came in online, he went and bought them at full price. In the early days he wasn't so concerned with making money immediately – more simply to test his proposition and see whether people were willing to buy shoes online.

A guide to these kinds of experiments and a new approach to technology start-ups based on this type of thinking can be found in Eric Ries's influential book *The Lean Startup*. Ries points out how:

> If Zappos had relied on existing market research or conducted a survey, it could have asked what customers thought they wanted. By building a product instead, albeit a simple one, the company learnt much more:

1. It had more accurate data about customer demand because it was observing real customer behaviours, not asking hypothetical questions.
2. It put itself in a position to interact with real customers and learn about their needs. For example, the business plan might call for discounted pricing, but how are customer perceptions of the product affected by the discount pricing strategy?
3. It allowed itself to be surprised when customers behaved in unexpected ways, revealing information Zappos might not have known to ask about. For example, what if customers returned the shoes?[11]

This or That Testing

Some time ago, *Wired* magazine ran an experiment where for one issue they had one cover that ran on the West Coast of the US and a different cover that ran on the East Coast. As the issue was the same except for the cover, they could see the relative success of each cover and learn something about the preferences of their readers.

And while this experiment is interesting, it required a lot of effort to run in return for just one result: the sales of Cover A in West Coast USA versus the sales of Cover B in East Coast USA. Online, it is possible to run tens or even hundreds of similar experiments in the course of a day. These are called split tests or A/B tests, as some people are given version A and others version B of the product, and the results are collected online.

The web allows you to do this on a scale, at a speed and with a precision that has never before been possible.

If you run a large website with hundreds or thousands of visitors, you can serve some of them one picture and others who visit another picture, and then measure how many respond to each. And thus you can test artwork, the way products are described or even which products are most popular with different groups of your customers.

You don't even have to have any customers. For example, I used Facebook advertising to run a series of experiments to explore alternative titles for this book. I found that *Online Gravity* was the most popular with hundreds of people based in the US, UK and Australia. It only cost me a couple of hundred dollars to do, and I didn't have to travel or run focus groups and am very confident it has now demonstrated it is the best title for the book.

Many leading tech companies now do this routinely, using a number of online services to help manage these tests (see below). And, indeed, many new online products and services are being developed in small steps that are guided by results from tests like this.

Do customers prefer a blue sign-up button or a green one? How much can I charge for this product? How should I describe the main features and benefits? Does this photo work better or that photo? What if I bundle this product with that product, offer free shipping, and so on? It's a marketing dream come true, as you can experiment with offers in a way that has never been possible before.

Search-Term Frequency

In addition to A/B testing campaigns that you instigate, there's already a vast treasure trove of data available in historic search queries.

The first thing many people do now when they think of something is type it into Google. Simple analysis of the frequency of different search terms can be another really valuable tool for understanding the current demand for goods and services.

You can learn all sorts of information about your market and your customers by examining this data. So, for example, if you are entering a new market that is seasonal, you can learn the timing of demand with a high degree of accuracy from this publicly available data in about five minutes.

By typing 'ski hire' into Google Trends, I discovered that in France the peak demand for tourists looking to rent skis (I know they are most likely tourists as they are searching Google in English) is in February each year.

I can see all the data from 2008 to now. I can also see that the town of Annecy in the Rhône-Alpes region is where English-speaking people looking to hire skis in France is most popular. I can also see that the demand for ski hire in France was in decline but appears to have picked up to roughly twice what it was in 2011, and it continues to be growing. Great information if I was interested in investing or starting a business in this area.

Now, if I overlay 'bike hire' into Google Trends, I can see there's a nice countercyclical demand. As may be expected, demand for bike hire in France is more popular in summer and non-existent in winter. Bike hire reaches its peak demand in July each year and is most popular in the neighbouring region of the Côte d'Azur.

You can see how, with tools like this, some simple modelling of the likely success of a proposed combination of a bike-hire and ski-hire business could be done in a matter of minutes.

This kind of information has been available to large companies for some time to help them plan where to optimally build shopping malls, service stations and supermarkets, but never has it been available in such an accurate and easy to access form to so many individuals and small business.

Online Tools to Help You with Testing

There are now a number of online services that help you manage your experiments in what customers want. Optimizely is one of the leaders in this space. *The Guardian* tested different variations of the homepage, landing pages and navigation menu of its dating site Soulmates using Optimizely. After making tweaks based on the test results, it increased its sign-ups by 46 per cent.

Two others in this online A/B testing market are Unbounce and Visual Website Optimizer. These offer the ability to test differing words and pictures online without requiring any programming skills from you, and they can also create 'heat maps' that show where people on your website have clicked, where they've hovered their cursor, how far down they've scrolled in their reading, and more.

5. Enable easy DIY 'product placement' for your products and services

Allowing others to easily help themselves to your content and services so they can feature in other places online is one of the best ways to virally spread the message and your brand.

YouTube has made it easy for others to embed YouTube videos in your own website and blogs by simply cutting and pasting fragments of HTML code thus spreading the reach and impact dramatically. LinkedIn enabled its members to optionally publish their profiles and make them public and thus generating a monster catalogue of material to be found directly via search engine queries. Online fashion social media platform Polyvore enables designers to contribute information about their products and brands which in turn become part of the vocabulary of user-generated 'edits' created by its tens of millions of users.

Ask yourself: is there a part of your product or service that could be cut up and served as a fragment on someone else's website or platform? Automated syndication via the web is a new and powerful kind of distribution and channel marketing strategy for the online era.

6. Manage Your Social Media and Email Newsletters All in One Spot

Social media is vital to any successful growth hacker's toolkit, but, as we all know, it soon becomes a full-time job managing it, which is especially a problem for small businesses. Fortunately, there are some great online tools that enable you to manage all your social media and email marketing from one spot.

Two leading platforms in this space are HubSpot and Marketo, which allow you to manage and optimise your inbound marketing – in other words, dealing with incoming traffic from customers who want to hear from you, because they are already interested in your products or actively on the hunt for help. The founders of both HubSpot[12] and Marketo[13] have written books on online marketing.

These platforms can also optimise your outbound marketing efforts, from making sure your website works on mobile platforms and its landing page is well designed through to optimising its discoverability for people searching on Google for the services or products you offer (search-engine optimisation) and registering details of the people coming to your website.

7. Engage the Envelopment Strategy

When Airbnb was faced with the challenge of scaling its global business in the highly competitive travel space with limited marketing resources, it came up with a cunning plan.

Airbnb worked out a way of automatically cross-posting listings on its site to the established gravity giant of local classifieds, Craigslist. It also promoted this idea to people potentially looking to advertise vacation rental properties on Craigslist, offering them a two-for-one service: advertise with us and your listing will appear on Airbnb *and* Craigslist.

This is a very simple form of 'platform envelopment', which has been put forward by Professors Thomas Eisenmann, Geoffrey Parker and Marshall Van Alstyne as a way of competing with gravity giants or dominant platform companies – by enveloping their features and then offering more. An example they give is the way the smartphone offered all the features of an electronic notepad or portable digital assistant (PDA), such as calendaring and the address book, but also much more, and thus the market for PDAs evaporated.

Airbnb clearly isn't looking to replace Craigslist, but it certainly wanted to dominate the worldwide market for private vacation rental advertising, and this cunning growth-hacking trick got it a big leg up in its early growth phase.

KEY POINTS

Online Gravity is accelerating change in our lives at all sorts of different scales. On a global scale it's speeding up the development of knowledge especially our cumulative knowledge in science and technology. It is also contributing to the rapid growth in economic prosperity of developing nations by reducing barriers to direct international trade. At a local scale Online Gravity is opening up new opportunities for small businesses to quickly connect with customers anywhere and expand in ways previously impossible. And at a personal scale Online Gravity holds the potential for us to improve productivity in our private lives – as the example of Chris McKinlay OkCupid hacker demonstrates. With better data (more about that in the next chapter) we can learn more about our environment and present our best selves to the world.

Online Gravity is accelerating growth in the following key spheres:

- *The economies of emerging nations.* By opening the doors to cross-border trade, online education and global markets.
- *Trade, industry and the world of commerce.* Particularly in platform markets and financial markets.
- *Scientific and academic knowledge.* There will be a billion scholarly articles online by the end of this century.
- *The global buying and selling of assets.* In particular, real estate and stocks.

- *Personal, corporate and national transformation.* By giving us easy access to detailed, real-time data about our social and environmental context and how we can best position ourselves in light of this data.
- *Small businesses.* By hosting a variety of online tools for 'growth hacking' and rewarding those who use them effectively.

LAW 5

ONLINE GRAVITY IS REVEALED THROUGH DATA

Data is the stuff that makes the effects of Online Gravity visible. In the way that the movement of stuff in the physical world is our key to understanding gravity, the pathways and clustering of data in the online world is our key to understanding Online Gravity.

A friend of Sir Isaac Newton's, William Stukeley, remembered a conversation where Newton said, 'there must be a drawing power in matter . . . and the apple draws the earth, as well as the earth draws the apple'.[1] Just as matter attracts matter, data attracts data. Massive, networked data collections such as Facebook or Wikipedia attract millions of small data contributions from you and me because it is more useful to contribute to a global collection than to a smaller or unconnected collection.

This is, in part, due to the network effects and in part due to the scale and comprehensiveness of the data collection. Networks have a property where their value increases dramatically with the number of participants on them.

Consider, for example, a new type of social media that lets you speak with one other person at a time – let's call it a telephone network. Initially, it starts with just you and me – there's only one possible connection. If three others join in, we now have ten possible connections, but if eight of our friends also join in we can now can make 45 different one-to-one connections. If everyone in your suburb – say, Beverly Hills, Los Angeles, where there are about 35,000 residents – is on the network, there are now a staggering 600 million different connections possible!

WHAT IS DATA?

Data is originally a Latin word meaning 'facts worth taking into account'. More recently, because of its use in computer terminology, data has come to mean a special category of facts – that is, facts that are or can be represented by numbers or digits.

Your fingers are sometimes also known as digits, as they can be used for counting. They were the original digital computers.

While many people think of computers as very complex machines, in reality they are not that complex. At the heart of all computers is the ability to store information using a very simple number system. So simple, in fact, that there are only two numbers in the system – one and zero – which are represented by on and off in an electronic circuit. This is very much like a light switch in your house.

You could, in fact, use your bedroom light switch to store facts and send a message to someone across the street in the same way a computer does. Say, for example, your elderly deaf neighbour kindly offers to bake you an apple pie. You could arrange to use your bedroom light to record and communicate your response to her invitation 'Would you like some apple pie?' like so:

- Light on means 'yes'.
- Light off means 'no'.

Imagine you also used your living-room light. Now you have doubled the capacity of your 'home computer' and can store four different pieces of information. You can turn both the lights on or both the lights off, or you can turn the living-room light on and your bedroom light off, or you can have your bedroom light on and the living-room light off.

Four pieces of information are more useful than two, as you could store the answers to more questions or the answers to more complex questions. Imagine your neighbour knows you would like some apple pie but wants to know 'Would you like ice cream or cream with it?' You could record and communicate your response to her as follows:

- 'Ice cream, please' – by turning your bedroom light on.
- 'Cream, please' – by turning your living-room light on.
- 'Ice cream and cream, please' – by turning both lights on.
- 'Neither cream nor ice cream, thanks' – by turning both lights off.

If you have a third light switch – say, in the dining room – you now have double the combinations, or eight pieces of information you can store and communicate. Each time you add a room and a light switch, you double the amount of information you can store.

Now, say you live in a house with eight rooms, each with one light switch. Maybe you have three bedrooms, a kitchen, a dining room, two bathrooms and a study. And say you used all the lights in your house to store information and share it with your neighbour. You now have the ability to store and communicate 256 different patterns of rooms with their lights on or off.

This is equivalent to one unit of storage in computer terminology, known as a byte.

With 256 combinations, you could, for example, turn your lights on in such a way as to represent any letter, number or symbol in the English language, including: all the upper- and lowercase letters, a–z and A–Z (52 combinations); all the numbers, 0–9 (10 combinations); and all the other common symbols we use, such as !'#$%&'*+,-./:;<=>?@[\]^_` {|}~: (another 42 combinations).

And, with the cooperation of your neighbours in a street of similar houses, you could spell out any word. On a longer street, you could spell out whole sentences. With all the light switches in each of the 130 million houses in the US at your command, you could store 120 megabytes of information. With all the houses in the world, you'd have a little over one gigabyte.

Using simple patterns of lots of on and off switches is how computers work to store and communicate complex information involving words, music and video.[2]

Below is a row of houses in a street, each with a different pattern of lights left on. These patterns represent a number between 0 and 255, which translates into letters and spells . . .

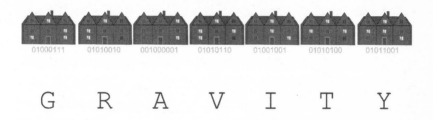

01000111   01010010   001000001   01010110   01001001   01010100   01011001

G   R   A   V   I   T   Y

I thought it was worth explaining this because it illustrates the fundamental nature of data – it is very simple at its heart, made up of discrete, digital building blocks, like Lego bricks. By combining with other data, it becomes more interesting and meaningful, allowing you to do more and more with it.

THE BLAST FURNACES OF ONLINE BIG DATA

To better understand the nature of data online, it may be worth contemplating for a moment where it comes from. It's born out of activity. It is simply a record of people and machines doing things over time.

As activities online are recorded, there's a process of transformation that happens. Like when you choose to bank what's left over from your pay cheque and it becomes savings and no longer income. Or when companies have surplus income and they use it to buy new tools or equipment and it becomes assets.

The engines that drive the transformations behind online data can be likened to the blast furnaces used to create steel from iron ore pellets. There are three such big data furnaces in the online world, which burn hotter and brighter by the day. They are:

- The interaction furnace.
- The transaction furnace.
- The automation furnace.

And ever cheaper computer power and storage are the fuels stoking the fires of these furnaces.

The Interaction Furnace

The first major source of online data is from our interactions with automated online services such as Google, Facebook and Wikipedia. I call this the interaction furnace as it is the site of all the interactions we have online – all the clicking, browsing and mousing around we do all day and night, at home, at work and now, increasingly, on the move too.

Every time you go online, you're connecting your computer, smartphone or tablet to other computers around the world. And each time you do a Google search, book a flight, do some online banking, check the weather or read the news, you're effectively having a conversation with a computer or a number of computers around the world.

Many of these may be very simple conversations, a bit like ordering a Coke from a vending machine in a swimming pool, but nonetheless they are conversations. Online, unlike with the vending machine, the information in these conversations is typically recorded. It is retained by the people providing the services (like the vending-machine owner), as well as by your internet service provider (the bus driver who took you to the pool), and sometimes by others too (say, for example, the landlord of the swimming pool complex). With a growing number of services available online, in the areas of media and entertainment, health, education and employment, and with over three billion people around the world now online, you can imagine the amount of data this relentless activity is creating. It's an awful lot of Coke conversations!

As we now spend most of our working days online, this is a huge new source of data. We are on a computer, smartphone or tablet, serving customers, collaborating with colleagues, researching competitors, working with suppliers, communicating with government, and so on. All this, by default, is logged in some way as data in various computers. That's hundreds of millions of person hours of work that are being recorded.

The Transaction Furnace

The second major source of data is the record of business itself. I call this the transaction furnace, and at its heart are all the people-to-people trades, deals and negotiations that take place online.

We all engage in business of one sort or another. Whether it's using Craigslist to sell an old pair of roller-skates we've outgrown or investing in technology stocks on E*Trade for our grandkids' retirement. And online is the ultimate marketplace. It's proving to be the ideal place to meet and do business – especially global business.

In the 1600s in Europe, before there were formal stock exchanges, merchants met in coffee shops to trade. By the time the 1700s arrived, there were several formal fully operational stock exchanges, in Amsterdam (1602), Paris (1725), London (1773) and Philadelphia (1790). At each of these venues, instead of business-people buying and selling directly, there were agents or brokers whose job it was to buy and sell parts of companies or other types of financial products on their behalf.

During the 1980s and 1990s, most major stock exchanges around the world moved from this model of a noisy room full of brokers buying from each another to the silent world of electronic trading. And, in the late 1990s, Charles Schwab and E*Trade both offered retail stock-market investors the opportunity to buy and sell shares themselves online.

Today, all trades in shares are conducted online – whether this is for individuals or for massive pension funds. But while the venue for this activity has changed, the nature of the business has not. Someone wants to sell and someone wants to buy, and if together they can agree on price, a sale or transaction takes place.

What is radically different, however, is that all these transactions are now archived at a level of granularity never before seen, and this is enabling a new kind of machine-assisted learning on a scale never before possible.

On today's global financial markets, there are now over two million of these transactions every second. And they are all logged and kept in massive archives, which are analysed by banks, stockbrokers and regulators to understand and regulate the market, and to inform future trades.

And while the price of the final sale is an important aspect of the business, there are many others that are of great interest, including the bids and offers in the lead-up to the sale, the number of buyers and, of course, the conversation prior to and after the sale. These too are being recorded and accommodated in the online world. And, in fact, the social aspect of online share trading – dating back to the table talk in the coffee shops of seventeenth-century Europe – has found a new form in online discussion forums such as Motley Fool, Silicon Investor and HotCopper.

In addition to being about money and financial transactions, business is a form of communication, and a key part of communication is stories. Often, the way we frame what we do and how we act is established by a series of stories: stories others have told us, stories we retell and new stories we create along the way. Some of these are fiction and some are non-fiction.

One of the most fascinating stories in the making is that of business through the lens of massive online data. While there are abundant and amazingly detailed online records of the price, time and location of most things sold on the planet now – from T-shirts to gold futures contracts – what's less explored is why people bought and sold these items. The stories behind the sales and purchases are fascinating ones, and I think there's a lot more we can expect to see in this space in the decades ahead.

Large, publicly owned companies that are listed on stock exchanges around the world tell their stories in part through their annual reports, where they report their sales, costs and profits for the year. The numbers in these reports, however, tell only some of the story. In fact, most savvy investors and analysts will tell you that the secret to reading company annual reports is to focus on the notes – the real story is often in these words, rather than the numbers.

The stories of business and the stories of society in general are being told, and have been told, through a variety of media, including books, magazines and newspapers, radio, television and film, and now online. What's different about online is that it offers us the potential to have access to the current story plus an incredible archive of backstories.

The Automation Furnace

The third and last major source of online data is machines communicating between themselves, with no human interaction needed. This I refer to as the automation furnace. There is a growing army of devices that detect phenomena and report back via the web to a computer. Some people refer to this as 'the internet of things'. The devices may report their location, climate conditions, movement and so on. In fact, any physical phenomenon that can be measured is being measured. Sensors are included in smartphones, in cars and even in consumer goods packaging. You find them on farms, measuring agricultural conditions, in shopping malls, measuring people flows, and even in space, using satellite imaging to ensure remediation of mining sites is successful.

In most of these systems, the data is recorded locally by the sensor, device or camera then transmitted to the web to be stored, processed and archived in a shared cloud-computing environment.

Cloud-computing is simply a name for online shared, remote computer services such as Amazon Web Services, Microsoft Azure and Google Cloud Platform. These services have lots of benefits including cost (as they are very large in scale and you only pay for what you need), scalability (so you can get extra capacity if you need it) and reliability (as they are backed up automatically). You can use cloud computing to store information, run software and provide secure access to shared networks. And when you connect sensors to cloud computing the electronic sensors need only be able to transmit their information to the 'cloud', and you can run software in the cloud to automatically take care of the rest.

There are now billions of electronic sensors around the world, in our pockets, in our homes and in our environments. Of these, firstly, our pocket devices perhaps spring most readily to mind. Most of us now have smartphones, and these have incredible power when it comes to data recording. Not only do they know where they are but they can also sense movement, direction and acceleration, allowing such apps as Find my iPhone to work.

Increasingly, our home too is filled with devices connected to the internet. Not just computers but everything from televisions to weighing scales to baby monitors. We are very aware of the benefits of this connectivity, such as the wave of movie-quality television drama that has been powered by online video services such as Netflix – *House of Cards* being a case in point. And we're perhaps less aware of some of the risks. One family's online baby monitor was hacked by a stranger who had gained access to it and was regularly logging on to watch and talk to their baby.

Lastly, our environment, both in the city and in the country, is increasingly being connected by a network of low-cost sensors, cameras and other mechanisms that can share data online. In cities, all kinds of details are being automatically recorded, from foot traffic and road traffic to air quality.

Automatically recorded data is developing rapidly in the car industry, where it is easy to log and track every movement of a car over its life: where it goes, how fast it goes, what routes it takes, and so on. This data can be used individually or in tandem with other vehicle movement information to improve car design and road safety, and to reduce insurance premiums. The practice is known as telemetry.

In the country, farmers are capturing microclimate data to enable them to buy cheaper insurance premiums and more effec-tively use fertiliser and irrigation. Also in this space, a whole new generation of companies is emerging to provide data services that combine remote-sensing technologies with big data and cloud-computing capability. Even in the jungle, remote bushland and national parks, conservationists are dutifully using digital sound recorders to automatically capture frogs' croaks, birdsong and snake slithers to better understand biodiversity and the health of our planet.

Due to the three blast furnaces of big data, there is now a huge and growing mountain of high-grade data on our doorsteps. The questions are what can we do with all this data and how can we use it to learn more about the behaviour of individuals, society and the environment?

WHAT CAN WE DO WITH INTERACTION DATA?

Our interactions with computers and other machines are growing daily. Think about the number of times you interact with your phone. One study suggested that people checked their smartphone on average every six minutes, or around 150 times per day.

Many online interactions such as a Google search have a clear and immediate benefit to the user – you get what you're looking for – but the traces left by the interaction itself are also, on aggregate, immensely valuable. By storing all the search queries typed into Google, we can get an amazing window into what people all over the world are looking for, and where and when they are looking for it. By looking at LinkedIn data in aggregate, we can learn things we would never have been able to access on this scale previously – such as which companies people are leaving from and which they are going to.

Health Monitoring

A generation or two ago, in an unconnected economy, it used to be common for coin-operated scales to sit on the platforms of train stations or in pharmacy entrances. For a small amount of money, you'd be able to weigh yourself accurately – something that may not have been possible for many people without scales in their own homes.

Now, with a set of web-connected digital bathroom scales, you can not only measure your body weight accurately but also monitor your readings over time and have them added, anonymously, to the pool of weights recorded by the online scales manufacturer, thus allowing the manufacturer to take the weight of the nation.

In addition to weight, of course, there are a myriad of other things that can be measured digitally about your body and your health. Philips in the Netherlands has created a simple but very sophisticated app called Vital Signs that uses the camera on your iPad or iPhone to measure your heart rate.

How is that possible? The camera on these devices is very sensitive – and can see some things better than we can with our eyes. It turns out that, every time our heart beats, we blush ever so slightly (known as 'micro-blushing'), and the camera can detect these changes. The clever software to interpret this was created by Vincent Jeanne, senior scientist at Philips Group Innovation, along with his colleagues. As a fun extension, the team also created a Valentine's Day edition that enables two people's heart rates to be monitored simultaneously.

Again, with appropriate permissions and privacy, data from home heart-monitoring apps like these could be uploaded with accompanying location and other demographic data to give a global picture of people's heartbeats in different countries over time. This kind of data could ultimately prove invaluable for medical-science or public-health researchers.

In a similar way, many people around the world are now publishing data from their exercise regimes with a myriad of fitness-tracking devices and accessories from Nike, Fitbit and Jawbone. These digital pedometers are measuring the movement of a generation.

Also in this market is Moves, a general-purpose move-ment-monitoring application for smartphones by Helsinki-based start-up ProtoGeo. It was a surprise hit on the iTunes Store and was acquired by Facebook in 2014. Moves collects and logs activity data on how you get about – whether you're walking, cycling or running, as well as calculating the energy you burn, mapping your routes and counting your steps.

Using these types of digital health data as a basis, we can train computers using a process known as machine learning to look for patterns and then go on to predict when people are under physical stress or likely to suffer illness before you become sick allowing you to take preventative action. Already elite sports teams such as the Leicester Tigers, the most successful profes-sional rugby team in the United Kingdom, are using this kind of technology to predict muscle fatigue, rotate players and thus avoid injuries.

Machine learning is a powerful general purpose computer technology that is one of the cornerstones of data revolution and helping us make sense of mountains of online data.

In addition to predicting trends, such as in health, another key application of machine learning is being able to accurately recognise and categorise things – both simple things we can see and spot but also others beyond our level of expertise. Next we'll explore this in more detail.

Digital Déjà Vu

In addition to uploading our heartbeats and footfalls to the cloud, we are now teaching online services how to do simple things we take for granted, such as recognising the songs we hear on the radio.

Shazam is a simple app that will be familiar to many readers. It can detect and identify what song is playing in a café or restaurant by listening with the microphone on your smartphone and comparing it with an online database of over ten million songs.

SoundHound offers a similar service but will also recognise songs that you hum or sing to it. So, when you can't get a mysterious tune out of your head, you can at least work out what it is. There are even applications to recognise and identify bird calls (Merlin) and frog croaks (Whatfrog).

A brilliant use of recognition is, of course, speech recognition, which gets better and better by the year. I just transcribed this sentence in one take on my iPhone using Dragon Dictation: 'The ultimate game [of] snap is when computers can recognise people's voice and transcribe that quite accurately.'

One of the grand challenges of computer science is to be able to create an application that can translate telephone conversations in real-time from one language to another, and dictation apps are halfway towards achieving this goal. Skype recently released a beta of its first attempt at a real-time online translation tool starting with English and Spanish. So it's not far away.

While applications such as Shazam, SoundHound and Dragon Dictation are getting better at identifying tunes and words from sound recordings, there are a growing number of applications able to automatically spot things in digital video and photos. For example, there are now applications to work out:

- what breed a particular dog is (Dogsnap); what type of plants are in your garden from their leaves (Leafsnap) and what bird it is that you see in your field trip (Birdsnap)[3]
- which friends and family are in photographs you take (a built-in feature of Facebook and photo library management tools Picassa and iPhoto);
- what fonts are used in packaging, streetsigns or book covers (WhatTheFont)

The technology in Amazon's mobile app known as Flow points the way to the future in this area of 'thing identification' as it can automatically recognise all sorts of things simply by pointing your smartphone camera at them – books, DVDs, videos, posters and even household groceries – and then adds them to a shopping list if they stock the identified item.

The research scientists at SRI International who were behind the Apple voice recognition technology Siri are currently working on an app that will be able to automatically identify, record and analyse the food you eat from photos you take on your smartphone of your plate.

Collectively, these applications and many more like them have huge potential to create geocoded archives of what people are doing, where they're doing it, all around the world. The implications (both good and bad) are staggering. In the next decade, we will have windows into the habits and behaviours of our populations like never before.

Measuring Customer Demand

In addition to being able to log and then later classify and analyse people's movements and behaviours, you can also see what they are thinking.

Google and other search engines keep count of every query that is typed into them. This results in a phenomenal data collection of what people are thinking (particularly, what their desires are and what they are looking for), at what time of day, where and how often. And the best thing is that this data is open and available for you to use.

In addition to providing targeted opportunities to advertise to people looking for flowers, dentists and handbags, the data can be used as a goldmine for marketers looking to better understand the demand for their products and services more generally. And they can even derive insights into what's on everyone's minds – keeping them up at night.

A practical application of this is measuring customer demand. One of the great challenges of any traditional retail business is management of stock. Keeping the right amount of the things people want and not too much of the stuff people don't is a key success factor. Australia's leading online retailer, Kogan, has a cunning new approach to this problem. They simply use the number of times people type '24-inch TV', '32-inch TV', '40-inch TV', '42-inch TV' and so on into Google to know how many TVs of each size to order. The founder, Ruslan Kogan, says this works very effectively in having the right numbers in stock.

There are many examples of search-traffic data being used for all sorts of other purposes, including accurately predicting the global spread of influenza. Google Flu Trends is an online tool that attempts to predict flu trends in 25 countries. It works by using a combination of historic data and a basket of words they've kept secret that people are currently typing into Google when they display symptoms. It worked brilliantly for five years from its launch in 2008, but – as a warning about unchecked hype in the big data space – its accuracy began faltering in 2013, when it began overestimating the number of people with the flu. A possible reason as to why the predictions started to overshoot was the introduction of 'autosuggestion', where Google tries to anticipate what you're trying to type and gives you a number of pre-typed likely alternatives. Given the service's previous track record of success, it probably just needs a good tweak.

Like most museums today, the Museum of Old and New Art (MONA) in Hobart, Tasmania, offers visitors an iPod tour guide that provides information about the artworks, commentary and maps. At MONA, however, the device also records your journey through the museum, and a map of this is then emailed to you as a memento of your visit. These maps remind me of the famous Ancient Greek hero Theseus, who used a ball of string to retrace his steps and escape the Labyrinth after defeating the Minotaur.

MONA curators, too, use this visitor information to move and remove any works that people spend too much time with and are too popular. This is in keeping with the humour and reverse logic that guides much of the thinking behind this beautiful, enigmatic and very contemporary art gallery.

WHAT CAN WE DO WITH TRANSACTION DATA?

Just as there is huge potential to better understand individual behaviours from interaction-based data, there is huge potential to better understand social systems by looking at the mountains of transaction-based data recorded online.

Stock-Market Research

In 1960, prior to the World Wide Web, a group of academics at the University of Chicago started a new data collection – something unlike anything that had been attempted previously. It was a data collection of stock prices from all companies traded on the US stock markets. In those days, there were records kept but there was no comprehensive archive of the history of stock-price returns for investors.[4]

What was then a massive data collection job took over three years and was mainly a labour of love. Once completed, though, it enabled remarkable, never before understood, insights into the workings of the stock market.

So powerful was this data that it led subsequent professors at the University of Chicago to become the pioneers of an emerging field known as financial economics, and in the process they developed many of the theories that are fundamental to the workings of finance and investment theory today.

Chicago scholars, for example, used this data to demonstrate how best to allocate assets in an investment portfolio in publicly traded stocks and how to price a special type of asset known as a derivative that provides a form of insurance for investors for various future risks. As a result of this groundbreaking work, an amazing seven Nobel laureates for Economics have been awarded to the faculty of the Chicago Business School since 1968.[5]

In 1960, Harvard University led the world in the emerging field of stock-market research, but, partly as a result of Chicago's powerful data collection and the talented faculty and scholarship that ensued, the University of Chicago today leads Harvard as the top university for stock-market research.

This historical example from the University of Chicago demonstrates the power of archival transactional data to reveal the underlying dynamics of markets and social systems more broadly. So in other words we can understand how systems like stock exchanges work and remarkable new theories can be informed and importantly tested by using data collections like the Chicago one in its day.

Today vast treasure troves of online data from all kinds of transactions, from retail data, to market data to social data, are being archived automatically thus producing an Aladdin's Cave of opportunity waiting to be explored for us to better understand what makes our society work the way it does.

Spotting Gravity Giants on the Stock Exchange

Thanks to online data, stock-market research is no longer the sole preserve of the experts. It is not only Online Gravity that is revealed through data but also the gravity giants it creates. And we can use this data to do our own targeted stock-market research, to invest in gravity giants in the making.

Imagine if you could have predicted that Google was going to be the success it is today during the early days of its stock-market listing. Or Apple when it launched the iPod and iTunes Store. Many early-stage gravity giants are loss-making and profitability is often not the marker of long-term success that stock market investors are looking at; instead, the key factors are revenue growth and user growth. This is also often what technology venture capitalists want to see when investing in early-stage companies, such as Facebook before it was profitable.

One comprehensive study by McKinsey & Company that looked at the successes and failures of 3000 technology companies from 1980 to 2012 found that revenue growth – not cost structure or profits – was the greatest single predictor of ongoing success and the likelihood of the company reaching $1 billion in revenues. Once companies are listed on public stock markets, both their accounts and how the market views the company, as reflected in its price, become visible. Using this data, it becomes easier to see which companies may grow into the gravity giants of the future. The market already 'knows' about these companies and prices them accordingly, and that is how you too can identify them for greater analysis and up-close inspection.

Here are a few tips for those interested in hunting down tomorrow's gravity giants from companies already listed on public stock markets. While there is no hard and fast formula, and certainly no guarantees, there are two simple accounting metrics that many contenders in this space share: highly valued intangibles, and expectations of high sales growth – or, for more mature companies, a history of massive sales growth. From an investor's point of view, these characteristics often combine to distinguish potential future gravity giants from other companies. In closer detail, the potential clues look like this:

- *Giants are built on intangibles, so look for a high 'price to book ratio' (as in, the company's current market price against the total net assets recorded on its own balance sheet).* The market tends to value the intangibles in gravity giants very highly, and usually this is at a very high multiple of the value of their tangible assets. TripAdvisor, for example, at the time of writing, has a market value of more than ten times its book value, which means investors think the business is worth more than ten times the tangible assets the company owns.

- *Would-be giants are scalable and have a high 'price to sales ratio'.* Some businesses, such as consulting companies, have very high value compared with their tangible assets but the market doesn't expect them to grow very rapidly. Gartner, for example, which is a global leading technology market advisory firm, has a price to book ratio of over 20 – as their services are all people-based – but the market value of the company is less than five times total annual sales, so there's not an expectation of rapid growth. Rather, the market value suggests that, due to the nature of their business, future growth will involve lots of new hires, which would add to their cost base. TripAdvisor, in contrast, is valued at over ten times its annual sales – which indicates that the market thinks it is well positioned to continue to grow its revenue base significantly without the need for additional staff.

- *Today's giants have a trailing revenue-growth story.* Some mature giants, such as Amazon, may not currently have double-digit price to sales ratios as they have already scaled. These giants will, however, be visible by looking at trailing revenue growth with double-digit per annum sales growth over the past three to five years.

As an example of this approach, have a look at the table below of ten listed companies. At the time of writing, investors rated all ten of these companies as highly knowledge-centric, because the market value of each of them is more than seven times the net tangible assets as measured by the price-to-book ratio. This means the people, intellectual property and brand assets are the keys to future value creation in these enterprises.

Seven of the companies also enjoy high expectations from the market as shown by their future sales growth potential being valued at over ten times their current sales in their price to sales ratio.

Gartner and IBM, however, don't enjoy the same price to sales ratios, indicating the market doesn't expect much in the way of dramatic short-term or mid-term sales growth, and this may be due to the fact that both are very much mature professional services businesses and at the moment the revenue they earn is largely a function of how many employees they have – something that is slower to grow than web services.

Spotting Gravity Giants on the Stock Exchange

Selected publicly listed technology companies, many gravity giants and potential future gravity giants enjoy double-digit Price-to-book and Price-to-sales ratios.

Company	Price to book ratio	Price to sales ratio
Demandware	7	20
Facebook	13	28
Gartner	22	4
IBM	7	2
LinkedIn	11	19
Salesforce	12	9
Shutterstock	13	10
TripAdvisor	12	11
Workday	13	19
Yelp	8	16

Source data: Google Finance, 20 December 2014

WHAT CAN WE DO WITH AUTOMATED DATA?

Now let's turn to automatically generated sensor data – the third furnace of online big data – and the potential it gives us to better understand our enviornment.

Tracking Environmental Change

Sensor data on a scale never before contemplated is being captured in our urban, rural and natural environments. The potential impact of this is huge and yet to be fully appreciated. Sensor data provides us with feedback that can improve the design of practically every aspect of everything we use in today's society.

Since the early 2000s, our understanding of climate change has been informed and continuously updated by the Argo global network of over 3000 floating sensors from over 30 different nations that measure the Earth's oceans' temperature, salinity and currents. Most major cities around the world are now covered by security cameras, recording 24/7 vision of our streets and the movement of people upon them. Traffic cameras, too, record car, bus and truck movements in real-time, and are being used to help manage traffic flows. Within many new cars and trucks are an array of sophisticated sensors that measure every movement of the vehicle – every gear change, steering-wheel turn and pressing of the brakes. In-vehicle sensors measure fuel consumption, acceleration, rotation and vibration in real-time. Many leading vehicle companies, such as Tesla Motors and Volvo Trucks, are collecting this treasure trove of data from their vehicles and storing it centrally for analysis, to better inform their design of safer, more efficient and more reliable cars and trucks of the future.

Spillover Uses

One of the interesting effects of this kind of en masse data collection is the potential spillover benefit from its original purpose. If, for example, the different trucks of one fleet were to all contribute data to a central data collection, this data could be used to better understand not only the trucks but also the road network itself, along with the performance of individual drivers.

NEW THREATS FOR ENTERPRISES FROM ONLINE DATA

We are all aware of the massive changes that technology and the new business models it enables have brought about in every industry. Traditional business and, indeed, entire industries have been turned on their heads by high-growth global companies that have digital information and the web in their bloodstreams.

Kodak once dominated the photography industry and, along with its challenger Fujifilm, pretty much ruled the waves in terms of photographic image making on Planet Earth for nearly a hundred years. As *The Economist* recalled on 14 January 2012, very shortly before the company filed for bankruptcy protection, 'By 1976 Kodak accounted for 90% of film and 85% of camera sales in America. Until the 1990s it was regularly rated one of the world's five most valuable brands.'[6]

In the nineties, the world began to embrace digital photography, and in the noughties it fell in love with smartphones. By 2012, Kodak's fortunes had well and truly faded. Kodak still continues to trade today as a highly respected specialist professional-imaging company, but in terms of scale it is a shadow of its former glory, operating at around a twentieth of its size in its heyday.

Why did this happen? Many have asked this question, and the overly simple answer is that it wasn't able to keep up with movements in technology and the marketplace. Kodak – and many others who have endured a similar fate – has been painted as the slow, out-of-touch incumbent.

This is far from the truth. Kodak had a huge technology research division. In 1997, it spent $1 billion on research and development from the $14 billion it received in sales, and it had on its team some of the best executives that money could hire. On the board, it had a professor of economics from Berkeley, a director of media and technology from Massachusetts Institute of Technology (MIT), the retired CEO of the New York Stock Exchange and the retired CEO of the German tech giant Siemens.

A better explanation as to why it faltered is offered by the author and thinker Professor Clayton Christensen. He suggests that companies facing changes in their market respond rationally and logically, but they are simply not equipped to deal with dramatic, ice-age-scale ones.

Christensen's *The Innovator's Dilemma* is probably the most influential and important book about company strategy in the last 20 years. It was written in 1997, the year Steve Jobs returned to Apple. And, according to Jobs's biographer Walter Isaacson, the Apple leader said it was 'deeply influential' to him. In it, Christensen outlines his theory as to why large, established companies routinely fail in the face of what he calls 'disruptive' technologies. Here's how it works: New market entrants use new generation technology to create lower-priced products, then existing market players' response is usually to go upmarket – or, in other words, to abandon lower-price segments of the market. These segments are less profitable, so they let the new entrants have them and instead focus on higher-price, more profitable products and customers.

Personally, in my work advising boards, I have heard experienced and wise board members recite this same mantra first-hand: 'we need to go up the value chain', they say. And this dominant mode of thinking applies to consumer businesses as well as businesses selling to other businesses.

And this is what Kodak did. It moved out of 'low-end' consumer photography and increasingly into 'high-end' professional services. Despite having an early foothold in digital consumer photography, it didn't work out in the way the company had hoped. It was number two behind Sony in digital-camera sales in

2001 and acquired Ofoto, a California-based online photography service later rebranded Kodak Gallery. However, its online and digital activities never grew fast enough to replace the decline of its core business of photographic film and photofinishing services. And there was always an inherent tension about digital cannibalising that core business.

Kodak behaved rationally. What happens, says Christensen, is that the new entrants start with cheap products or services on the new technology platform, and they too make an upstream journey in the value chain, eventually usurping the existing industry players.

Christensen makes the point that this has also happened in many traditional industries, such as car making. Toyota, he argues, didn't start their entry into Western markets by selling luxury cars and SUVs; instead it started by selling very cheap, small and simple cars – an entry point that it came to dominate – then moved up from there. Where markets under the influence of Online Gravity differ, however, is that while Japanese car makers such as Toyota have been hugely successful in expanding their global market share, they still face strong and very robust competition from domestic players in the US and Europe. And in the case of Kodak, the double punch of the transition to digital cameras and then the smartphone, with the ability of these technologies not only to take photographs but also to publish them online, nearly killed it stone dead.

The transition of the photography industry to the online sphere exposed it to the forces of Online Gravity, which creates its own winners and losers, writ large. In early 2004, Kodak was delisted from the Dow Jones Industrial Average index, having been a member for 74 consecutive years. Also in 2004, a new company was formed in Canada called Ludicorp, which created the much-respected online photo-sharing community Flickr, and one of the first 'social' photography services that allowed for tagging, groups and public browsing.

In January 2005, Kodak acquired the Israel-based OREX, a digital X-ray company for medical patients, for $50 million in cash, and Creo, a Canadian company that provides technology for the high-end commercial printing industry, for $980 million cash. And also in 2005, Yahoo!, in an effort to revitalise by diversifying into amateur photography and user-generated content, acquired Flickr for $35 million. Flickr is now the worlds largest photography community and among the Top 100 web properties in the United States and among the Top 200 worldwide.[7]

In late 2010, as Standard & Poor's removed Kodak from its S&P 500 index in New York, a new company was born in San Francisco, named as a combination of 'instant camera' and 'telegram'. Instagram was a huge and rapid success, aligned with the growing number of iPhone users worldwide. It went from zero to 35 million active users in less than two years.[8] In April 2012, Instagram was acquired by Facebook for approximately $1 billion in cash and stock, to provide an expanded mobile footprint for the company. In 2014, Instagram had grown to over 300 million users, making it larger than Twitter.

Flickr in the online space and Instagram later in smartphones were both created with different business models to provide a new generation of digital services for this era. Shutterfly, another venture capital-based start-up emerged to dominate the 'conversion' part of the business – making prints and photobooks from digital images – leaving very little space in the consumer photography business left for Kodak.

IS DATA THE NEW GOLD?

They used to say that those who have the gold make the rules. In other words, those with the valuable, scarce resources that others want or need can leverage their position to set the terms of engagement for any business.

Throughout history, the things that are in most demand have changed. In the first days of globalisation in very early modern Europe, spices such as pepper, ginger and cinnamon were hugely sought-after commodities that were imported from the East Indies (South-East Asia) by the very powerful Dutch East India Company. Pepper was even known as 'black gold' and occasionally used as a form of currency by traders.

The late Peter Munro, emeritus professor of economics from the University of Toronto, has shown that there was huge demand for these spices at this time, and their cost was 40 to 70 times what it is today. And sugar was 500 times as expensive. So, to buy 100 grams of pepper in London in 1438 cost about half a day's pay for a master carpenter. To give you a sense of perspective, the average hourly rate for a master carpenter in the US today is around $25 per hour, which would mean that 100 grams of pepper would cost in today's money about $100. A kilogram bag of sugar would have set you back nearly a full week's wages. You couldn't afford to have too much of a sweet tooth at those prices.

The price of most spices has obviously come down, thanks to greater efficiencies in production and transportation, and greater competition in trade. When comparing the cost of spices from 500 years ago in Europe to today's prices in your supermarket, however, saffron is the odd one out.

Saffron was expensive then and remains expensive today. I understand that's because its production is a very manual process, as the spice comes from flowers that produce only three saffron threads each. So the supply, even today, remains very constrained.

Supply of some online data is also constrained. A good example of this is sales leads (as in the first step of the sales process, whereby likely customers are identified). In David Mamet's brilliant play and movie *Glengarry Glen Ross*, the most promising sales leads are finite and rationed out as a form of power distribution. In the online world, there are some sales leads that are hugely valuable and also finite. For example, the number of people with lung disease contracted from asbestos poisoning is small and finite (thankfully) and extremely valuable to the compensation lawyers who make a living representing these people. As a consequence, 'mesothelioma' is one of the most expensive keywords you can buy on Google AdWords, at over $300 per click. Lawyers know that, when people type this into Google, they or someone in their family has most likely just had a diagnosis.

Online data is like gold as it is reusable, malleable and has the potential to be transformed into very valuable and actionable information for a multitude of purposes. Unlike gold, however, the value of online data is cumulative. One kilogram of gold is worth the same to you and me. It is even worth the same to someone who has a lot of gold, say the Federal Reserve Bank of New York, who have 7000 kg already in an underground safe in Manhattan. Data however is different. One gigabyte of data can be worth a lot more to Facebook or Google than to you or me and many other companies. Why? Because they can connect and combine it with other data in infinite combinations with mountains of other data to produce new value both for its users, advertisers and commercial partners. This leads to a positive feedback cycle where the organisations with the most data are best positioned to take advantage from and prepared to invest in new data and data services. And so we have another key force influencing the formation of gravity giants – data aggregation.

KEY POINTS

Data is what makes the effects of Online Gravity visible, along three main lines:

- *Nature.* Online data is simply a record of people and machines doing things over time, digitised into discrete building blocks that can be usefully put together.

- *Sources.* Online data is generated from three sources: from people browsing the web and interacting with online services like Google search; from people transacting with each other like eBay purchases and increasingly from machines and sensors automatically recording data like Tesla cars, that can automatically log where each of them drives. Each of these sources is acting as a huge global data furnace generating more and more data every day fuelled by ever cheaper computer power and storage.
- *Uses.* Online data, especially when aggregated, can be very valuable and used for health monitoring, digital recognition, measuring customer demand, stock-market research, spotting gravity giants on the stock exchange, tracking environmental change, and much more. The context-sensitive nature of online data means its potential value increases dramatically with scale.

LAW 6

ONLINE GRAVITY IS NETWORKED NOT TRIBAL

Many businesses in the traditional economy enjoy ongoing loyalty from customers, who may even have bought their products for generations.

Brand loyalty relates to our tribal roots. In pre-industrial times, many of us lived together in rural villages, communities or tribes with shared histories, habits and tastes. Think of the Scots – they've established one of the clearest and most distinctive identities on the planet by their choice of tartans, bagpipes and offal-based smallgoods. Over time, this regional taste-making and tribalism morphs into intergenerational loyalty.

Consider cars – many families have a preferred brand of car that has served them for generations. Some families have in effect become *Ford families*, for example. Farmers have a loyalty to tractor brands that is phenomenal. Some brands, such as the leading John Deere (they are the green ones, for the city dwellers), enjoy repurchase rates of over 75 per cent for some lines.

Online Gravity, however, obeys different laws – it's less tribal and more networked. Because many products in the online world have built-in benefits related to the network, customers may choose between online brands on taste and features initially, but once one of them reaches a planetary scale, its pull becomes irresistible. No matter how big a Myspace fan you are, it is unlikely you would not have migrated to Facebook once it reached critical mass. You may have loved the search engine AltaVista in its heyday, but you probably didn't use it in its last years (it finally 'closed' in 2013).

This is why there's no Pepsi or Avis-like companies that are large established and successful rivals to the leaders in cyberspace. Myspace didn't go on to become a large credible rival to Facebook as Pepsi is to Coke or Avis is to Hertz. Instead, once they've reached maturity, online markets are characterised by a leading brand dominating with room only for a number of small niche brands but no large, tribal rivals, such as (coming back to tractors) Massey Ferguson (the red ones), Caterpillar (the yellow ones) and New Holland (the blue ones).

This chapter looks at these ideas from a variety of perspectives, and explores how Online Gravity connects people to services and products in different and new ways from those of traditional industries. And, at the end, we look at how you can use the network powers of Online Gravity to better navigate valuable new collections of personal health information and where these networked online services are heading.

WHERE DOES BRAND LOYALTY COME FROM?

In traditional industries, brand loyalty and the confidence it gives the companies that enjoy it has enabled and supported long-term investment, growth and diversification of many businesses. Many companies have developed reputable brands, both for them and the products they produce, which have become hallmarks of excellence in their industries and that have spanned many decades. So where did brands come from?

In the early farming economies, where you lived was very important to your survival and prosperity. Everyone was tied to one bit of land or another – whether you owned it or were part of a community who worked on it. Identification with the distinctive features of the land and its agricultural history was important, as it was a way of sharing information that could later be useful to your kids and future ancestors. Many people's family names reflected their particular geographical origins.

As travel and trade grew, tribal distinctions were important in demonstrating your identity to other tribes. The Scots, the Irish and their ancient Celtic cousins developed sophisticated heraldry and tartan clothing to indicate which tribe they belonged to – especially for battle or ceremonial use. As more cities arose and replaced villages as the main centres of social activity, the quality and quantity of trade grew. As trade grew and truly globalised, with goods taking to the high seas, federations of cities soon made more sense than solo cities, and there was a need to centrally fund a naval force that no one city could afford on its own, and so nation states emerged.

From the Renaissance onwards, there was a series of European, colonial, sea-based empires that defined their nation sponsors back home and whose successes and failures were based on a combination of the host countries' naval power and their capability and value as trading partners. As trade became more international, brands were no longer simply a mark of superior quality compared with local rivals but also started to become tokens in a bigger board game.

The greater the number of people living in cities, the lesser their need to identify with specific regional origins and customs. Nonetheless, people still felt a deep need for belonging. In place of local costumes, dances and cuisine arose a new system of signs more suited to the emerging industrial economy: brands. So, instead of showing your neighbours which clan you belonged to by the pattern on your kilt, you could now show them the cut of your jib by which local inn you chose to frequent or which local football team you supported.

Advertising, like the tribal customs it replaced, started out very local. Brands were important signals for the fledgling marketplace of consumer goods. They told consumers which companies were behind the goods they were buying and became a shorthand for quality and origin. But, from the 1700s onwards, international trade really started to take hold, as the industrial era got into full swing. The world's first global brands began to emerge from each successive European empire, and many are still around today, such as Stella Artois (from Belgium), Schweppes (from Switzerland) and Twinings (from England).

Tea is fascinating, as it has become the basis of self-identification for the British Empire. It was also, of course, used as a wedge by the new world in the Boston Tea Party of 1773 – a key historical moment in the lead-up to the United States asserting its independence. An entire shipment of tea by the East India Company to the United States was destroyed over what the Americans saw as unfair taxation imposed by motherland England. This has entered our cultural consciousness, and the English-speaking world now strongly identifies tea with Britain and coffee with the US. That's tribalism on a grand scale.

During the American Revolution and in the year of the United States Declaration of Independence, 1776, the number of times the word 'coffee' was mentioned in all novels published in English overtook mentions of 'tea' for the first time. Soon after, 'tea' regained its crown in the English-speaking fictional imagination, until 1968, when 'coffee' forged ahead again, and it has remained in front ever since.[1]

While coffee and tea are de facto national brands through the habits of millions, global car makers know their products are less and less aligned to the nationality of the car maker and are increasingly about the brand. Buyer habits, however, still play a very important role, with some families continuing to remain loyal to the same make of car or brand of laundry detergent for generations. This is tribalism in a new format.

Some families, it would seem, are Coke families, while others are Pepsi drinkers. Strong brand loyalty largely explains decreasing returns in the traditional industries, and why it is very difficult or nearly impossible to convert the disciples of certain products over to the rivals' camps.

And, from looking at online data from both Google and Facebook, it appears to me that, if you are American and of German parentage, you are more likely to drink Cola. In fact, German speakers worldwide are more than twice as likely to be Cola drinkers. This is perhaps not that surprising, but what I found more interesting is that, if you're a German-speaking American, you're actually much more likely to prefer Pepsi over Coca-Cola. And even more so if you live in Ohio, North Dakota or Montana – where it's 30 per cent more likely, if you're a German-speaker, that you prefer Pepsi to Coke. I don't understand what this connection is but I am curious to find out. This analysis is based on a correlation uncovered in Google search data between people who search for 'Pepsi-Cola' and those who search for 'German family', which was then cross-checked with Facebook data, which has demographics on how many members are German speakers, where they live and who likes Pepsi or Coke.

Do you see a connection here?

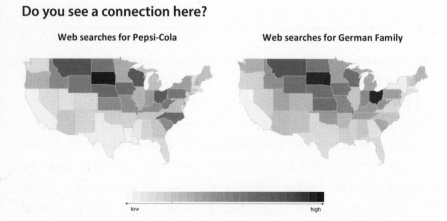

These maps of the United States represent the number of people searching online for 'Pepsi-Cola', on the left, and 'German family', on the right (Data source: Google Correlate, January 2015)

Advertising makes sense in a social context, and our brand preferences are often shared by our friends, neighbours, family and community. Many social groups are loyal to the same brand of car, beer and soap powder, as it's felt they say something about the kind of people they are or the loyalty is simply born out of habit, perhaps passed on from parents, friends or other influential people in your circle.

And because online is not tribal but networked with a tendency for one network to dominate each domain, we can use the power of online networks to better understand offline tribal behaviours. So, because nearly everyone is on Facebook for social, uses Google for search and Wikipedia for reference, these data sources become invaluable field guides for brand loyalties, and large-scale buying behaviours offline. The charts on the previous page are a simple example of doing this, but there is a huge array of opportunities to do more in this vein.

THE BIG DATA OF DOING

Action speaks louder than words but not nearly as often, lamented Mark Twain. What if actions could speak more often?

While there's been a lot of discussion about the massive amounts of information – the big data – held by the gravity giants such as Facebook, Twitter, LinkedIn and other social-media companies, much of this is what we choose to present to the world. It's the photographs we want to share, the status updates we want to represent us. In other words, it's a record of what we say rather than what we do.

As we all know, there's often a big difference between these two things. In the excellent book *Freakonomics* – which I'd recommend to anyone who finds this book interesting – the authors, Steven D. Levitt and Stephen J. Dubner, show how what people say and what people do on online-dating sites couldn't be more different. On one online-dating website they studied, half the white women and eight out of ten white men said on their profile that the race of potential dates didn't matter. Despite their professed positions, the white men who said race didn't matter sent 90 per cent of their email responses to white women, and the white women who said race didn't matter sent 97 per cent of their responses to white men.

There are now, however, lots of records not just of what we say on Facebook, Twitter and LinkedIn but also of what we do. This is another category of big data: the big data of doing. Every time you turn on your smartphone, it records where on Earth you are. If you have an iPhone and you have GPS turned on (most people do, as it is very handy) and go to Privacy/Location Services/System Services/Frequent Locations you'll most likely see a list of all the places you (and your phone) have been lately.

Everything you purchase on a credit card is recorded by the issuer or bank, and even with cash purchases supermarkets and department stores have a record of what people buy together in the same basket.

Supermarket experts have been working on this for some time. There's a much repeated tale of how marketers worked out that newborn nappies often appear in the same basket as beer. It would appear that new fathers like to reward themselves for their thoughtfulness in picking up nappies for their newborns. One UK supermarket chain found that, if they put the beer near the newborn nappies, sales of both would increase.[2]

It turns out that, just as we make brand choices at the level of our social groups, we also display group behaviour in our purchasing patterns, even when we're on our own. And we will hear many more stories like this resulting from big data observations over the coming years. The Australian minister for communications, Malcolm Turnbull, called them quite poetically 'Anecdata' – anecdotes from big data.

We need to be careful how we look at and think about these types of connections. Just because two things appear to be connected or happen at the same time and place, it doesn't necessarily mean one causes the other. There could be a third thing causing both phenomena. If we looked at raw data alone, we could find that people who suffer headaches take aspirin, but clearly this doesn't mean that aspirin causes headaches. But still there are some amazing insights ahead. And this is just the beginning.

THE SOCIAL CHEMISTRY OF ONLINE GRAVITY

Behavioural data from thousands of people combined with machine learning (as seen in the previous chapter) holds enormous potential, and illustrates the difference between online networking and the tribalism of offline brands. Whereas traditional car makers may look to craft brands and advertising to appeal to the aspirations of their target groups, an Online Gravity-savvy car maker such as Tesla can offer tailored, personal feedback on owners' driving performances compared with those of their peers and offer tips for improvement. Online driverless cars are definitely on their way too – Google have them working in the lab, and it's just a matter of time and acceptance before they roll them out.

Again, with this next generation of cars, the network will inevitably be the key point of difference, and the first company to gain traction in this marketplace will no doubt become a huge enterprise – perhaps the first car-maker online giant. The current intense tournament for personal-driver transport (Uber, Lyft et al.) may be the forerunner for this.

In a broader sense, beyond products at the intersection of the data of doing and machine learning, there's also potential here for a new kind of discipline – a kind of social chemistry of Online Gravity. Chemistry is the science of matter. It shows how all matter is made up from 118 different types of atoms and each of these in its pure form is an element. Elements include gold, silver and copper and gases such as oxygen, hydrogen and nitrogen. These elements can be organised on a structured grid or table known as the periodic table where each row represents the number of rings of electrons each atom has.

From this organisation, chemists have developed a very good understanding of possible ways these elements can be combined to produce other forms of matter that are a mixture of elements like water, a mix of hydrogen and oxygen or brass, a mixture of copper and zinc.

Perhaps there's the equivalent of a 'periodic table of social interactions' comprising fundamental elements and a framework that explains how they can combine – like chemistry. This could be an extension and amplification of the fascinating work already done over the last two decades in examining the way in which we frame and make our decisions (like the example given earlier where people in a supermarket when presented with too many choices of jam don't buy anything) in an area of research known as behavioural economics.

A great example of this at work is the fascinating studies that Navneet Kapur at LinkedIn has done ranking universities based on their database of 300 million candidates worldwide. Have you ever wondered how you or perhaps your kids could land a job at an iconic employer that leads its field? Kapur's research suggests the university you attend could improve your chances of finding work at these companies.

Say design is your thing and you want to work at Apple – who wouldn't? Based on graduate hires in the past eight years, you may then want to consider the Academy of Art University in California. While it's clearly no guarantee of a job there, Apple has hired more designers who are graduates from this school than any other. Perhaps you'd like to work at the hot international ad agency R/GA. Then studying at the School of Visual Arts in New York is probably your best bet. If working at the Walt Disney Company is your dream gig, then you could do worse than enrol in the Art Center College of Design in California.

If investment banking is more your speed and you're hankering for a job at one of the most sought-after firms in the biz, such as Citi, JPMorgan and Goldman Sachs, then you may want to consider Georgetown University ahead of Harvard.

First, Kapur and his team at LinkedIn identified the most 'desirable' companies to work at in each industry by looking at actual job movements using data analytics. So, for example, if software engineers are leaving Google to work for Facebook, then Facebook is more desirable, and vice versa. They also looked at turnover rates and its flip-side, retention rates.

Then they ranked universities based on those that produced the most graduates who landed jobs at these most desirable companies in each profession.

Fascinating. The initial release of the US rankings covers eight professions: accounting, design, finance, investment banking, marketing, media, software and software at start-ups. And there's also a version for the UK and Canada, each of which features a subset of five from the above.

You can examine outcomes from a variety of perspectives too. You can look at the professions as well as the individual companies in each of these professions to work out which universities and colleges most employees in certain roles attended. You can also look at the career path of graduates from each university and see which companies they ended up working for and then filtering by type of work or field of study.

Lastly you see examples of individual people who followed these paths, both from your network and more broadly. There's also a list of notable alumni from each university. This is great data. And only the beginning of a new world of insights to come from the treasure trove of data on LinkedIn.

A different but equally innovative source of dynamic social chemistry data is from the Seattle-based start-up called Polis (pol. is). It has developed an open-ended online survey that allows groups of people such as newspaper readers or students to interact in real-time in a town-hall or classroom setting based around a series of free-form questions. The audience can vote on questions as well as add their own comments and feedback, all via their smartphones. The results are summarised and mapped online, conveying a quick sense of the whole group's points of agreement and disagreement.

This is a new, networked form of interaction. And, after the fact, it offers a kind of data-enabled *tele-vision*, using the digital-data footprints to distil and visually represent the views and preferences of the participants.

What's interesting is how it dynamically represents people spatially based on their responses to each of the questions posed, enabling both the participants and organisers to gather insights into which issues were most important and which issues are most divisive.

Over time systems like these could be used to better inform public policy formulation at a grass-roots level or at a larger scale at a state or national level.

GRAVITY SHIFT TOWARDS INDIVIDUALISM

By the middle of the twentieth century, a rising Western middle class meant a global system of brand families began to emerge that spoke not only about the origin, nature and quality of the product itself but also about the values, discerning taste and affluence of the purchaser.

And so consumption increasingly has become not about connecting with your geographic tribe but about asserting or inventing your identity as an individual and connecting with a new global virtual tribe defined by taste, consumption and attitude. This can be seen as a broader social movement towards individualism across the last century.

From the 1970s onwards advertising and media profession-als are increasingly grouping consumers according to how they spend their time, what they believe and what they are interested in ('psychographics') rather than just looking at their income, age and sex ('demographics').[3]

Online Gravity certainly supports this trend. Online companies can provide self-service applications you can tailor to your own interests, needs and aspirations. And smartphones have accelerated this further: as most phones are typically not shared, users can choose from over one million different apps suitable and configurable to their own specific needs and interests. For example, Professor Emeritus Ron McCallum AO, Faculty of Law, the University of Sydney, who has been blind since he was a baby, has set up his iPhone with a range of apps that 'see' with the camera and then 'read' to him out loud via its speakerphone, including the Money Reader app which tells him the value of notes in all major currencies, a colour identification application which tells him what colour things are, and TapTapSee which enables him to take a photo of anything, like labels on jars, and have them read out to him.

Sport has also similarly moved from a tribal enterprise to a game of global 'federated individualism'. Team sports such as cricket and rugby union were once very much extensions of the tribal organisation of society. Traditionally, players represented their local town, city or nation, and in the British Empire these games evolved as venues for international competition between England and her subjects. The fan base of each team was very much a voice for a region or specific geographic area.

Some former colonies of the British Empire have taken these tribal games very seriously and are now very good at them. New Zealand and Australia still revel in the fact that they often dominate England in the respective codes of rugby and cricket.

But the story of the last 100 years has been not really about team sport but about the rise of individual sports such as golf and tennis. As an aside, this may be a concern for some who feel that rugby and its derivatives are a modern form of proxy warfare, and indeed even preventative. Human rights activist and Nobel Peace Prize winner Nelson Mandela believed in the transformative power of team sports on a nation and its people, and he was an active campaigner for South Africa's international engagement through rugby and soccer.

Another broad trend related to the rise of individualised lifestyles is the broad and ongoing shift towards a global economy more heavily dominated by the production of consumer goods and services as opposed to industrial goods and services.

The economy of the 1950s and 1960s was dominated by transnational industrial corporations, such as US Steel, Amoco and Westinghouse, whereas today's digital economy is led by the technology consumer giants Google, Apple and Microsoft.

To thrive online, organisations need to provide automated, personalised services while at the same time allowing users to join a large network of like-minded and interested people. They need to understand the power and potential of online self-service tools like Delta Air Lines, for example, who went from being the worst-ranked airline to the top-ranked airline by introducing a range of interactive self-service tools online and at airports.

In a similar way, Australia's Commonwealth Bank went from the worst performing in terms of customer service to number one, again by implementing a series of automated customer-service measures using online, mobile and social-media technologies. One award-winning free smartphone application they produced enables you to find the most recent sale price of any house in Australia you point the camera at – a great research tool for home buyers and dinner party conversation starter!

PERSONAL HEALTH INFORMATION

The networked nature of Online Gravity presents us with many opportunities to improve our health in new ways. For many simple but often chronic health ailments, traditional or home remedies can have remarkable success, but access to information about these cures is often by word of mouth, unreliable and untested.

A few years ago, I had a wart appear on the bottom of one of my feet. It became increasingly painful to walk on, and I had never had warts appear anywhere on my body before. I learnt from my local doctor that this is known as a plantar wart, from the Latin word *planta*, meaning 'sole of the foot', and the standard treatment is to diligently apply a type of acid to it each day for a month – which I did, but with no success.

Then, like many people, I researched my ailment online. I soon found not only that thousands of others suffered this condition but also that many of them were also at their wits' end. I read of one mother who had her young children suffer for years with this problem, with none of the advised remedies helping to relieve their chronic pain.

Fortunately, that's not all I found in my research. I came across a website called Earth Clinic, which provides a way for thousands of people worldwide to share their ailments and report their successes and failures with trying different home remedies.

I found a couple of home remedies for plantar warts and began trying them. The second one, which involved gaffer-taping a one-inch square of banana skin to my foot for 24 hours, completely cured the wart, and it has not reoccurred since. I kid you not. And I have no shares in banana plantations! I promptly went back to the site and rated it a successful cure for me. I also told my doctor and pretty much anyone else who would listen.

The point is, this type of system works best by harnessing the cumulative insights and experiences of many people who are all experiencing the same issues. And while this approach is clearly not a replacement for traditional medical treatment for any serious or urgent health issues, for many simple, non-life-threatening physical ailments it certainly could be worth considering.

Another website, called PatientsLikeMe, provides a similar service but allows people to report on and share their own experiences as patients of more serious and chronic conditions. Patients and their families have the option to contribute real-world data over time on their own conditions, treatments, symptoms, weight, mood and quality of life over the course. This has resulted in a huge, community-contributed data set which includes field-based data on the relative patient-reported efficacy of different treatments, drug interactions and their side effects and much more. Because the data is collected in a quantitative and structured format, you can see the overall success rates of various treatments across an entire community with the same condition.

SCIENCE AND MEDICINE: THE FIRST FRONTIER FOR ONLINE GRAVITY

Science and medicine have always been a global and social enterprise, and, to some extent, these practices already followed the rules of Online Gravity prior to the internet. There's a consensus view among the experts in each branch of science about the wisdom of the day, which is defended until a rival theory comes along that proves to be better and so dislodges it. It's the kind of tournament business that is at the heart of Online Gravity.

People who challenge the establishment in science and medicine are generally not given much airtime at best and labelled crackpots at worst. That is until someone comes along who demonstrates there's a better way of understanding the world. In his philosophy of science, Thomas Kuhn calls this a paradigm shift – where an idea is so powerful, radical and effective that it provides a whole new way of looking at things.

Nobel Prize winner Professor Barry Marshall is famous for discovering that stomach ulcers and gastritis are caused by bacterial infection and are therefore curable by antibiotics, rather than being caused by stress, spicy foods and too much acid, as was the previously accepted medical wisdom. He is quoted on the website of the Office of the Nobel Laureates in Western Australia as saying:

> When the work was presented my results were disputed and disbelieved, not on the basis of science, but because they simply could not be true. It was often said that no one was able to replicate my results. This was untrue but it became part of the folklore of the period.
>
> . . . It was a campaign and everyone was against me. But I knew I was right because I actually had done a couple of years' work on it by then and I had a few backers. When I was criticized by gastroenterologists, I knew that they were mostly making their living doing endoscopies on ulcer patients. So I thought to myself, I'm going to show you guys, knowing that, in a few years from now you'll be saying, 'Hey! Where did all those endoscopies go to?' It will be because I was treating ulcers with antibiotics.[4]

Marshall has demonstrated there is no significant innovation without a disruption to the status quo. Some economists call this 'creative destruction'.

The internet has meant that the scientific and medical communities are better connected and able to share information more readily than ever before. This has the impact of promoting the prevailing viewpoint widely and quickly but also benefits those, like Marshall, who look to challenge the dominant theories of the day.

Marshall was a very early adopter of the internet, and in 1981 he used Medline, an online database created by the National Library of Maryland, to access medical-journal articles, printing them out with 20 pages of references at a time.[5] This helped him to better understand the current thinking around the world in ulcer research and thus understand his challengers.

After about a year into his now famous research he realised that, at its heart, medicine is an information service. And today, with a few clues, we can all find good health information online.

The networked nature of Online Gravity means it tends to send signals and propagate news in 'information waves', somewhat like diseases. Topics, trends and memes travel around the world very quickly – and some get retransmitted by millions of people. 'Going viral' is a term for when a television commercial or funny video is shared online over and over again to an ever-growing global audience. This is now such a powerful way to communicate with millions of people around the world that many advertisers pray for this to happen.

There are even ad campaigns designed to be infectious. Most are unsuccessful, but some, such as the tram public-safety commercial 'Dumb ways to die', turn out to be epic. This catchy video was viewed 2.5 million times within 48 hours of being released, and, like a disease, this nearly doubled to 4.7 million views within 72 hours. Within two weeks, the video had been viewed 28 million times. Today, the video has had over 70 million views.

In London in the 1850s, there was a massive outbreak of the deadly contagious disease cholera. By plotting the deaths on a map, Dr John Snow realised the cause was a contaminated community water source, not 'bad air', as was commonly thought in the day. In the future, as Barry Marshall suggested to me in an interview in April 2014, similar public-health scares could be detected by the clever use of social media.

For example, Twitter could detect major anomalies in public health, such as an unusual number of people suddenly waking up reporting headaches. The locations of the Twitter users could be triangulated to uncover the problem's source, such as a dead animal in the water supply. There's a huge opportunity here, Marshall says, to better understand public-health issues in real-time by examining people's tweets and where they are.

Google has already demonstrated how it can detect influenza outbreaks with great accuracy and timeliness by analysing the millions of people typing in symptoms around the world. This knowledge could prove vital in averting widespread plagues of the future.

KEY POINTS

Whereas the traditional economy can be described as 'tribal', meaning that people identify with and remain loyal to certain brands due to history or geography, the online economy is all about networks: the bigger the better. This has various implications and manifestations:

- *Network size trumps brand loyalty.* Once an online company or service reaches a planetary scale, its pull becomes irresistible.
- *Brands are a modern version of tribalism.* Both cater to our human needs for identity and belonging.
- *Tribal behaviour is revealed online.* And 'the big data of doing' shows that we don't always make the consumer choices that we think and say we do.
- *New understanding of social patterns online is emerging.* A new form of understanding or 'social chemistry' is emerging from analysis of patterns in our interactions and seen in the traces left from what we do online.
- *Brands are increasingly becoming about expressing individuality.* Online Gravity supports this trend, providing almost unlimited customer choices via low-cost automation (often via self-service) combined with the benefits of mass-market scale.
- *Online networks are doing great things for science and medicine.* The more people on these networks, the quicker new scientific ideas can be disseminated, and the more feedback users can get from the community on the success or failure of certain theories or medical remedies.

LAW 7

ONLINE GRAVITY LOVES RENAISSANCE TALENT

In fifteenth-century Renaissance Europe, people with skills that spanned both arts and science were commonplace. During this era, universities did not specialise in specific areas but rather trained students in a broad array of sciences, languages, music and art. Some celebrated people of this period, such as Leonardo da Vinci, were at the leading edge of both art and science – accomplished in drawing and painting as well as in anatomy, engineering and inventing.

In a similar way, talented people with a diverse range of skills are critical to the success of organisations looking to succeed in the age of Online Gravity.

Steve Jobs demonstrated how an unlikely mix of informal electronics and liberal-arts education could be put to great use. At both Apple and Pixar, Jobs created billion-dollar global enterprises led by teams of talented people with educational backgrounds in arts, design, engineering and computer science who created customer-friendly and highly desirable products and services.

One of the key differentiators of the first-generation Apple Macintosh computers was that they provided users with proportional typefaces. In other words, each letter on the screen had a different amount of space allocated to it – like regular printing.

Most other computers of the time only offered fixed-width or monospaced fonts like this, with an equal amount of space for each letter, which is much harder to read.

Proportional
Monospace

Steve Jobs credited this decision to the fact that he himself had taken a design course that looked at typography as part of his college studies. And, because of this distinctive feature, Apple computers immediately found favour with designers, artists and educators.

STEAM SKILLS

Computers have always been at the forefront of advances in science and engineering but as web-connected computers, smart-phones and tablets become part of nearly everyone's everyday lives, software is offering us enormous power to amplify knowledge in many social and cultural domains such as education, design and media.

You can see this in the extraordinary success of MIT Media Lab, the celebrated research facility for arts and science collabo-ration created by Nicholas Negroponte at MIT, originally from its School of Architecture, in 1985.

The foundation faculty of MIT Media Lab was like a renegade rock-star supergroup, comprising experts and leading thinkers from a range of arts and social-science domains including education, music, philosophy and design, all with a shared interest in computers and the digital realm.

The founding team included Seymour Papert – a leading mathematician and educational theorist who pioneered bringing learning theory to the computer domain. His ideas were instrumental in the creation of Lego Mindstorms – the hugely successful programmable series of robots for kids, which brought the toymaker into the digital age and revived its ailing fortunes.

Another foundation faculty member was the Kiwi-born electronic-music pioneer Barry Vercoe, whose ideas set the standard for digital-music creation for over two decades. Two MIT Media Lab students, Alex Rigopulos and Eran Egozy, combined their understanding of arts and science to invent the imaginative blockbuster console games *Dance Central* and *Rock Band*, which together have sold over 15 million copies worldwide.

Being able to understand the mechanics and social dynamics of fields such as entertainment then apply them more broadly to 'scale' in online games and education has never been more doable or valuable. And this is why an expertise in 'traditional' areas outside of computers combined with programming and other digital skills has never been at more of a premium.

Some of the world's governments are supporting a greater educational emphasis on science, technology, engineering and mathematics (STEM). America is in this camp, with President Barack Obama announcing at the Third Annual White House Science Fair in April 2013:

> One of the things that I've been focused on as President is how we create an all-hands-on-deck approach to science, technology, engineering, and math . . . We need to make this a priority to train an army of new teachers in these subject areas, and to make sure that all of us as a country are lifting up these subjects for the respect that they deserve.

However, there is also an emerging, perhaps less publicised, call for people with STEAM skills: science, technology, engineering, arts and mathematics. In China, many parents see the liberal arts as vital to the future success of their children, as this survey indicates:

Educational priorities expressed by Chinese and American parents

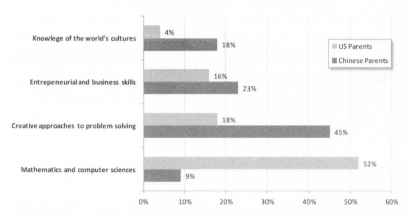

What skills do children need to drive innovation?
American and Chinese parents disagree.

Data source: Daniel McGinn, 'The Decline of Western Innovation', Newsweek, 23 November 2009.

SOUGHT-AFTER STAFF IN THE CONTEMPORARY WORKPLACE

A generation ago, employment specialisation was encouraged and rewarded. Depending on the industry you worked in, and the skills and background you had (or that others perceived you to have), the roles available to you were fairly rigid and predetermined.

The television drama series *Mad Men* reflects this phenomenon. It is set in a US advertising firm in 1960s America, and the characters are the embodiment of the industry. The roles and skills in this era, just like in our more recent history, are clearly defined. You have the wordsmiths (copywriters), the picture guys (art directors) and the business guys (client executives or 'suits').

In the last decade, as software envelops all industries, people with deep expertise in one area combined with the ability to collaborate with others in other fields have become increasingly sought after.

T-Shapers

One expression of this is the call for people with T-shaped skills. The vertical bar on the T represents a depth of skills and expertise in a single field (which is often technology-related), whereas the horizontal bar is the ability to have a broad but shallow understanding of a lot of different fields and hence be able to communicate and collaborate with experts in other areas. As David Guest describes T-shaped people in *The Independent* of 17 September 1991:

> These are a variation on Renaissance Man, equally comfortable with information systems, modern management techniques and the 12-tone musical scale.[1]

Another expression of this is people with pi-shaped skills, named after the Greek letter π. This refers to people with two areas of deep expertise combined with the ability to relate to others.

Slashies

In big cities around the world, we're seeing a new generation of young people who resist being defined by a single occupation or job title. Instead, they are using the 'slashie' approach to signal a portfolio of interests, capabilities and responsibilities.

The first combination of occupations separated by the 'slash' symbol that most of us became familiar with was actor/model/singer. Nowadays, the combinations are becoming more diverse, even Jekyll and Hyde-like: lawyer/photographer, union leader/band member or, one of my favourites, the 'Dub Dentist', who fills cavities by day and gets his DJ groove on by night.

Leading demographer Bernard Salt says, 'Gen Y is the first generation that have genuinely had the freedom to slash.'[2] With this in mind, though, this 'freedom' isn't necessarily always by choice, since more traditional, permanent employment is dominated by Baby Boomers and Gen-Xers – but even so, Generation Y Slashies will most likely be able to adapt better to the seismic shifts in the jobs market caused by Online Gravity.

And, in a professional sense, we're seeing more call for versatile people with multiple skills who can traverse technology as well as other domains. And even within technology, having multiple skills is now seen as very desirable in many situations.

Global Passionistas and Uberslashies

A select few slashies have been able to convert their interests and passions coupled with their tech savvy into global businesses on a scale hitherto unimaginable.

Whereas previously a talented entrepreneur interested in fine art could at best create a commercial gallery in a major metropolitan city, Carter Cleveland, a computer-science graduate from Princeton University, has created Artsy, a global platform for art discovery and purchase which is today one of the largest online collections of contemporary art. It features 200,000-plus artworks by 30,000-plus artists from 2500-plus leading galleries and 300-plus renowned museum and institutional partners, serving 200,000-plus registered users around the world.

Other examples of online successes that were founded by passionistas include Houzz (interior design), Pinterest (design inspiration), SoundCloud (sound), Spotify (music) and Goodreads (books).

Nocturnal Moonlighters

The rise of global marketplaces for online freelance talent such as Freelancer.com and oDesk is helping to accelerate the slashie phenomenon, as it means people can work in a more traditional role during the day and, if they want to moonlight, they can engage in freelance specialised work of their choosing at night – online.

Victors and Spoils is a new-generation creative advertising agency built around the principle of tapping into this deep and growing pool of night-time and freelance creative talent. One of its selling points to potential advertising clients is that, while any major advertising agency on Madison Avenue, New York, will have a small slice of the best talent in the business, Boulder, Colorado – based Victors and Spoils has access to around half of all the talent from all agencies – *at night.*

And those wanting to start a shop now have the option of beginning it online – also at night. Specialty online-retail stores using global platforms such as Bigcommerce and Shopify make it simple to create an online shopfront and manage it as a part-time job.

This applies not just to paid freelance work but also to volunteering, self-guided study and community engagement. Many of the army of people who voluntarily contribute to editing Wikipedia or writing software for open-source projects, for example, make their contributions in their own time on weekends and at night.[3]

Jack of All Technology Trades, Master of One

Traditionally, computer software roles themselves were quite separate, specialised and distinct. There were people who wrote code (programmers or developers), those who planned what it should do (analysts), those who tested it (quality assurance) and those who looked after its running once it was written (operations).

The rise of global online services that operate 24/7 and are continuously worked on and improved incrementally has seen the emergence of new, hybrid roles that combine these skills. One such hybrid role is known as 'DevOps' – a developer who looks at quality assurance and also manages live operations. And these people are among the most sought after in the tech world. The concept is less than five years old, yet there are already over 20,000 people on LinkedIn who mention DevOps in their skills profile.

Online Gravity means that lean global start-ups that serve millions of people online can be created with a relatively small staff who perform lots of differing roles. In the early days, WhatsApp Inc. had many people performing multiple roles, including one whose job title was 'German/Spanish/Android guy'. With a team of less than 100 staff, it was able to grow to support a live 24/7 global messaging service now used by over 450 million people around the world.

XYZ Combinations

Y Combinator is the most famous and prestigious 'academy' for aspiring technology start-up companies. Established in 2005, over five hundred fledgeling companies have now been through the program and 'graduated' including Airbnb, Adioso and Dropbox.

Importantly, the Y Combinator accelerator has influenced the technology sector and set best practice in terms of what works when forming new enterprises. One key trend is that companies with co-founders are more likely to succeed. Establishing a technology company with two or more founders with complementary skills has become the accepted wisdom for many people in the technology start-up community.

When I first heard the term Y Combinator, I thought it must refer to preference for duo-founded companies – with the two arms of the letter 'Y' coming together to form a company. Turns out that's not the case; instead, it refers to a term in computer software. A 'y combinator' is a computer program that can initiate another computer program in a loop to enable very large-scale repeatable processes to be created in a simple programming language.

So instead, I'm coining the term XYZ Combination for when multiple people with diverse, complementary skills come together to create something new, such as a start-up. One such combination is reflected in the trinity of catchy new job titles used by many start-ups comprising 'the hipster' (the domain expert or product person) and 'the hustler' (marketing, finance and management) and of course 'the hacker' (software and technology leadership).

ONLINE GRAVITY FAVOURS COMPANIES WITH MORE THAN ONE FOUNDER

While there are exceptions, such as Jeff Bezos at Amazon, most of today's leading Online Gravity giants were established and led by two or more co-founders, including Facebook (Mark Zuckerberg, Dustin Moskovitz, Chris Hughes and Eduardo Saverin), Google (Sergey Brin and Larry Page), Wikipedia (Jimmy Wales and Larry Sanger), Pinterest (Paul Sciarra, Evan Sharp and Ben Silbermann), WhatsApp (Brian Acton and Jan Koum), Atlassian (Mike Cannon-Brookes and Scott Farquhar) and Xero (Rod Drury and Hamish Edwards). One analysis of leading technology companies in 2012 indicated that only one in four had a sole founder.[4]

The proposition that co-founder or multi-founder start-up technology companies are more likely to succeed than those with a single founder was also validated by a study done by David Lee and Ron Conway of Silicon Valley Angel in 2011. As over 95 per cent of the returns for investors in tech start-ups come from only five per cent of the companies, looking at the stats on all companies makes no sense. Instead, they chose to look at the patterns of the successful ones. They defined two levels of success: ones that were big successes and sold, or could have sold, for more than $25 million, and those that were huge successes and sold, or could have sold, for over $500 million.

Their research showed that 84 per cent of those that were big successes had multiple founders, and 89 per cent of those that were huge successes had multiple founders.

In a similar way, David Court, a leading authority in the entertainment and finance businesses, has observed that this trend of team founders is consistent with leading film-production companies. Starting famously with the Warner brothers, many of the most successful movie-making businesses are run by siblings, including Joel and Ethan Coen (*The Big Lebowski, Fargo, No Country for Old Men*), Lana and Andy Wachowski (*The Matrix*), and Bob and Harvey Weinstein (*Pulp Fiction, The King's Speech, Django Unchained*).

Due to the highly competitive and cut-throat nature of film production, it's vital to be in business with someone who 'has your back'. With siblings already fulfilling this role, Court figures, it's no surprise that this has emerged as a successful pattern of production-company formation.

RENAISSANCE HIRING

In addition to Online Gravity favouring a differing mix of skills within individuals and teams, gravity giants have a mixture of skills that offers a 'talent signature' that differs from that of traditional multinationals.

Naturally, organisations looking to take advantage of Online Gravity will employ a significant number of people with computer skills and qualifications. What's less immediately evident is that many of the most successful online companies also favour other skills and qualifications. These hiring patterns result in a kind of digital talent signature, and, while every company is different, there are some patterns that many leading companies share.

The talent signature of digital titans includes:

- *More economists.* Mature gravity giants have about twice to three times the number of economics graduates than the traditional multinationals. At Amazon, for example, over a thousand of its employees have studied economics – twice the number that the world's other top retailers, Walmart, Tesco and Carrefour, employ. This is despite the fact that Walmart employs roughly three times the number of staff that Amazon has. Many companies, including Google and Amazon, have their own chief economists too – perhaps not surprising given these companies are of the scale and complexity of many nation states.

- *More statisticians.* Statistics is growing in significance and popularity with the major online enterprises. Students recognise this, and enrolments in statistics courses at university are skyrocketing. At Harvard University, for example, statistics enrolments have experienced a tenfold growth in the past five years, overtaking economics as the most popular undergraduate course on campus.

- *More artists and musicians.* Graduates with arts, social-science and humanities degrees are surprisingly well represented at today's leading gravity giants. Sixteen per cent of Apple's staff, for example, have visual-arts, social-science, communication and literature degrees. This is about seven times the number of people with the same types of degrees at IBM, where they constitute two per cent of all staff. While many people would not be surprised to learn that lots of senior staff at Apple are computer-science graduates from Stanford University and MBAs from the University of California, Berkeley, for example, it is perhaps more surprising to learn that many studied fine arts at places such as the Pratt Institute in New York City or music at Berklee College of Music in Boston.

Immigrant Advantage

As the legendary technology-industry commentator Mary Meeker has astutely pointed out, more than half of the largest global technology companies are founded by first- or second-generation immigrants to the United States.[5]

Among the companies that are titans of the online world, this trend is even stronger. Almost all of the gravity giants are US-based and have migrants to the US among their founding teams:

- Google's co-founder Sergey Brin was born in Russia.
- YouTube's co-founder Jawed Karim was born in Germany, and another co-founder, Steve Chen, was born in Taiwan.
- Facebook's co-founder Eduardo Saverin was born in Brazil.
- eBay's co-founder Pierre Omidyar was born in France.
- Yahoo!'s co-founder Jerry Yang was born in Taiwan.
- Of PayPal's co-founders, Max Levchin was born in Ukraine; Peter Thiel was born in Germany; Elon Musk was born in South Africa; and Luke Nosek was born in Poland.
- LinkedIn co-founder Konstantin Guericke was born in Germany.
- Amazon's founder Jeff Bezos is the son of a Cuban immigrant.
- WhatsApp's co-founder Jan Koum was born in Ukraine.

There's a natural alignment here with the increasingly global direction of the web. Today, over nine out of every ten people online live outside the United States, compared with a decade ago when more than half of all the people online lived inside the United States.

The early hires of companies such as WhatsApp included many people who doubled up in their roles – as, say, software engineer and tester as well as translator for the version in the country of their native tongue.

World-readiness – which is the Microsoft term for designing software and online services to suit differing calendar systems, currencies, languages and other localisations – is emerging as a key factor for companies looking to serve a global customer base, so employees with this sort of specialised knowledge are at a premium.

Several leading universities, such as Imperial College, London, and the University of Washington, are now offering continuing or postgraduate education in internationalisation and localisation of software, and some, such as the University of Illinois, are offering these courses from their linguistics faculty.

LESSONS FOR PARENTS AND STUDENTS

A Renaissance Education Starts Early in Life

A surprising number of the founders and leaders of many of today's technology giants share one little-known fact in common: they attended Montessori schools.

Montessori is a method of education developed by Maria Montessori in the early 1900s originally to help disabled children at a school in Rome, and later applied to teach all children at private and public schools around the world. There are now more than four thousand Montessori schools worldwide, each following the approach that Maria Montessori outlined over a hundred years ago. While it is still not mainstream, it is by no means marginal either.

Some famous technology pioneers who were graduates of Montessori schools include the founders of Google (Sergey Brin and Larry Page), Digg (Kevin Rose), Amazon (Jeff Bezos), Wikipedia (Jimmy Wales) and Maxis (Will Wright).

The Montessori method of encouraging children to choose activities within set constraints seems to enable today's global computer-science-powered technology entrepreneurship. In fact, inventors Thomas Edison and Alexander Graham Bell were early supporters of Montessori education – both helping to establish early schools.

Looking into this idea a bit further, it turns out that folks who attended a Montessori school are four times more likely to go on to study computer science at university than those who didn't. They are also three times as likely to study natural science.

Where did this data come from? It comes from the magic of Online Gravity and one of the gravity giants: LinkedIn, which now has the detailed résumés of over a hundred million people worldwide.

Of all the people registered with LinkedIn, around one per cent of people in countries such as the United States, the United Kingdom, Australia and Canada have studied computer science at university, whereas four per cent of those who have mentioned their Montessori school experience went on to study the subject.

The Twenty-First Century Is an Independent Learner's Paradise

If ever there was an age for people who like to teach themselves things, this is it. Never has there been a better time for the curious and self-motivated learner. Learning resources have never been more abundant, accessible and affordable.

The Library of Alexandria, in Egypt, was hailed as one of the great wonders of the ancient world. Destroyed by fire over two thousand years ago, the library was stocked with what was no doubt one of the most astonishing collections of human knowledge and reference material in the world. Today, the amount of educational and reference material readily available online to most people with an internet connection dwarfs this collection by well over a hundred times.

There were reputedly up to half a million scrolls in the Library of Alexandria, representing a collection of a few hundred thousand individual books. As you can imagine, it was only a small number of educated scholars who would have had physical access to this collection and would have had the education to be able to read these scrolls.

By way of comparison, there are 50 times this number of 'scrolls' on Wikipedia. The online encyclopaedia has over 30 million articles, with over four million in English, all of which are freely available for anyone to read and are being read by over 50 million people in the United States alone each month.

Open Library, by the Internet Archive, provides over a million classic books in ebook format for free, as well as access to over

200,000 books from the 1900s to borrow in a traditional lending-library model, but again as ebooks.

On the question and answer website Quora, there are over two million questions posed for its audience of around 400,000 curious readers and responders.

Apple's iTunes U provides free access to audio and video lectures and other content from over 800 universities, including material from most of the world's leading institutions including London School of Economics, Harvard University and MIT.

And at a school level the free global online educational portal Khan Academy is helping millions of kids around the world with their homework. Khan Academy has over 5000 online 'mini-lecture' videos and over 100,000 practice problems as well as easy-to-use tools for teachers, parents and tutors, to allow them to monitor, coach and reward students as they progress at their own speed through exercises and topics. The non-profit service began in 2006 when founder Salman Khan was tutoring his cousin in mathematics on the other side of the United States and recorded some videos to help him with his studies. With donations, it has expanded rapidly to now cover many fields in many languages including medicine, finance, physics, chemistry, biology, astronomy, economics, music, and computer science.

Online educational videos such as those provided by the Khan Academy have been used successfully around the world as part of 'flip the classroom' strategies, where students do schoolwork at home and their homework at school. In other words, they watch video lectures from teachers for their homework and work on problems while receiving personalised tutoring by teachers at school.

KEY POINTS

Online Gravity favours the following types of entrepreneurs and employees, all of whom display 'Renaissance talent':

- *Employees with a diverse range of skills.* Gravity giants are often looking to employ people with an arts background (for example) as well as expertise in computer science.
- *Employees educated in the 'STEAM' subjects.* For this reason, it pays to study an arts subject at college, as well as the 'STEM' subjects of science, technology, engineering and mathematics.
- *T-Shapers.* Those with a depth of experience in a technological field and a broad range of experiences and interests in non-technological areas.
- *Slashies.* Versatile people with multiple skills, defined not by a single job title but by many, separated by 'slashes'.
- *Passionistas.* Those who can combine tech savvy and their passions to innovate in the digital sphere.
- *Nocturnal moonlighters.* People who find fulfilment beyond the realms of their day jobs by pursuing passion projects (often on behalf of gravity giants) by night.
- *Jacks of all technology trades, masters of one.* Being able to perform several technology roles at once, such as the DevOps function – a developer who looks at quality assurance and also manages live operations.
- *XYZ combinations.* When multiple people with diverse, complementary skills come together to create something new, such as a tech start-up.
- *Economists and statisticians.* Because online giants take statistical analysis very seriously and data is the new gold.
- *Immigrants.* Because the biggest online companies are global, and they need the specialised local knowledge of people from other countries.
- *Montessori-educated entrepreneurs.* The Montessori system results in a greater than average number of people going on to study computer science.

THE FUTURE

WORK AND MONEY
IN THE ONLINE AGE

The web as I envisaged it, we have not seen it yet.
The future is still so much bigger than the past.

Sir Tim Berners-Lee, inventor of the World Wide Web[1]

What does the future hold for ourselves and our children in terms of employment and finance in the age of Online Gravity? On the one hand, the explosive growth of global online information and services offers us a great deal of opportunity, and on the other it presents us with lots of new and emerging challenges. This chapter contains some thoughts and reflections on both, along with my observations of what I am tipping as the major upcoming trends and developments in these areas.

ARTHUR C. CLARKE'S IMAGINED FUTURE IS HERE

One thing I'd like to share with you before we begin is something I came across a long time ago but still love. It's Arthur C. Clarke's set of predictions for the future of technology. *It was written in 1962* – yet, with surprising accuracy, he predicted many of the key communication and information technology trends of our time:

- 'Personal radio' – surely this is the iPod/Spotify/Pandora.
- Artificial intelligence – online machine learning now powers algorithmic trading and self-flying helicopters.
- Global library – which sounds exactly like the web.
- Telesensory devices – the 'internet of things' by another name.[2]

And there is still time for his other predictions to come true, as he cast them further into the future than today. These are: contact with extra-terrestrials (2035); memory playback (2055); and mechanical educators (2060). I'll leave those to your imagination!

WORK IN THE AGE OF ONLINE GRAVITY

The mechanics of finding work, the type of roles available and even the nature of a career itself are all changing rapidly in the age of Online Gravity. Following is the whistlestop tour.

X-Ray Work-Goggles

Like physical gravity, the effects of Online Gravity cannot be shielded against, and one of these is the way it automatically encourages the stockpiling of new collections of information about both us and our potential employers. This provides us and our employers, current and future, with a kind of X-ray vision, granting access to more of our personal details and history than ever before.

Dick Bolles is the author of *What Color is Your Parachute?* With over ten million copies sold, it is the most popular book about job-hunting and careers ever written. Since 1970, when it was first published, Bolles has completely rewritten the book in light of developments in the global economy, including mass unemployment in Southern Europe and what is happening online.

Chapter Two is now titled 'Google is Your New Résumé', where he points out that job-hunting has been online since 1994 but has accelerated rapidly in recent years. And that,

'Sometimes – 29 per cent of the time, it is claimed – an employer will offer you a job because they were impressed with what Google turned up about you.'[3]

And you can use this to your advantage by curating your online identity to present your best face to employers. You can even use your Twitter profile as a mini-résumé, Bolles reminds us. Using the same logic, it makes sense to be careful about what you and others post online via social media, as employers increasingly can and do learn more about their employees' or potential employees' private lives from Facebook than they'd intended to reveal.

Potential candidates can put on X-ray specs too and learn a great deal about potential future employers via web services such as Glassdoor, which provides a popular forum for anonymous and candid insider commentary about conditions, salaries and people's experiences of what it's like on the inside of most companies – large and small – from an employees' perspective.

LinkedIn provides the ultimate in X-ray technology when it comes to seeing into workplaces and indeed even entire economies. Previously, it was very difficult to learn about some companies – especially private ones. In some industries, there are whole categories of publicity-shy companies that avoid the attention of their competitors and the media. This is often because they worry about their trade secrets being stolen, having their staff poached or drawing unwanted attention because of how much money they are making. Some boutique hedge funds and high-technology companies adopt this approach, operating in 'stealth mode'.

Now, most companies in the Western world of any scale are visible via their employees' profiles on LinkedIn. While not everyone is on the network, a lot of people are, from a lot of different industries, offering great insights to employees, employers and analysts. Companies and recruiters can purchase a complete licence to see all profiles on LinkedIn: not just those they are connected to. Now this is the ultimate X-ray vision, as it allows people to see across the whole economy – worldwide.

LinkedIn is using this data to help inform governments about large-scale trends in employment, and it contributed to a 2012 US Presidential Report about future jobs,[4] outlining areas where they could *see* new jobs emerging. LinkedIn is calling this the economic graph – as distinguished from Facebook's creation of a worldwide social graph.

Jobs growth in the US economy by type and industry

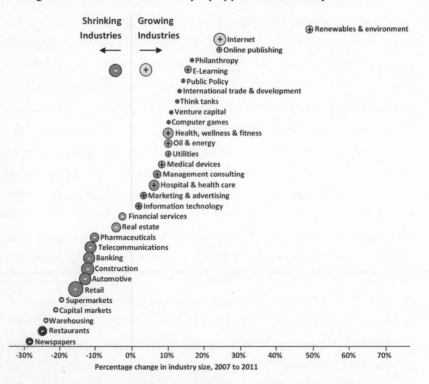

Each circle represents the number of jobs lost or gained in each industry – larger circles means more jobs gained or lost. Data source: LinkedIn, February 2012.

LinkedIn is one of the most valuable of the gravity giants and central to the future of work in the coming era. If you've not tried it already, I'd urge you to investigate this valuable and fascinating service.

Casualisation of the Workforce

One of the clearest employment trends in the West in recent years has been the growth of part-time and self-employed workers. In the United Kingdom in the last decade, the number of self-employed people has risen by about 25 per cent, and the number of part-time workers has grown by about ten per cent.

There is debate about whether or not this is a good thing, and whether it's a sign of a stronger economy or one in distress. Clearly, for some individuals, self-employment is preferred, while in other cases it will be an option of last resort, as full-time employment was not forthcoming.

In the UK and Australia, this is referred to as the 'casualisation' of the labour market, as 'casual' positions are jobs that are not ongoing or permanent in nature, because they are temporary or contract hires.

One thing for certain is that employment – whether it is full-time or part-time or permanent or freelance – is becoming increasingly broken down into more and more specialised roles, and in many cases these roles are becoming segmented further and further into the tasks that make them up.

This is like the logic that dominates current best practice in the development of online services. Each component is designed as an autonomous part that does as small and as simple a task as possible, and reveals its costs to those interacting with it. It's a transaction-based logic.

Work, however, is for most of us more than simply a trans-action, and Online Gravity has huge implications, both positive and negative, for the future of work. On the plus side, it means more and more people may be able to find fulfilling roles that use and value capabilities that traditional roles currently don't. It also means that there may be opportunities for some to create more of a portfolio career, with multiple part-time roles combined with a series of project-based jobs. However for others it may mean less stability, less certainty and more periods of underemployment or unemployment.

Outsourcing and Specialisation

There is a growing number of ways to make money by doing things online: buying and selling on eBay, writing computer software, writing articles, graphic design. You can also find others online to work for you and do these things. Now, there are numerous online marketplaces for all kinds of work that can be done online. Some of these marketplaces are specialised, but there are two big global general ones: Freelancer.com and oDesk.

Much of today's momentum for activity on Freelancer.com and oDesk is the still massive disparity in wages in different parts of the world. Five billion people have yet to access the internet. They currently live on $10 a day. And they want to earn $10 an hour. You can find people to create a website for $200 on Freelancer.com that would cost $5000 if sourced locally.

While many people in the West look down on these services as they see them as undermining local work and wages, they could ultimately turn out to be the best form of direct foreign investment in developing economies the world has ever seen. Matt Barrie of Freelancer.com says, 'Developing countries like Malaysia believe that micro working online is the solution for the bottom 20% of earners. We have contracts with the Malaysian government, teaching people to use websites and learning trades.'[5]

Another trend that Matt Cooper, vice president of oDesk, reports on is an increase in clients hiring from within their own borders – so, Muscovites are hiring freelancers from remote Russia and people in Los Angeles are hiring freelancers from the rural Midwest.

As well as these global labour marketplaces, there are smaller online markets emerging for very specialised skills. One example of this is the online service Kaggle. Companies use Kaggle to find solutions for tricky technical challenges, such as earlier detection of driver drowsiness for Ford, better and broader identification of talent for Facebook, and increased effectiveness of click-through rates for Chinese gravity giant Tencent.

Kaggle frames these challenges as games, offering cash prizes for the best solutions. These competitions are then put to a growing global army of elite, talented scientists, engineers and mathematicians, who compete to win the prizes and the prestige.

Automation

An inevitable outcome of hyper-specialisation, though, is automation. Any job that you can imagine being done by a machine today *will* be done by a machine in the near future. Ben Hammersley, the UK futurist and noted author, has a great quote about this: 'Anything that can be flow charted will be automated.'[6]

Indeed, online automation is everywhere, and its implications for the future of work are profound. Just think of the last time you visited a movie-rental store. These stores, along with bookstores and record stores, used to be major employers – there were three on every high street in most parts of the developing world. Now, they are very few and far between.

Local Meets Global

Many are concerned that Online Gravity is creating two-tier economies and two-tier cities. The top tier is composed of people whose skills are increasingly in demand and connected to the global value chain, which sees them employed in highly paid, interesting jobs. The bottom tier, meanwhile, is made up of those who are out of this loop, whose skills are being marginalised, outsourced and automated. And there is certainly an element of truth to this.

One consequence of our increasingly busy lives is that personal and domestic services are on the rise. Those lucky enough to be employed in global jobs are trading cash for time doing domestic chores such as washing and cleaning. In the global online outsourcing marketplace, in addition to by-the-hour and project-based work offered via Freelancer.com and oDesk, we now see labour marketplaces emerging for small, local micro-jobs such as cleaning, shopping and assembling furniture. Examples of these marketplaces are TaskRabbit (US and UK), Airtasker (Australia) and Sooqini (UK).

Online Unions for Freelancers

Unions have played a vital role in protecting the rights of individual workers around the world and balancing power in the democratic West, providing a countervailing force to large-scale, capital-intensive industrial businesses.

Many traditional labourers have become individual contractors, and the level of trade-union membership and power has declined in many industries. One area where there has been a growth in union members and power, however, is in the above-mentioned domestic services.

The National Domestic Workers Alliance, formed less than a decade ago in the United States, has already got the state of New York to adopt America's first bill of rights for people working in family homes. *The Economist* reports this is 'guaranteeing overtime pay, protection from discrimination and harassment, a minimum of one day's rest a week and a minimum of three days' paid leave a year – not much, but better than nothing'.[7]

Another interesting development in this space is the emergence of unions for freelancers, such as the Freelancers Union in the United States, which now has over 240,000 members. Its founder, the self-described 'practical revolutionary' Sara Horowitz, says on its website:

Nearly one in three working Americans is an independent worker. That's 42 million people – and growing. We're lawyers and nannies. We're graphic designers and temps. We're the future of the economy.

As most of its members don't work for large employers and many are temps, the Freelancers Union doesn't engage in traditional wage bargaining. Instead, it offers members a range of other benefits, such as health care, insurance and retirement savings plans. In the United Kingdom, the Professional Contractors Group (PCG), which has over 20,000 members, offers similar services.

Where's My Four-Hour Work Week?

Tim Ferriss's bestselling book *The 4-Hour Workweek* presents a lifestyle design strategy that interestingly he developed during a three-week break from running his business, in which he travelled around Europe, Asia and South America. It struck me when doing research for this book that the founders of WhatsApp also took a long break after leaving work at Yahoo! to fly frisbees in South America before starting their $17 billion mobile messaging business. Maybe this should become a trademarked success strategy: the unplugged sabbatical.

During Ferriss's time away, he learnt how to automate much of the activity of his company, and, with self-discipline (such as checking his emails only once a day) and a range of online productivity strategies (such as hiring an online personal assistant), he was able to minimise the amount of time he spent on this business when he got back from his vacation and simplify his life.

Ferriss's book is very compelling and contains some practical, up-to-date advice. And who doesn't like the thrust of its subtitle: 'Escape 9–5, live anywhere and join the new rich'? But the promise of a life of leisure around the next corner is not new. There has been a steady stream of pundits saying it is within our reach since the 1920s.

Distinguished British philosopher and mathematician Bertrand Russell, in his famous and brilliant essay 'In Praise of Idleness', argued that a four-hour working day (not quite four hours a week, but still not bad) would be possible with the technology and productivity of his era, and indeed was proven to have worked during the First World War:

> The war showed conclusively that, by the scientific organisation of production, it is possible to keep modern populations in fair comfort on a small part of the working capacity of the modern world. If, at the end of the war, the scientific organisation, which had been created in order to liberate men for fighting and munition work, had been preserved, and the hours of work had been cut down to four, all would have been well.[8]

Despite many predictions of a life of more leisure, this has not yet materialised for most of us. Despite many predictions of a life of more leisure, this has not yet materialised for most of us. Respected Australian scholar and former parliamentarian Barry Jones is sceptical about such predictions. In his 2007 book, *A Thinking Reed*, Jones says that as 'service employment has almost infinite capacity for expansion' this would prevent a total collapse in work as we know it.[9]

Predictions of an oncoming era of leisure have been a bit like predictions of the apocalypse. So far, they've all been wrong, but they keep on coming. Why is that, and will Online Gravity change anything?

Attitudes towards work have varied throughout the ages. The Ancient Greeks thought that, along with illness, it was an evil that sprung from Pandora's box, prior to the opening of which man was 'free from ills and hard toil'.[10] And at various other times in history it has been seen as a virtue and a duty.

The web certainly means we can all do so much more than ever before. Yet the working week has been shown to be expanding, not shrinking – especially among the best-paid workers. A comprehensive national survey of full-time workers by the largest economics research organisation in the United States, the National

Bureau of Economic Research (NBER), looked at how many hours per week people worked over the last two decades and how much they earned. It found the number of people regularly working 55 hours a week or more has grown dramatically among the top wage earners but shrunk among the lowest earners:

> This shift was especially pronounced among highly educated, high-wage, salaried, and older men. For college-educated men, the proportion working 50 hours or more climbed from 22.2 per cent to 30.5 per cent in these two decades ... There was no increase at all in work hours among high-school dropouts.[11]

Unlike high-school dropouts, who are typically paid direct overtime for their extra work, the highest earners in the survey are salaried and are not. So why work another 20-plus hours above and beyond the 40 you are paid for? Because they are worried about losing their shirt:

> The long hours may enhance their prospect of keeping their current job if the firm decides to lay off workers in the future. Studies suggest that perceived job insecurity has risen substantially among highly educated workers.

And because Online Gravity means the stakes are getting higher for both companies and employees alike, NBER economist David R. Francis concludes:

> It could be that longer-than-normal work weeks help firms to produce better products and services in 'winner-take-all' type of markets.

FINANCE IN THE AGE OF ONLINE GRAVITY

The global banking and finance sector has only recently started to feel the full effects of Online Gravity. In media, travel and retail, the effects are obvious, but, to a large extent, financial services has been a late arrival to the party. This party is now in full swing, so we will see some dramatic transformation in the decade ahead.

The subcategory most visibly transformed by Online Gravity so far has been online payments, led by PayPal. We're also seeing the rise of a new generation of companies who offer mobile and online payment services for small retailers such as Square, Stripe and Braintree (acquired by PayPal in 2013).

Online Lending

Today, online-lending clubs, led by Zopa in the United Kingdom, SocietyOne in Australia and Lending Club in the United States, offer a platform for investors to pool money online and lend it to others who are seeking personal loans.

Others, such as Funding Circle, offer peer-to-peer loans to small businesses in the United Kingdom and United States. There are even peer-to-peer lending services that offer interest for investors using the leading crypto-currency Bitcoin, including BTCJam, BitLendingClub and Bitbond.

In Germany, Friendsurance is offering lower premiums to insurance customers by harnessing Online Gravity. The way it works is that part of your premium can be reduced by agreeing to cover a small part of someone else's risk directly in the event they need to claim – the more connections you have, the greater your discount.

To date, most of these loans and insurance platforms are low-risk and offered only to people and businesses in the same country they are operating in. Kiva, on the other hand, provides a platform for people to offer small loans online in a peer-to-peer lending service designed for the developing world. It has facilitated more than $400 million in loans in its first decade of operation and is currently lending about $4 million a week. These loans are going to farmers needing to buy supplies and livestock, retailers looking to buy stock to resell, students needing to fund their education and pay for housing, and lots of other good causes.

The Kiva platform is really the thing that makes this amazing service work, as it presents the stories of individual loan applicants in a format that people can understand and relate to. Individual lenders can act like bank managers of yesteryear and assess who they think is most creditworthy and/or in greatest need. Kiva collects and displays historical and statistical information about lenders, borrowers and the field charity organisations that help distribute and manage the loans. And, by the statistics reported on the site, the overwhelming majority (98.94 per cent) of all Kiva's loans are repaid.

Once borrowers have repaid their loans to Kiva, lenders have the option of withdrawing their cash via PayPal, reinvesting in new loans or donating the money to Kiva. And, to date, 70 per cent of all lenders have re-lent their money.

Online Gravity Provides a Safe Haven for Barn Owls
In Nicholas Taleb's brilliant book *The Black Swan*, he talks about rare, high-impact events that many of our current ways of thinking are not well equipped to deal with. These 'black swans' can be positive events, such as the birth of the internet, or negative ones, such as the start of the First World War – but, Taleb argues, they are all unexpected.

In contrast to black swans, I'd like to put forward the 'barn owl' theory. Barn owls are predictable but still infrequent, high-impact events, such as student loans and work-related injuries. Because they are predictable and repeated, there are market mechanisms to deal with them, and the web extends the power and reach of many of these risk-and-reward-sharing mechanisms and puts them in the hands of more individuals.

So, for example:

- Education has an impact on earnings and well-being, yet many people in the developing world don't have access to student loans required to fund their education – here, crowdfunding via web portals such as Kiva may be able to help.
- New ideas for products and creative projects can have a big impact, yet many inventors and artists lack access to capital to pursue them. Here, project crowdfunding services such as Kickstarter can help.
- Work-related injuries – they are infrequent but still happen, and they have a big impact when they do. And many workers, especially in the developing world, lack basic insurance for their health and livestock. Could forward-looking online insurance services, such as Friendsurance, offer more people access to low-cost insurance?

Where's the Apple of Banking?

While Kiva is focused on small loans – so-called 'microfinance' in the developing world – up the other end of the lending chain are large loans to purchase property in the West. This is a very lucrative part of retail banking, and just emerging – and a clue for the decade ahead – are peer-to-peer marketplaces for mortgages, such as LendInvest in the United Kingdom.

In the next decade, there will most likely be rapid growth in this space, just as we saw with the rise, demutualisation and consolidation of building societies in the 1980s and 1990s. In the last two decades, 37 banks in the United States have merged to become four – though we've yet to see the same degree of consolidation across borders.

What is less certain but more interesting is whether we will see a rise in transnational peer-to-peer lending. In the way that there's a clear global leader in online payments, PayPal, could a global player emerge in both in-country and cross-border mortgages?

PayPal has around 94 per cent market share of online payments across the entire web.[12] And the total global market for residential mortgages is about $20 trillion, or about 25 per cent of the entire total world GDP for a year.[13] Total interest on all these mortgages at five per cent is $1 trillion per annum, or roughly around ten times the current revenue of the world's largest retail banks, such as HSBC, Bank of China and Bank of America.

Imagine a company that had a leading role in the online global mortgage business. Apple was for some time the largest company in the world, largely by inventing and selling the planet's most popular smartphone to over half a billion people. Think for a moment how much you spent on your smartphone and how much you spend on your mortgage, and imagine now an Apple of online mortgages. How large would this company be?

What would a global online market for peer-to-peer mortgages look like? If one were to emerge, how large could this grow? What are the regulatory and other constraints on this happening?

Another radical future for mortgages that Online Gravity could facilitate is the bold proposal put forward by leading global economist Nicholas Gruen for central banks to consider running their own online loan books, lending directly to individual residential investors. In a report for the United Kingdom Government's National Innovation Agency, NESTA, Nicholas Gruen calls on the country's central bank, the Bank of England, to offer the services it currently only offers to other banks directly to individuals. Using the power and cost-effectiveness of the web, Gruen suggests that the Bank of England can and should offer cheap online deposit and savings accounts as well as online mortgages directly to the public.[14] The fact that the web offers the ability to offer automated transactions at almost no administrative cost is behind the innovative zero commision online stockbroking service Robinhood discussed earlier and could form the basis for many other large-scale financial market innovations ahead.

Crowdfunding Follows Online Gravity

Online marketplaces for raising money for projects and companies are known as crowdfunding services. There are two main types of platforms: those that aim to raise money – usually small amounts from lots of people – for a project, artwork or new product; and those that look to raise money to start a business and offer investment in that business.

While crowdfunding has been around for a while and there are many players, such as Indiegogo, Crowdtilt and Quirky, Kickstarter is the early leader in the project-funding arena because it has reached critical mass in backers, innovators and funded projects. Kickstarter enables people to fund projects and new product ideas, many of which are in the creative spheres of music, film and theatre. In 2014, it had attracted over $1 billion in pledges and facilitated funding of over 50,000 projects from over five million backers, around two million of which have backed more than one project.

Most projects are small and look to raise less than $10,000, seeking relatively small pledges of $25–$50 per contributor. Typically, these projects offer backers pre-orders of the product, T-shirts and kudos. There have also been a number of Kickstarter projects that have become very high profile, such as the design and production of a Dick Tracy-style LCD smartwatch called the 'pebble', which raised $10 million in 2012. OUYA, a new type of open-source video-games console, raised $8 million in 2012, and the movie of the TV series *Veronica Mars* raised $5 million in 2013.

Many of the projects are experimental, and many project backers don't necessarily expect much in return but are willing to make a contribution to support creative endeavour.

A range of other services, such as CircleUp, Crowdfunder and AngelList, provide online platforms for investment in young growth companies. These platforms offer a way of investing small amounts of money alongside other investors in groups or syndicates.

Crowdfunding is a way of broadening and deepening many people's access to capital on a more global and meritocratic basis. However, many of the same Online Gravity dynamics apply to both project-based and investment crowdfunding. So, for example, on Kickstarter, less than half of all projects put forward are funded, but this varies greatly by type. At the time of writing, 70 per cent of dance and 64 per cent of theatre projects were funded, but only 29 per cent of fashion and 33 per cent of technology projects. And, as a reminder on the website, they say:

> Funding on Kickstarter is all-or-nothing in more ways than one. While 12% of projects finished having never received a single pledge, 79% of projects that raised more than 20% of their goal were successfully funded.

In other words, once the funding ball gets rolling and crosses a certain threshold, its momentum becomes unstoppable, often at the expense of other competitors in the market.

Gravity Investments

Index funds – where you can invest in a basket of leading stocks that is automatically rebalanced as the market ebbs and flows – are probably the biggest revolution of managed investments in the last 50 years. The first index fund was started by John Bogle in the United States in 1975 through his company The Vanguard Group, which is now the leader in this space. In the 1980s, index funds became exchange tradeable – so you can buy and sell the 'whole market' or selected aspects of it just as you can shares in any listed company. They trade like regular stocks and even have their own ticker codes.

In addition to exchange traded index funds – where one share represents a portfolio of different assets – there are also a growing category of online investment products known as 'Synthetics' which don't invest in the underlying assets such as companies, commodities, currencies as such but instead aim to simulate this process by investing in related financial instruments known as derivatives. Synthetic traded funds are emerging as one of the most significant and interesting new professional investment trends enabled by greater connectivity and critical mass of people online. Big businesses are increasingly investing in this way, while at the same time the idea is being democratised by companies such as Motif Investing, which offers the ability for individual investors to develop a thematic investment strategy or policy that they can then turn into their own tradeable stocks.

You can have an idea and create a 'motif' on the site, comprising a basket of up to 30 weighted stocks that represent an investment idea or theme – for example, shale oil, Chinese internet or ethical retailers. You can then publish your motif online and share or follow others. The website provides information about the financial performance of each motif. And, if other people follow or invest in your motif, you receive a royalty. Already, over 5,000 motifs have been created by the website's customers, which is more than all exchange-traded funds in the United States.[15]

KEY POINTS

We can expect to see the following developments (and more) in employment and finance, many of which have already begun:

- *X-ray vision in the jobs market.* Employers will be able to find out much more about us than ever before, and vice versa, owing to online data.
- *Casualisation of the workforce.* Growth in the numbers of part-time and self-employed workers, many participating in the online freelancer economy.
- *Outsourcing and specialisation.* Concurrent growth in the numbers of freelancers and specialists, and also of trade unions for freelancers.

- *Automation and self-service.* Technology is replacing many jobs involved in customer service through automation and self-service but creating many others in economics, technology and the product design of innovative new online service platforms.
- *A local support economy for busy global workers.* Online micro-job marketplaces opening up for global workers looking for people to do the things they no longer have time for, such as cleaning, shopping for groceries and assembling furniture.
- *Paradox of greater productivity but longer working hours.* Because Online Gravity creates highly competitive work and business environments.
- *Online small loans.* Growth in the number of small online loans via peer-to-peer money-lending services, crowd-lending services for third-world development and discounted insurance services based on users covering small parts of other users' risks.
- *Online large loans.* Emergence of peer-to-peer marketplaces for mortgages signals the potential for a transnational mortgage-lending gravity giant.
- *Almost free transactions costs.* At scale, the administrative cost of online transactions is almost zero. Innovators in online investment such as Robinhood and Motif are already demonstrating the potential power of this.

STRATEGIES FOR SMALL BUSINESS OWNERS AND COMPANY EXECUTIVES

Whereas the previous chapter looked mainly at the future of work for employees and aspiring entrepreneurs, this one is for those already in business – small business owners as well as executives and decision-makers in larger enterprises. Here, I set out the challenges and opportunities facing both groups of people, and suggest seven ways you can turbo-charge your small business online, and also seven strategies for senior executives of larger companies to reposition your business to take advantage of Online Gravity.

LESSONS AND OPPORTUNITIES FOR SMALL BUSINESSES

In many practical ways, there has never been a better time to be in small business. Many small businesses can now benefit from the kinds of services that previously only global companies had access to.

Anyone in small business knows that much of your time and energy is spent not on the things that make your business special but on the daily grind of admin and other things that all businesses have to do – things such as managing suppliers, managing

236

staff and contractors, chasing accounts, finding new customers, filing tax returns and complying with other government requirements. Many of these things don't make your business special or help you to stand out from the competition. Often, your customers don't even see them.

To hang out your shingle and start a new business has a big price. And whether your business is a florist, garage or ice-cream parlour, there'll be lots of work that is not about arranging beautiful flowers, fixing cars or creating delicious new flavours of ice cream.

Fortunately, things are changing. If you run or work in a small business and learn to play your cards right, using the forces of Online Gravity to your advantage, you should be able to increase efficiency and spend less time doing the things you're not so passionate about. Pretty much all of the world's smartest tech start-up companies are already working in this way, and we can all look to them and learn a great deal. Even if your aspiration is not to be the next Google, Facebook or Atlassian, your small business can benefit enormously from the many lessons and 'secret sauces' these clever operations use to make their businesses run so well.

Pretty much all start-up tech companies now use a range of new online services to do everything from managing their payroll and finding the best new recruits through to raising capital for new projects. As we've seen, venture capitalists who invest millions backing these high-risk, high-growth technology companies have a good expression in this area: *avoid any undifferentiated heavy lifting*. In other words, they're saying, 'Don't spend your time and our money doing things that others can do better and cheaper.'

The expression 'undifferentiated heavy lifting' was popularised by Jeff Bezos, founder and CEO of Amazon, who said in a 2006 interview with tech-industry publisher and luminary Tim O'Reilly:

I believe that for most companies, and it's certainly true at Amazon, that 70% of your time, energy, and dollars go into the undifferentiated heavy lifting and only 30% of your energy, time, and dollars gets to go into the core kernel of your idea.

I think what people are excited about is that they're going to get a chance to see a future where they may be able to invert those two. Where they may be able to spend 70% of their time, energy, and dollars on the differentiated part of what they're doing.[1]

So, if you can find a way to automate it using the web or have others do it for you online, then that's what you should do. Many venture capitalists want to see the founders of companies they invest in spending as much of their time and energy as possible on things that make them special.

Many of the traditional internal functions needed to run a business have now been broken apart and turned into low-cost, simple, self-customisable online services. This means small businesses today have more flexibility and power than ever before.

All aspects of business are being transformed in this way. Professional communication, for example, used to require a war room of office machines including laser printers, photocopiers, telexes and fax machines, and most of this can now be done more efficiently, more professionally and much more cost-effectively online.

But when was the last time you got a fax? Email is one of the fundamental productivity tools of our generation. As Bill Gates, founder of Microsoft, knows well, it's the most efficient way of communicating in business. In 2006, before he left the company to focus on philanthropy, he said:

At Microsoft, email is the medium of choice, more than phone calls, documents, blogs, bulletin boards, or even meetings (voicemails and faxes are actually integrated into our e-mail in-boxes).

I get about 100 emails a day. We apply filtering to keep it to that level . . . email comes straight to me from anyone I've ever corresponded with, anyone from Microsoft, Intel, HP, and all the other partner companies, and anyone I know.[2]

And while all start-up tech companies use email, many no longer run email servers themselves. Instead, they choose to use an online service such as Gmail, Zimbra, Zoho or Office 365.

Now, no matter what business you are in, a better understanding of Online Gravity can make a big difference to your prospects, and here are some practical ways to get started.

Seven Ways to Turbo-Charge Your Small Business Online

1. Getting Started Online

Starting a business, registering a business name and lodging all the paperwork needed is much easier these days. Most governments now provide the ability to search for an appropriate business name and fill out the required documents online.

In addition, there are a number of low-cost, third-party company registration and lodgement services online, such as LegalZoom in the United States, United Kingdom and Canada, Rocket Lawyer in the United States and United Kingdom, and LawPath in Australia. Many of these also provide access to other standard small-business legal agreements, such as confidentiality agreements.

Filing for trademarks to protect your brands is now a straightforward and simple process online too. And while many governments suggest you should consider hiring an attorney before starting the process, if you read the instructions on the website, you can file online yourself directly with the relevant government authorities in your jurisdiction:

- the United States Patent and Trademark Office;
- the Canadian Intellectual Property Office;
- IP Australia;
- the European Office for Harmonization in the Internal Market;
- the UK Intellectual Property Office.

I applied directly online to the United States Patent and Trademark Office for a US trademark for 'Online Gravity'. It took me a while – about 40 minutes – to complete the application and cost $325 in fees.[3] A simpler approach can be to use one of the many commercial online filing services, which offer more support and feedback. To give you a sense of the growing impact of these third-party services, LegalZoom filed more US trademark applications in 2010 than the top 20 law firms combined and has handled over 20 per cent of all new limited liability company incorporations in California in 2011.[4]

If you haven't done so already, you can register an internet domain name (web address) for your business at one of the many online registrars, such as Go Daddy, Melbourne IT or names.co.uk, and build yourself a simple WordPress website for your business out of the box. All you need are a couple of hours and your credit card and away you go.

Even simpler than a hosted WordPress site is to use a hosted website-building service such as Wix, Squarespace or Weebly. These services offer very easy-to-use, point-and-click configurable templates that are automatically set up to work well and look good on a variety of web browsers such as Internet Explorer, Chrome and Safari as well as most commonly used smartphones and tablets. They are also automatically tuned to be well formatted for indexing and discovery via Google and other search engines or to use the jargon 'Search Engine Optimized' (SEO). Lastly they offer a range of additional web site management services such as visitor statistics and simple integration of online payment services.

If you're a retailer, you may consider using Bigcommerce or Shopify, which offer similar simple tools to create your own online retail presence with built-in shopping-cart and product and inventory-management features. Shopify also offers a point-of-sale view that turns a touch screen tablet into an online 'cash register'. Or you could create a store on eBay or Amazon, which is how many successful online retailers begin their journey.

A simple, free way you can carefully monitor the number of visitors to your website is with Google Analytics, which will give you detailed information about how many people visited, when they visited, where they were from and more. Importantly you can also connect this to your payments system so you can better analyse and understand trends in the 'conversion' process – when and how browsers become shoppers.

If you are selling goods online, a 'no questions asked' refund or exchange policy is strongly recommended.

2. Organise Your Events Online

Offline events are central to every organisation. Online event-organisation platforms such as Eventbrite, Cvent and Amiando make it a breeze – whether it's a ticketed event or simply a free customer event where you want to ensure that everyone RSVPs.

3. Advertise Your Business Online

Online direct marketing has never been easier and more accessible for small businesses. Google and Facebook provide an easy way for anyone to advertise with small budgets and, importantly, experiment with their outbound promotions. You can also target only the customers you are looking for by geography, interests and age, so you can really speak to those people who are most likely to buy your products or services. And you can target advertising to be timed to display to people who are in the mood for buying.

Facebook, for example, allows you to target people who have recently moved houses and, for example, may need new furniture, and Google, of course, allows you to target by search keywords, so you can advertise to people looking to buy engagement rings right at the time when they first type that into Google!

4. Stay in Touch with Your Customers

Online tools such as MailChimp and Campaign Monitor enable small businesses to keep in touch with their customers via simple, beautiful graphic newsletters. These tools also provide ways for small businesses to get valuable feedback on how many of their customers read their mail, which products are most popular and which customers are most interested in them by logging and reporting on the number of people who open and read the newsletters you send out and which articles or images your customers click on. Campaign Monitor is also a joy to use and I've learnt a lot with using it in a variety of different contexts with many clients.

5. Source Supplies Globally

Companies that rely on third-party suppliers can now source supplies globally and readily – everything from basic office stationery to specialist business inputs. If you can buy it online globally, you probably should. Google Shopping provides a simple price-comparison service across a number of suppliers.

The China-based Alibaba is one such global supply marketplace of staggering scale. Amazon and eBay also each have a huge range of global suppliers.

6. Get the Best People Working for You Anywhere

Anything that can be outsourced is being outsourced. Freelancing marketplaces such as oDesk and Freelancer.com provide easy access to global talent. Each now have millions of people buying and selling services such as website design, computer programming, market research and finding new sales leads.

Also, with over 300 million people around the world now on LinkedIn, hiring longer-term or permanent staff has become a lot simpler. For a small fee, you can reach people in a targeted way never before possible – including many people who are not currently actively looking for work.

7. Run Your Whole Business Online

You can now pretty much run your whole business online: your IT, your customer service, your sales – the works. Below is a list of things you might be doing already, but, if you're not, I can recommend all of them from personal experience.

Now you may think this is risky – what about technical failures, hackers and power outages? There are always risks in business and yes these are still there. The reality is, however, working with large-scale reputable online service providers many of these risks are very low – much lower than if you do them yourself as their systems are more reliable, backed-up and more bulletproof than any small business could build or maintain themselves. The real risk for many small businesses may be not adopting many of these online services and being left behind by your more nimble competitors who do.

Outsource Your Basic IT

Using online office productivity tools for word processing, spreadsheets, calendaring and email is a simple way of lowering in-house IT costs and improving the reliability of your service. Google Apps, Microsoft Office 365 or Zoho Office are the leading products in this space and each offer complete suites of tools. I've always used Gmail, and I've found it to be brilliant. I also use Google Slides to create all my presentations now – which can be easily converted to PDFs for offline presentation or handouts if required.

To back up and synchronise your files across different computers, use a cloud-drive system, such as Dropbox (the market leader), Microsoft OneDrive, Apple iCloud or Google Drive. I have used Microsoft Word – the offline, PC-based version – combined with Google Drive to write this book and have found it brilliant, as I can have the latest version synchronised with other computers anywhere, and I can share it with others.

Develop Your In-House IT Online

If you develop any of your own in-house IT systems or run, say, a customer database, you can also use cloud-based service providers such as Amazon Web Services, Microsoft Azure or Google Cloud Platform for amazingly good value, flexible and reliable online computer storage and processing services. For those looking to migrate to developing online, GitHub is like the Dropbox of programming. It provides a way of collaborating and ensuring all your code is synchronised and up to date.

Manage Your Projects Online

Keeping projects involving teams of people on track and having people work together efficiently who work at different times and even at different locations has never been easier. Online tools such as Atlassian's hugely successful product Confluence allows you to work with others on shared projects using a model of collaboration like that which underpins the hugely successful Wikipedia, but in your own company. Using services like these, people can work at their own speed independently with systems to help organise contributions, record revisions and see where everyone is up to. Another online tool for group communication and managing called Slack is rapidly growing in popularity.

Keep Your Books Balanced in the Cloud

Making sure customers are invoiced and staff and suppliers paid is the most fundamental part of running any small business. And this has now become something that can be done online with easy-to-use cloud accounting solutions such as Xero, Fresh-Books and Intuit QuickBooks. These also offer online solutions for invoicing, payroll and bookkeeping. For larger companies with more employees there are also more comprehensive online solutions focused on people management and payroll specifically, such as Workday.

Accept Payments Online via the Web or In Person

To accept and process online credit card, Bitcoin and Apple Pay payments, you may want to consider using one of the leading online payments providers Stripe or Braintree – these services simplify and streamline the process of taking payments securely and seamlessly and integrating this with your online business. If your business is mainly about in-person payments either on the go, in store or at a market, you may want to consider Square, the mobile online payments company established by legendary Twitter co-founder Jack Dorsey, or Invoice2Go which enables you to issue professional invoices from your mobile phone.

Manage Your Own Foreign Exchange

Companies for whom export and import of goods are an important part of their business previously needed to rely on banks to provide them with bespoke and often expensive foreign exchange services. Now, small companies have the option to buy and sell foreign currencies with relative ease *online* with services such as OzForex and Currencies Direct.

Here's a table of some other very interesting services that can help your business.

Key global tools and online services for businesses

Aspect of doing business	Type of service	Name of service
Advertising, communications and sales	Advertising	Google
	Communications	Campaign Monitor
	Events	Eventbrite
	Sales	Salesforce
	Surveys	SurveyMonkey
New products and services	Goods	Alibaba
	Services	Freelancer.com
Operations	Accounting	Xero
	Collaboration	Confluence
	File-sharing	Google Drive
	HR & Payroll	Workday
	Legals	LegalZoom
	Online sales	Shopify
Strategy and innovation	Expert advice	Quora
	Quantitative prediction	Kaggle

ONLINE GRAVITY STRATEGY FOR THE COMPANY EXECUTIVE

If you are the CEO, managing director or other pivotal executive in a company (or in a position to advise such executives), here are some questions and strategies you may be able to use yourself to better position your enterprise in an age of Online Gravity. The questions are not quantitative ones, which may seem odd considering that Law 5 is 'Online Gravity is revealed through data', but, as Malcolm Gladwell points out in his outstanding book *Blink*, focusing first on a mountain of data can often impair important decision-making. Sometimes, we need to step back from this and look at the whole picture.

Let's look at the questions first, which I've formed through my own experiences as a senior executive at IBM and a strategy consultant to many organisations. Then I will offer seven successful strategies that have worked for executives at companies in markets under the direct influence of Online Gravity.

Know Thyself

The Ancient Greeks had a saying that they carved into the Temple of Apollo as a reminder of the power and benefit of self-awareness: *know thyself.* And while this is true in our personal lives, it applies equally to life in business.

In times of change and crisis, companies can draw strength and guidance by reminding themselves of their founders' original purpose. Specifically, they can ask themselves the following questions:

- Why did we get started?
- Who started us?
- What kind of company are we?

Companies are formed for a purpose, and those that endure and thrive are usually there to do more than deliver above-average quarterly profits and dividends to shareholders.

Steve Jobs established Apple Computer in 1976 and was CEO until he was ousted from the company in a boardroom coup in 1985. Twelve years later, he was reinstated as CEO, after Apple bought the company he built after leaving: NeXT Computer.

During Jobs's second stint as CEO at Apple, from 1997 to 2011 – just as with his first – the company paid no dividends to shareholders. Zero. Zip. Nothing.

What he did do, of course, was turn around the company he co-founded 21 years earlier from being unprofitable and on the brink of disaster to becoming the largest company in the world by market value, with over $183 billion in annual revenues in 2014.

The growth of public stock markets over the last century has meant that many of the world's largest companies are now run by independent, professional management and governed by independent, professional directors representing the interests of large and diverse groups of shareholders. Yet many of the most successful and iconic companies of the last 50 years – including Bloomberg, Virgin Group and News Corporation – are those led by their founders. The personal vision, energy and tenacity of Michael Bloomberg, Richard Branson and Rupert Murdoch have made their companies the leaders in their industries.

Online gravity giants Amazon, Facebook and Google are clearly in this mode too, with Jeff Bezos, Mark Zuckerberg, and the duo of Sergey Brin and Larry Page all still firmly at the helm of the great companies they founded.

And Steve Jobs's own approach to transforming Apple from 1997 onwards was to return to the purpose of the company he'd co-founded and have it refocus on building great products. He is quoted in Walter Isaacson's biography as saying, 'Everything else was secondary. Sure, it was great to make a profit, because that was what allowed you to make great products.'[5] Jobs saw this too in other successful, founder-led companies, and, like them, he wanted to create something to last:

> I hate it when people call themselves 'entrepreneurs' when what they're really trying to do is launch a start-up and then sell or go public, so they can cash in and move on. They're unwilling to do the work it takes to build a real company, which is the hardest work in business. That's how you really make a contribution and add to the legacy of those who went before. You build a company that will stand for something a generation or two from now. That's what Walt Disney did, and Hewlett and Packard, and the people who built Intel. They created a company to last, not just make money. That's what I want Apple to be.[6]

When I worked at IBM during the 1990s, I was certainly conscious of the legacy of Thomas J. Watson Snr and his son, Thomas J. Watson Jnr, who successively ran the business from 1914 to 1971.

Watson Senior 'invented' IBM as we know it today when he renamed it from the Computing-Tabulating-Recording Company in 1924. You could almost hear them in the corridor. The culture of customer respect, equal-opportunity hiring and sincerity was very much alive 20 years on from when Watson Jnr left the building.

At IBM at that time, there was also a deep culture of reflection – a rare thing in a contemporary corporation. Watson's Snr's famous slogan of 'Think', encouraging reflection among its employees, dated back to 1911 prior to his arrival at IBM and he brought it with him in his kit bag. In 1935, IBM filed 'Think' as its first US trademark, 14 years before the company filed for a US trademark on the name 'IBM' itself. It was used for the internal company magazine *Think*, as well as the hugely successful ThinkPad Laptop, introduced in 1992, and on a series of signs that adorned the desks of IBM and its customers in the 1960s.

I attribute the company's values, as embodied by its founders and then passed on to successive generations of staff after they left, as being responsible for a large part of IBM's achievements.

Seven Winning Strategies to Take Advantage of Online Gravity

The following are my observations of strategies that have worked for companies looking to reinvent themselves during periods of great digital disruption, and which you can consider applying to your company to position it for ongoing success in the era of Online Gravity.

When it comes to such strategies, there is no 'one size fits all'. Looking at what others did and attempting to copy it to the letter is almost certain to fail. There will be an approach, however, that can give you exactly what you need. It is just a matter of finding it.

As well as being informed by your company's history and the original intentions of its founders, the strategy you apply also depends very much on what level of influence Online Gravity has already had on your market. If your company is in the midst of a duel to the death with another global contestant for the crown in your segment – say, for example, the battle under way between oDesk and Freelancer.com, or Uber and Lyft – a different approach is needed to if, say, you're in an emerging market where a clear tournament is yet to begin.

So, with those notes of caution, here are the seven strategies.

1. Airlock Innovation at IBM

This idea is adapted from Professor Clayton Christensen, author and inventor of *The Innovator's Dilemma*. I call it the 'airlock' approach.

IBM, along with General Electric, is one of the few major companies to survive several ice-age-scale generational changes in technology. One was the move from mechanical computers (tabulators) into the electronic era. This was followed by the move from mainframes into minicomputers, and from minicomputers to PCs.

In the 1970s, IBM had seven competitors in the business of large computers for large companies, which were known as mainframes. This group of eight companies was sometimes referred to as 'IBM and the Seven Dwarfs', as IBM's market share was much larger than the others – in a pattern akin to the Online Gravity comets described previously in this book. The seven 'dwarfs' were Burroughs, UNIVAC, NCR, Control Data Corporation, Honeywell, RCA and General Electric.

In the 1980s, two whole new technology categories emerged that began to form part of the ever-changing computer landscape:

- minicomputers, targeting medium-sized businesses; and
- microcomputers, targeting businesses and personal users.

Each of these segments had different technologies, customers and cost bases, and a whole new generation of companies emerged within them to compete with IBM. As Christensen has pointed out, importantly, each of these segments also had very different levels of profitability:

- Mainframes were 60 per cent gross profit.[7]
- Minicomputers were 45 per cent gross profit.
- Personal computers were 25 per cent gross profit.

IBM's solution to serving these markets and preventing the existing, more profitable segments from killing off the emerging but less profitable new segments was to create 'airlock' businesses, which ran with a high degree of autonomy their own culture and authority in different locations. So, while IBM's mainframe business was in Poughkeepsie, New York, it established mini-computers in Rochester, Minnesota, and personal computers in Boca Raton, Florida.

When minicomputers disrupted the mainframe business, the only survivor was IBM, and when the personal-computer business later disrupted the minicomputer business, IBM was again the only one in that sector not to fall. *Forbes* magazine contributor Steve Denning commented on the success of IBM's personal-computer operations thus:

> IBM survived the threat of the PC by setting up a special business unit in Florida with authorisation to bypass normal company restrictions. The team abandoned established IBM practices of doing everything in-house and built the machine with 'off-the-shelf' parts from other manufacturers. They used an existing 'off-the-shelf' IBM monitor and an existing Epson printer model. They also decided on an open architecture, so that other manu-facturers could produce and sell peripheral components and compatible software without purchasing licenses. The new PC was delivered amazingly quickly – in about a year. The commercial results from these bold and rapid changes were extraordinary. IBM took over the entire PC market.[8]

In 1993 – the year I joined IBM – the company reported the largest ever single-year loss in corporate history: $8.1 billion. It clearly had some challenges. IBM was facing a new generation of competitors that had a gravity of their own – not at that stage Online Gravity but personal-computer gravity.

The newly minted 'outsider' CEO, Louis V. Gerstner, reversed the previous management decision to split the company into pieces to mirror its growing army of nimble competitors in microprocessors (Intel), operating systems (Microsoft), databases (Oracle), storage (Seagate), printers (Hewlett-Packard) and networking (Novell). Instead, Gerstner decided to focus on the one thing IBM could do that none of these companies could: integration. Splitting the company would have destroyed that unique IBM advantage – being able to pull together whatever technology was needed to make large computer systems work.

So the company created a new 'airlock' business – IBM Global Services – which had the freedom and autonomy to pick and choose technologies from third-party providers, including competitors, to meet its customers' needs. This was a spectacular success, which turned around the company's fortunes.

2. Bolt-on Disruption at Google

A large part of Google's signature innovation strategy is to buy early-stage companies that are or have the potential to disrupt large global markets like word processing, mapping and advertising and integrate these into the existing Google product and user ecosystem which of course is centred around their core product, web search. I call this bolt-on disruption.

Marrisa Mayer, prior to her roles as CEO of Yahoo! and on the board of directors at Walmart, was a vice president at Google responsible for global products in a number of areas. Each year, Mayer famously took 20 or so new product managers in her team on a tour of Asia to complete their internship.

I was fortunate enough to see her give a public talk with her flock of newly minted product-innovation managers in Sydney at NICTA – Australia's leading technology-research organisation. At the end of her talk, I asked what she considered was the next most important product innovation developed at Google after search. And she said Google Maps, which incidentally was developed in Sydney. The thing that struck me was not that this product had been developed in Australia but that it came not from their own research efforts but in fact from a company they'd bought.

Google Maps was created by a Danish-born software developer called Lars Rasmussen, his brother Jens Rasmussen and two Australians, Noel Gordon and Stephen Ma. In 2003, the four of them formed Where 2 Technologies in Sydney. A year later, it was acquired by Google and Google Maps was born.

In fact, when you look at it, despite Google spending nearly $10 billion[9] each year on research and development, nearly all of its major business innovations outside of search are in large part the result of acquisitions:

- Blogger – via the acquisition of Pyra Labs in 2003.
- Photos – via the acquisition of Picasa in 2004.
- Maps – via the acquisition of Where 2 Technologies in 2004.
- Docs – via the acquisition of Writely in 2006.
- Video – via the acquisition of YouTube in 2006.
- Display advertising – via the acquisition of DoubleClick in 2007.

You have to ask yourself, why did Google pay $1.65 billion for the then loss-making online video-sharing service YouTube when it could have easily built an equivalent technology and service itself?

I think the answer is that Google understands Online Gravity and knew that online video in this form had reached a tipping point. Buying YouTube was a lower risk and perhaps its *only* chance of entering this market.

One thing Google has really excelled at is the integration of many of its acquisitions. So maps, documents, video and advertising have all been beautifully incorporated into a relatively seamless suite of online applications.

Google has also demonstrated, like IBM, that it has a repeatable and scalable approach to expanding into new markets as they emerge. And this gives confidence to the market that the gravity giant will be able to continue to expand its ecosystem and chart a stable course on the sea of large-scale disruptions and opportunities ahead.

3. Plug and Play at Amazon

Amazon has to be one of the smartest businesses in the world right now. And it's clear that it also understands the nature of Online Gravity.

That's why the stock-market investors also love Amazon. The stock is valued at a price to earnings ratio that is more than ten times that of Google, Microsoft and IBM, and a price to book ratio that is double these companies. What this says is that investors expect future profits to grow big time, and they put great faith in Amazon's intangible assets to be able to deliver on these expectations.

So what's so good about Amazon? Many of you will already know the company from experience as a customer. Starting as a humble online bookstore just over a decade ago, Amazon now sells everything under the sun. Its major categories of online retail include computers and electronics, home and garden, health and beauty, toys, kids and baby, apparel, shoes and jewellery, sports and outdoors, tools, auto and industrial, and digital devices. In the United States, it is also now offering groceries, with AmazonFresh.

But it's not just the colossal retail machine that excites investors. It also has its own cloud-computing service, called Amazon Web Services (AWS). Launched in 2006, AWS offers other companies the ability to use Amazon's own amazing computer power *online*.

What Amazon realised is that, in order to power its online retail business, it needed to run one of the largest and most sophisticated computer-operation businesses in the world. Amazon's herculean computer system needs to be big enough, tough enough and fast enough to cope with the peak retail demand in the lead-up to Christmas but then is massively underutilised for the rest of the year.

Offering this spare computer power to other people would not only provide a greater critical mass for the platform and thus increased Online Gravity but also lower the unit cost and prevent further competition in this space.

Massive corporate computer facilities such as Amazon's are expensive to build and run. While some of the costs are variable (the more people who use the service, the larger the network charges, the more electricity used, and so on), a lot of them are fixed. You need to buy or lease lots of land, build a huge data centre, fill it with football fields' worth of computers, and then write and maintain millions of lines of computer code. With these large fixed costs, the more Amazon can share its computing power with other external users, the more competitive it becomes.

Technology-industry insiders have known for some time that mass-audience software often means better quality and wins out over niche-audience software. Anyone who has been involved with computer software for some time realises that low-end consumer products often win out over high-end professional products (as in, the cheaper it is to buy, the more users it gathers and the better the software becomes as development is essentially a fixed cost). So where there's potential for any overlap, general purpose beats specialist, and consumer wins out over enterprise. This is another example of Clay Christensen's brilliant *Innovator's Dilemma*, as producers of simpler, low-cost mass market products often end up the ultimate victors.

As a fan of 3D computer graphics and animation in the early nineties, I, like many others in the field, looked on with awe at the advanced capabilities of specialist computers made by Silicon Graphics (now SGI), and specialist high-end animation software such as the Canadian Softimage. Softimage was released in 1988 and was used to create advanced visual effects on feature films, such as Steven Spielberg's *Jurassic Park* and James Cameron's *Titanic*. Microsoft acquired Softimage in 1994; Avid acquired it in 1998, and Autodesk in 2008.

At the bottom of the market was a far more affordable product called 3D Studio, which ran on the ubiquitous and cheap DOS-based, and later Windows-based, personal computers. Because the product was more accessible to a much larger audience, there was a generation of people who learnt how to use it and later became its advocates.

With a much, much larger user base, there developed a market for 'plug-ins', or small pieces of software from independent developers that could extend the functionality of the primary software. This created a very active and growing ecosystem, which added more value to the product in a virtuous cycle. It was a kind of online marketplace for small apps, like the iTunes Apps Store.

Over time, the more affordable and ubiquitous 3D Studio (rebranded 3ds Max after an acquisition by Autodesk) got more features and won more market share. Today, 25 years later, Autodesk owns all three major computer graphics creation environments: 3ds Max, Maya and Softimage. The company recently announced that 2015 would see the last release of Softimage and it was migrating users to its other, much more popular, products: 3ds and Maya.

So here we have a prime example of the high-end product losing out over the long run to what was the low-end market entrant. You may want to consider this option for your company too – one of building an outward-facing marketplace that third-party developers can build plug-ins or apps for.

AWS, however, takes a different approach to 'plug and play', which seems to stem from a broader idea that Jeff Bezos has about online services. I understand that Bezos holds that every business can and should break up its offerings into smaller pieces wherever possible – creating services that can be offered to others for a price online via a computer interface, so other computer-mediated services can be built on top of each service. If they can be consumed separately, services should be offered as separately priced purchases.

This is a combination of good economics and good computer science. If you follow this logic, your company becomes a kind of box of Lego bricks, broken down into its most basic units. An example may be a simple online customer satisfaction survey tool, built initially for your company's customers, which could be designed in a way that it could be flexibly re-configured and reused, with different types of questions presented in different contexts as inputs in another part of the company, say for example, as an online supplier survey or employee satisfaction survey. Because of the open and reconfigurable design approach this 'survey engine' could potentially then be offered to other companies to use for their own surveys as well. Conversely, because the inputs and outputs are clear, spelt out and measurable, it could be swapped-out without too much fuss if a say, better, faster or more flexible tool comes along.

This approach has some serious benefits. Namely, your company can become:

- more agile – you can plug the services into one another and recombine them in new ways to create new services, because each service has a standard and known computer interface;
- more efficient – you can share services across the company to avoid duplication and make sure you have the best possible fundamental building blocks;
- more reliable – you can better maintain your business and, if one service is faulty, get a new one – either from inside the company or outsourced;

- more measurable in its cost basis – you know the exact cost of each service for each transaction (in terms of computer usage, storage, dollars, staff time etc) and hence the total costing, as none are bundled with other services and the costs are simply added up.

And you can do as AWS does and offer your box of Lego bricks for others to use. This way, when others build their business using your Lego bricks, you create a broader user base, lower cost base and also a new business stream.

Renowned internet futurist Mark Pesce outlines this idea in his online book *Hyperbusiness: The Next Billion Seconds*. Pesce points out that 'service disaggregation' has been going on for some time.[10] Think of hotels: usually, hotel-room rental is bundled with services such as air-conditioning, television and bath-towel laundry. And there are other services that you usually pay for separately on a usage basis, such as a minibar, room service and massage. In super-discount air travel, we're seeing services such as in-flight meals and extra baggage, which were once included in the price of a ticket, now being offered as paid-for extras.

A large hotel group may well employ a plug-and-play strategy for in-sourcing traditional services – say, some extra laundry from private clients to provide their own internal laundry services with greater scale and efficiency – but you'd reach a limit pretty quickly in terms of the local demand and the fixed cost of labour in doing the laundry.

A plug-and-play strategy for online services, however, where the operating costs approach zero, has no such limits. A large hotel group could, for example, offer the use of its online reservations system at almost no extra cost to hotels on the other side of the world and derive extra revenue for the use of this platform, which could be reinvested in improving and maintaining it for their own customers.

AWS does just this and now acts as the platform for many leading online marketplaces, such as Etsy, Spotify and Netflix.

A plug-and-play strategy means you can spread the cost of your vital infrastructure across many other users, reducing your outlay, lowering your risk and increasing returns from a new business stream.

4. Radical Product Innovation at Sony

While easier said than done, a product innovation that radically moves the market forward a generation in terms of technology can galvanise the forces of Online Gravity, disrupt the existing players and make way for new entrants.

An example is the PlayStation 2 (PS2) computer-games console, which at its launch in March 2000, with advanced graphics and processing power completely trumped the existing generation of games consoles released around five years earlier – known as the fifth-generation consoles. It had a built-in DVD player, and so offered Sony a bundling strategy as well (see following). DVD players were at that stage expensive and in many cases more expensive than the PS2 so many bought it on that basis alone.

Although not part of the initial functionality, Sony importantly provided internet connectivity later via a network adaptor to allow people to play with or against each other online and connect to games publishers. This became an important part of Sony's strategy as owning a console grew in value with a growing network of online players and the PS2 went on to become the bestselling video-games console in history, with over 155 million units sold from its launch in 2000 to when it was discontinued in 2012 and superceded by the PS3 and PS4.

The PS2 had been so successful that Sega announced the discontinuation of its rival console, the Dreamcast, in March 2001, just 18 months after its promising launch. As a result, the PS2 was the only sixth-generation console remaining in the market for over six months, before Microsoft launched its rival Xbox and Nintendo launched its GameCube.

Sony has a long and proud history of breakthrough personal-entertainment and media products, with products such as the Walkman (1979) and Discman (1984). These were huge global successes that helped to redefine the market for portable personal audio worldwide. If your company can produce anything as game-changing as the PS2 or these, it is of course on to a winner.

5. The Lasso at Microsoft

Disrupting or dislodging Online Gravity giants once they are established is nearly impossible – indeed, I think it *is* impossible.

Microsoft knows this more than anyone. Having been the lead technology giant in the personal-computing era, and despite Apple becoming the largest company in the world, Microsoft still owns the desktop, and even today enjoys over 90 per cent market share of the operating system that runs on all desktop computers.[11] What has happened, however, is that with the rise of smartphones and tablets, which Apple clearly dominates, the personal-computer desktop has become less relevant.

So, looking to dominate in a completely revolutionary category of product such as the smartphone is one approach – as Apple have done – but another is to lasso or bundle the innovative features of other products into your existing platform.[12]

There are two pieces of software that are essential to all online marketplaces: the browser software that runs on your customers' computers and the server software that runs on the computer running the website.

Netscape, which was the poster child of the early web from its formation in 1994 up to its sale to AOL in 1999, provided the leading software of both types. Its web browser was Netscape Navigator, which commanded more than 80 per cent of the browser market, and its server software was Netscape Enterprise Server, which also enjoyed the majority share of the market.

The Netscape Navigator web browser initially retailed at $49 a copy, and Netscape Enterprise Server sold for between $995 and $3995, depending on how big your website was and how many users you had. Technology investors of the day felt that Netscape had the keys to the online kingdom, and the company enjoyed a spectacular stock-market debut on the tech-heavy NASDAQ exchange on 9 August 1995, as recalled by Alex Planes of The Motley Fool website in 2013:

> Shares were offered at $28 apiece before Netscape's IPO [initial public offering, or stock-market launch]. At the opening bell, the price shot up, and by the end of August 9, Netscape closed at $58.25 after reaching as high as $74.75 during the day. This meteoric rise valued the 16-month-old company at nearly $3 billion.[13]

Microsoft was keen to capitalise on this momentous shift of value to the web and spent over $100 million per year on developing a rival browser, Internet Explorer, in the late 1990s.[14] According to one team member's recollection, it had more than a thousand people working on it by 1999.[15]

Microsoft released its initial version of Internet Explorer in August 1995, and, unlike Netscape Navigator, it was offered for free. From December 1995, Microsoft began bundling Internet Explorer 2.0 with computers that had Windows 95 pre-installed. In August 2006, Microsoft also bundled a number of features in the release of its major server operating system, NT, including an internet server called Internet Information Server (now Internet Information Services, or IIS), to compete with Netscape's offering, and a music streaming service for Windows Media Player. The music streamer decimated the leading player in this field at the time: RealNetworks, which was previously sitting on a 90 per cent market share. Again, this was included for free.

As the majority of the world was running Windows-based PCs, these two moves by Microsoft, coupled with internal problems at Netscape, caused the latter's market share to go into massive decline.

Another example of this happened in the corporate local-area-networking market. Before the arrival of Windows NT Server, Novell claimed 90 per cent of the networking market for PC-based servers, but because its system was late to adopt the open internet networking standard and was tied to an older, pre-Windows operating system, DOS, it rapidly lost market share.

When Windows NT arrived on the scene, it offered much of the functionality of Novell NetWare, as Igor Jazbec, leading networking consultant at the time, commented:

> I agree NT did kill NetWare, but not because NT was a better product. NT wasn't very good at doing the same task as NetWare at the time of initial release – file/print servers. Windows NT did app servers. App servers never took off on NetWare for some reason – I don't think they bothered pursuing it really. In the end it's similar to the way Mosaic [predecessor to Netscape Navigator] was killed off by Internet Explorer – it didn't actually matter that it was the better product – once its functionality was incorporated into the higher-cost higher-complexity system (the desktop/server OS), even if it isn't as good, why fork out for a separate product when you no longer have to?[16]

The lasso strategy is one where you launch a new product or service that includes or bundles the functionality of a competitor's and uses your existing customer base to make the incumbent redundant.

It is worth noting that Microsoft has also executed some of the other strategies mentioned here, such as radical product innovation (Kinect) and bolt-on disruption (Hotmail and Skype).

6. Autonomy Insurance at Workday

Workday is the gravity giant that provides online-payroll and financial-management software to large companies. The company was established in 2005 by David Duffield, the founder and former CEO of the enterprise-software giant PeopleSoft, and former PeopleSoft chief strategist Aneel Bhusri, following the hostile takeover of PeopleSoft by rival Oracle.

The sale of PeopleSoft to Oracle was an opportunity for Duffield and Bhusri to start again from scratch and build a cloud-based enterprise-services company that leveraged the power of Online Gravity to its full extent. Cleverly, from the beginning, they focused on new techniques meant to make it easy for businesses to use the service and integrate it into their pre-existing technology.

The company listed its shares on NASDAQ in 2012, valuing the company at $4.5 billion, and at the time of listing the two founders collectively held 67 per cent of the company's voting shares. This voting structure and ownership makes the threat of a hostile takeover much more unlikely and provides them with 'autonomy insurance' to continue with their mission of providing online-finance and human-resources apps built for the future. By 2014, the company had more than trebled in value from its initial listing and is now worth over $16 billion.

Many other successful founder-led public companies, such as News Corporation, have paid close attention to the design of their voting and ownership structure to ensure that they can keep hold of the reins.

In a sign of trusting its own staff with a degree of autonomy, Workday now enables its employees to take 'unlimited' personal and sick leave with the okay of their manager. This trend of offering employees unlimited leave has been promoted at other tech companies, including another gravity giant, Netflix, which pioneered the concept and whose success with this has inspired other entrepreneurial companies such as Virgin Group to follow suit.

7. Market Revolution at Apple

From the outside, Apple appears to have the best company strategy, but perhaps it is the hardest one to replicate. Or it seems that way, as not many others have managed to.

Apple is rare in its ability to repeatedly create breakthrough, novel products from within and take those with great success to market. So what is Apple's secret strategy when it comes to Online Gravity?

Opposite is a chart of Apple's share price from its huge initial listing on NASDAQ in December 1980[17] through to 2014.

What do you notice about it, apart from wishing you had a time machine handy to go back and buy stock? At the bottom, above the years, there are two rows of flags with the letter 'D' – this means the company paid a portion of its profits to its shareholders at this time: a dividend.

As we've seen, the company never paid dividends when Steve Jobs was around (1976–1985 and 1997–2011). What does that tell you? It's a reflection of Jobs's style and approach. And part of his strategy was to create value for the customer first and not the shareholder.

Regular dividend payments are the hallmark of clockwork-like precision, focused on delivering the predictable company results expected by Wall Street analysts and the army of professional company CEOs that eagerly look to impress them, along with the fund managers they represent.

At Apple's 2010 annual general meeting, Jobs told fellow share-holders who asked about the dividend policy:

> Our goal is to increase enterprise value. Which would you rather have us be? A company with our stock price, and $40 billion in the bank? Or a company with our stock price and no cash in the bank?
>
> . . . When you take a risk, you jump in the air, and it's nice to know that the ground is still there.

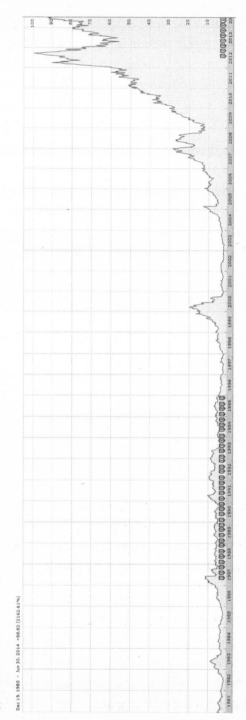

Apple's share price from 1980 to 2014

Apple Inc. (NASDAQ:AAPL)

Dec 19, 1980 - Jun 30, 2014 +88.82 (2162.61%)

> . . . You never know what opportunities lie around the corner.
> We are a large company now. So to move the needle, we need
> to think big.[18]

John Sculley said recently, reflecting back on the time when he
ousted Steve Jobs from the company he created:

> I did not have the breadth of experience at that time to really
> appreciate just how different leadership is when you are
> shaping an industry as Bill Gates did or Steve Jobs did, versus
> when you're a competitor in an industry, in a public company,
> where you don't make mistakes because if you lose, you're
> out.[19]

And this industry-shaping leadership, where you are fearless and
have a vision for where you want to take things, is how to create
your own planet in Online Gravity. It's kind of like space engineering – not for the faint-hearted or for everyone.

To put the company's achievements under Jobs's leadership
into perspective and to give a sense of scale of the resultant gravity
giant, Apple sold more iOS (mobile operating system) devices in
2011 than all the Macs it sold in the previous 28 years – now that's
using the force!

KEY POINTS

Small business owners and company executives may benefit from
employing the following proven strategies, which are already used
by established gravity giants as well as many savvy gravity giants
in the making.

Small business owners

- *Avoid undifferentiated heavy lifting.* Outsource anything that
  can be outsourced, so you can play to your strengths.
- *Register your business, file for trademarks and set up your stall
  online.* There are many online tools to help you to do this.

- *Organise your events online.* Again, online tools, such as Eventbrite and Amiando, make this easy and efficient.
- *Advertise your business online.* Facebook and Google allow you to target your advertising very specifically by audience, time and location.
- *Stay in touch with your customers online.* MailChimp and Campaign Monitor are two very useful tools in this regard.
- *Source supplies globally.* You can often get them cheaper from overseas.
- *Get the best people working for you anywhere.* When you out-source tasks, you can recruit based on expertise, rather than geographical proximity.
- *Run your whole business online.* Much of your business needs, such as accounting, IT and foreign-exchange services, can be met via online services.

Company executives

- *Know thyself.* When facing business challenges or transforma-tions, ask yourself why your company got started, who started it and what kind of company it is.
- *Airlock innovation.* Use independent business subsidiaries to pursue innovation independently.
- *Bolt-on disruption.* Expand your offerings by buying and integrating innovative companies that have the potential to shake your industry, even if your company could replicate the technology itself.
- *Plug and play.* Break up your business offerings into smaller pieces wherever possible, which will grant your company greater flexibility and also give you a new stream of revenue in offering these components to other companies.
- *Radical product innovation.* Aim to make products that can trump the competition and redefine the market.
- *The lasso.* If you can't beat other technologies, replicate them and bundle them into your own offerings, ideally for free.

- *Autonomy insurance.* Selling part of the company such as via a venture capital round or stock market listing is a great way to raise money to fund global expansion, growth and innovation but be mindful that founder-led and controlled companies are often the most successful in the long run.
- *Market revolution.* Aim to please the customers rather than the shareholders, by continually outpacing competitors and by reinventing the market.

SOCIETY: A TALE OF TWO CITIES

> It was the best of times, it was the worst of times, it was the age of wisdom, it was the age of foolishness, it was the epoch of belief, it was the epoch of incredulity, it was the season of Light, it was the season of Darkness, it was the spring of hope, it was the winter of despair, we had everything before us, we had nothing before us, we were all going direct to Heaven, we were all going direct the other way . . .
>
> Charles Dickens, *A Tale of Two Cities*

As our world becomes more and more connected by the day, is it becoming a better place? Some argue that it is, and that the online revolution is creating an open, collaborative and increasingly egalitarian global society, while others see our social systems as becoming increasingly inequitable and unstable. So is the online world a smooth, flat ground full of opportunity for all or is it an uneven, rocky land suited to the construction of huge castles in the sky for only a select few?

A WORLD OF SMOOTH CONNECTIONS

The web provides us with individual liberties never before enjoyed. It also provides us with powerful new ways to connect with others:

those we love and care about most, those in our broader circle and even those we don't know yet. And, importantly, it provides us with new ways to share stuff.

The future painted by Rachel Botsman and Roo Rogers in their book *What's Mine is Yours*, about what is becoming known as the 'sharing economy', is indeed a positive one. They present what they call the rise of collaborative consumption, which Botsman describes elsewhere as 'An economic model based on sharing, swapping, trading, or renting products and services, enabling access over ownership'.[1] The success of these collaborative systems, the authors argue, is dependent on four principles:

1. Critical mass – having a large enough user base to make the system self-sustaining. For example, a city-wide bike-share program needs enough bikes to meet the needs of all the people who want to use it.
2. Idling capacity – people's willingness to put lazy assets, such as drills or other power tools that they use only four times a year, to better use by sharing them.
3. Belief in the commons – by contributing to the group interest, our shared pasture, we all benefit, and the internet is the most robust commons in history.
4. Trust between strangers – collaborative consumption often removes authoritarian gatekeepers and requires trust among its users.

The authors hope that we look back on our current era and see one where our self-interest, greed and consumerism was transformed into a future of sharing, more meaningful interactions and intuitive social cooperation. Botsman and Rogers believe that, by a happy combination of the power of the internet and our better natures, this will come to pass.

There has certainly been a huge growth in online-enabled sharing-economy businesses. As *Wired*'s Jason Tanz wrote poetically:

We are hopping into strangers' cars (Lyft, Sidecar, Uber), welcoming them into our spare rooms (Airbnb), dropping our dogs off at their houses (DogVacay, Rover), and eating food in their dining rooms (Feastly). We are letting them rent our cars (RelayRides, Getaround), our boats (Boatbound), our houses (HomeAway), and our power tools (Zilok). We are entrusting complete strangers with our most valuable possessions, our personal experiences – and our very lives. In the process, we are entering a new era of internet-enabled intimacy.[2]

Others, such as Kevin Roose, suggest that the proliferation of these businesses is not due to us having any more trust in each other but simply due to a decline in full-time employment, which has led to people looking for alternative ways to make money. He says:

In a few cases, it's because the pricing structure of the sharing economy made their old jobs less profitable. (Like full-time taxi drivers who have switched to Lyft or Uber.) In almost every case, what compels people to open up their homes and cars to complete strangers is money, not trust.[3]

Whatever the motivation, there's no denying it's happening. In her book on *The Mesh*, online entrepreneur and author Lisa Gansky says she has uncovered over 1500 companies in the sharing economy: 'a world where access trumps ownership'. Gansky says the rise in sharing will result in better quality, more durable and repairable products, and turn the logic of throwaway culture on its head. She quotes her friend Saul Griffith, the maverick and respected MIT Media Lab alumni inventor, who has coined the beautiful term 'heirloom design' – something that's built to last for generations. Griffith explains in an interview with *GOOD Magazine* the importance of this idea:

GOOD Magazine: Why is it important that we design stuff to last longer?

Saul Griffith: An enormous amount of the energy we use [industrially] is locked up in 'embodied energy'. It's trapped, or embodied, in the materials our stuff is made of. It's the energy that we use to mine materials and process them into products. While we can choose materials that have less embodied energy for any given product, it's much better to choose objects that last two or three, or preferably 10 times, longer. As I see the climate change and carbon dioxide problem, it is one way of figuring out how to live the best quality of life while using much less energy. Heirloom products are one way to make a significant contribution. It probably means you will end up owning less junk, your life will be less cluttered, and your stuff will be more beautiful and serve you with more joy. [4]

A FLAT LAND OF EQUAL OPPORTUNITY

In the third major edition of his bestselling and compelling book *The World is Flat*, three-time Pulitzer Prize-winning author Thomas Friedman outlines how a series of ten digital-technology-related flattening forces are 'equalizing power – and equalising opportunity', and continuing to level the global playing field. [5]

The title of the book derives from a quote from the former CEO of Infosys, Nandan Nilekani, dubbed the Bill Gates of Bangalore. Friedman explains it in an interview with Daniel H. Pink for *Wired* magazine in 2005:

Wired: What do you mean the world is flat?

Friedman: I was in India interviewing Nandan Nilekani at Infosys. And he said to me, 'Tom, the playing field is being leveled.' Indians and Chinese were going to compete for work like never before, and Americans weren't ready. I kept chewing over that phrase – the playing field is being leveled – and then it hit me: Holy mackerel, the world is becoming flat. Several technological and political forces have converged, and that has produced a global, web-enabled playing field that allows for multiple forms of collaboration without regard to geography or distance – or soon, even language.[6]

In the introduction to the third edition, he goes on to clarify that when he says flat, he doesn't mean that the world is equal in terms of incomes, which clearly has yet to happen, simply that the basis for competition has been equalised and that many of the walls – literally (he starts with the Berlin Wall) and figuratively (traditional barriers to trade) – have come down.

Friedman says that globalisation has occurred in three phases and we're in the third of these:

- Globalisation 1.0 – where governments were the main actors;
- Globalisation 2.0 – where transnational companies led; and
- Globalisation 3.0 – where individuals armed with web-connected PCs are leading the way.

I'd agree with him on this, and it's in individuals and small businesses making purchasing decisions and outsourcing services globally where we'll see some amazing things happen over the next decade. And we're really only at the beginning of this cycle.

Ever since Friedman's book, other writers, subeditors and Friedman's critics have been riffing on his original title. That's a sign of sure impact! Professor Pankaj Ghemawat at the University of Navarra in Spain wrote a punchy article in response for *Foreign Policy* titled 'Why the World isn't Flat'.[7] In it, he made some great data points, claiming that:

- more than 90 per cent of all phone calls and web traffic is local;
- the number of long-term international migrants amounted to three per cent of the world's population in 1900 – the high-water mark of an earlier era of migration – versus 2.9 per cent in 2005; and

- the total amount of the world's capital formation that is generated from foreign direct investment (FDI) has been less than ten per cent for the last three years for which data was available (2003–05). In other words, more than 90 per cent of the fixed investment around the world is still domestic.

And Professor Richard 'Creative Classes' Florida wrote another great article in *The Atlantic* titled 'The World is Spiky', which is complete with an atlas of the spikes to illustrate his points.[8]

AN OPEN LAND OF PUBLIC DATA

In a June 2014 report for the G20, Nicholas Gruen highlighted the increasing opportunity that open data presents for governments looking to promote global growth, trade and employment.[9]

The Group of Twenty, or G20, is a group of finance ministers and central bank governors from 20 major national economies. It pledged at a meeting in Sydney in 2014 to pursue new policies aimed at growing the national incomes of its members' collective economies by over $2 trillion over the coming five years and in the process create tens of millions of new jobs. 'We will develop ambitious but realistic policies with the aim to lift our collective GDP by more than 2% above the trajectory implied by current policies over the coming 5 years,' the official G20 communiqué reads.[10]

Nicholas Gruen argues that government policies that accelerate the use of open government and publishing of public data could contribute more than half this growth target, or 1.1 per cent growth in GDP. Liquid information is the key to any market operating efficiently and effectively. Given governments are still the central information and data custodians in most countries, they are uniquely positioned to play a significant role in opening this treasure trove to create value for the community, business and individual citizens everywhere.

Types of datasets that could become public access

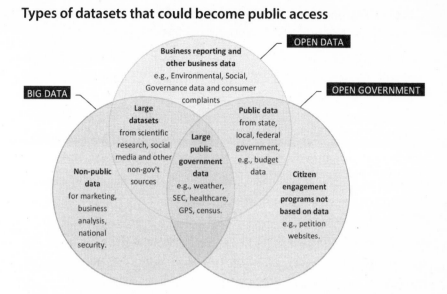

Figure based on: Joel Gurin, *Open Data Now*, McGraw-Hill, New York, 2014.

HAZARDS AHEAD FOR ONLINE EXPLORERS

So far, Online Gravity seems to be positioning us for a bright and rosy future: one of socially smooth sharing, full of rich and open information, and played out on an abundant, super-connected and level playing field.

Like the polar explorers of the twentieth century, there are many hazards facing Diginauts or fearless adventurers exploring the frontiers of work and business under the influence of Online Gravity.

There are two iceberg-sized issues that could put these smooth-sailing outcomes in jeopardy. These are that Online Gravity may be contributing to long-term declines in profitability, and also that it might be playing a part in a growing, longer-term trend of global inequality. Inequality on the worldwide scale has become a central point of discussion in economics lately, or, as Megan McArdle from Bloomberg Businessweek rather poetically put it:

Everyone, it seems, is worried we are shortly headed for a world in which a handful of rich people will own everything, and the rest are forced to rent their air and water from Mark Zuckerberg.[11]

The First Iceberg: Company Profit Evaporates

The first threat to our rosy future is an idea called the Big Shift, created and promoted by John Hagel, author and co-founder of the Deloitte Center for the Edge. The Big Shift sheds light on a number of long-term changes afoot in the global economy – many of which we've discussed in this book.

Hagel argues that the growth of digital technologies and global trade combined has radically increased competition in business over the past 40 years and made it more difficult for businesses to make the profits they used to.

There's one part of this in particular that I and many others have found fascinating, and that's the long-term decline in returns on assets – that is, in how much profit companies are generating on the things of value they hold. In a traditional business such as manufacturing, for instance, assets are the factory, equipment and the land the company owns in order to produce future products and income.

On aggregate, the return on assets of US firms has fallen to one-quarter of its 1965 levels. Profitability depends on firms finding new ways to generate value from their assets. Hagel argues that today, because of their short-term focus, many 'companies are broken, and many don't know'.[12]

One likely explanation for this is the rapid growth of intangible assets over the same period. The things that are the sources of future value for Online Gravity giants are not factories and fleets of trucks but their brands, talented employees and relationships with millions of customers.

In the 1970s, the structure of the Western economies looked very different and manufacturing was the dominant sector. Not surprisingly, in 1975, over 80 per cent of the assets of 500 of the largest companies in the United States – those in the S&P 500 index – was made up of tangible resources. Today, this situation has reversed, with over 80 per cent of the assets of these companies residing in intangible resources.[13]

The other explanation is that many of the online giants are still growing rapidly and short-term earnings are not their priority. Instead, they have their eyes on a much longer-term, larger prize.

In the risk sections of their annual reports, many gravity giants are clear with their investors about this. Zillow says in its 2014 annual report, 'We have incurred significant operating losses in the past and we may not be able to generate sufficient revenue to be profitable over the long term.'[14] And Amazon provides a similar warning: 'In addition, profitability, if any, in our newer activities may be lower than in our older activities, and we may not be successful enough in these newer activities to recoup our investments in them.'[15]

Online Gravity can be a high-stakes, high-risk game for investors and for employees of companies under its influence. Investors often willingly forgo earnings and dividends for the promise of future stock price growth and, likewise, employees and executives routinely forgo part of their salary and work longer hours than their peers in the hope of windfall gains from stock options.

And, of course, we know that not everyone is a winner in Online Gravity – in fact, it's the complete opposite. Necessarily, there will be many investors and employees whose sacrifices will not be met with windfall gains, future profits and bonuses. Many, if not most, may even lose their shirts.

So, while a very few of us are likely to thrive and do abundantly well under the Big Shift, many of us may also struggle to adapt to this new world.

The Second Iceberg: Kingdoms Return

In the middle of the seventeenth century, the French king Louis XIV created one of the most elaborate and expensive palaces in history. His private residence, the Palace of Versailles, is one of the largest and most spectacular palaces in history and can comfortably host the royal family and up to 600 guests.

This was clearly not a time of equality. The cost in the currency of the day was 91 million livres,[16] while the average skilled worker earned one livre per day.[17] In 2014, skilled bricklayers and plumbers earn around $200 per day, and on this basis Versailles is an $18 billion palace. Running of the palace is thought to have consumed between six and 25 per cent of France's total national income per annum![18]

The bloody French Revolution – which ensued not long after the completion of Versailles in the reign of his grandson, Louis XVI – proclaimed to end all this excess but perhaps wasn't as successful as its promoters had planned. French economist Thomas Piketty points out in his book *Capital* that inequity has been a structural flaw in our economic systems not just under the famously extravagant monarchies of the 1600s but also throughout the 1700s and 1800s – the settings for Jane Austen's famous novels – through a combination of inherited wealth and the rigid class systems in many parts of Europe.

Piketty's 685-page work has been described as the most important book in economics in many years and 'maybe of the decade' by Nobel laureate Paul Krugman. Piketty and his colleagues have compiled data on wealth and incomes for over 20 countries from 1700 to 2014 and found that structural inequality has been a factor in all Western economies throughout time, from the days of the Roman Empire until today, with the exception of the period between the First World War and now. During the last one hundred years, clearly economic inequity hasn't disappeared entirely but it has shrunk dramatically in many Western countries along with the post-war economic boom, waves of technology-led innovation and the growth of the middle classes. Piketty argues that the last century may however have been an economic oddity and predicts that the world is now returning to its long-term norm, where returns on capital are greater than overall economic growth, thus continuing to widen the gaps between rich and poor and between those with inherited wealth and those without.

Piketty's analysis is certainly thought-provoking. One area I question is that while he accepts technology has been a central driver of growth in the twentieth century but says we should not base ourselves on the 'caprices of technology', to which I'd say that the laws of technology are not capricious and it may well be we are in a new era of technology with irreversible growth built in – an era of Online Gravity.

On the other hand, one of Piketty's critics, Lawrence Summers, argues that diminishing returns on capital have been underestimated, which he believes will set an upper limit on inequality.[19] In Online Gravity, there are no such limits. In fact, as increasing returns apply, more inequity, not less, is likely to ensue.

Let us assume technology continues to deliver benefits at the exponential rate we've come to appreciate and even begun to expect. There still remains the question: who owns the robots?

KEY POINTS

What sort of future society will Online Gravity produce? This chapter expresses both optimistic and pessimistic forecasts:

- *A world of smooth connections.* Online Gravity engenders a 'sharing economy', whereby greed and consumerism are replaced by beneficial connectivity, meaningful interaction and social cooperation.

- *A flat land of equal opportunity.* Online Gravity levels the global playing field by removing geography, distance and language from the game.
- *An open land of public data.* Global governments boost their average national income by opening up their treasure troves of data to the public.
- *A spiky land of unequal opportunity.* The web's global nature fails to redistribute wealth along non-national lines, with the disfavoured nations becoming even more so due to low levels of migration and foreign investment.
- *A 'Big Shift' economy.* Decreasing returns on companies' assets means less prosperity on the whole, alongside huge prosperity for the runaway winners.
- *A return to 'kingdoms'.* The gap between rich and poor widens as the rewards for Online Gravity's big winners outstrip overall economic growth, heightening wealth inequality.

SUPERPOWERS AND RENAISSANCE 2.0

> Any sufficiently advanced technology is
> indistinguishable from magic.
>
> Arthur C. Clarke, *Profiles of the Future*

A final key aspect of Online Gravity's influence on our future is that it has the potential to give us 'superpowers', both on a personal level and within our institutions, such as health and science. Our personal superpowers will come mainly through new ways of interacting with the web-enabled technology increasingly surrounding us. We'll be typing less and less and swiping or using other gestures more and more, in a manner resembling futuristic science fiction. And we're already on a journey to the point where we no longer even need gestures.

Advances in health, education and scientific research are all now a product of the knowledge economy of the web, and the access it gives us to unprecedented amounts of data. We can become self-educators and armchair experts, and whole new professions may be born in online-data analysis for specific purposes, such as medical diagnoses and treatments.

Finally, a new, perhaps even more spectacular, renaissance seems to be on the cards, combining everything we've seen in this book, including advanced technology, automation, globalisation and big data, to produce potentially huge leaps forward in knowledge through a new era of data science. This chapter will cover each of these topics in turn.

COMPUTERS & HUMANS – A MARRIAGE THAT KEEPS DEVELOPING

One way to look at the major phases of computer technologies and their impacts is to consider the way in which we interact with them. In fact, it can be said that most of the money and impact in any computer-technology revolution occurs not where the rubber hits the road but where the tech touches the people.

The first generation of digital computers required experts to operate them. Computer programs had to be written that were converted into numbers for the computers to process. Typically, the only people who ever interacted with these machines were the scientists and engineers who built and maintained them.

Another generation along, computers began to be able to work with letters, and an 'operating system' was born that provided rudimentary user access via a keyboard. This enabled people to work with their own computers without the need to consult its maker.

As magnetic storage evolved, it became possible to store data and programs on portable, reusable magnetic disks. And the operating systems were tweaked to help take care of storing and retrieving information from these disks. One of the first such systems was known as the Microsoft Disk Operating System, or MS-DOS, which of course became hugely popular around the world and formed the basis of the company we know today. It had what was called a command-line interface, which allowed you to type words – a bit like today's search engines – in certain sequences to perform certain tasks, such as storing or running programs.

This era was one driven by text-based user interfaces, as the way you interacted with the computer was by typing various commands and using the function keys as shortcuts. Early word processors such as WordPerfect and spreadsheets such as VisiCalc all worked this way.

The next era was ushered in by the groundbreaking research done at the photocopy pioneer Xerox's corporate computer research lab in California, known as Xerox PARC (Palo Alto Research Center). Researchers at Xerox PARC invented most of the technologies that formed the basis of the personal-computer era – so the mouse, local computer networking and, importantly, the graphical user interface, or GUI, which meant you could now use visual icons and menus to make your computer do things, rather than typing in commands.

Steve Jobs saw what they were doing and realised it was the future. He offered Xerox a slab of pre-IPO Apple stock for the privilege of reviewing the inventions in their lab. Bill Gates also got the telegram. What resulted was the Apple Macintosh, Microsoft Windows and Adobe's vector graphics computer language called PostScript, and we moved into the era of GUIs, where computers were driven by windows, icons, mice and pointers (WIMPS). *That's a real acronym, in case you think I've made it up.*

The next major inflection point for our interactions with computers was with the launch of gesture-based interfaces, such as with the Nintendo Wii – the pioneering games console you could play without a controller. Some, including the former Microsoft researcher August de los Reyes, call this the natural user interface era. Hot on the heels of the Wii launch, Apple again seized the lead with the introduction of its touchscreen-based smartphone (iPhone), which allowed people to interact through that most simple and natural of human gestures, pointing and touching. It was also fully configurable, as the screen was glass and the buttons could be rewritten in the software.

NEXT-GENERATION INTERACTION

The next phase of this development is already under way on a variety of frontiers, all of which are directed towards making us feel increasingly at home with our devices. They will give us a new set of 'superpowers', which fall into three main groups:

- Metavision – the ability to see things in new ways.
- Invocation – the ability to use our voice as never before.
- Telekinesis – the ability to act at a distance.

Metavision – Enabling Us to See Further

We all know that, when we look around, we don't see the full picture. Imagine if we could. While closer inspection of the far (telescope), near (microscope) and under the surface (X-ray machine) have been central to our discoveries in modern science, being able to see at a distance (literally, television) is arguably the most important media innovation of the last century.

Now, Online Gravity provides a new dimension of being able to see in ways we never could before. At the supermarket, for example, with metavision, you'd be able to see as much or as little detail on each of the products as you wanted, and focus on whatever aspect was most important to you. Where did all the ingredients come from? How do the nutritional benefits fit with your special dietary needs? What are the company's policies on the environment and ethical treatment of animals? When holidaying in Europe, as another example, you will be able to 'see into' history in new ways that provide personal and engaging interactivity.

A visual overlay with extra information about the environment around us – or augmented reality – has been here for many years within the military, in the form of head-mounted displays for fighter pilots, and driving data is now being projected onto the windscreens of many new cars. Combined with the power of

Online Gravity, augmented reality gives us a kind of contextual and personal pop-up guide to everything we see and touch. Google Glass is beginning to explore this very exciting new territory which combines a set of clear glasses that incorporate a computer display overlay with a camera and voice recognition to produce a Smartphone-like experience on a new consumer wearable technology platform.

We're also seeing Samsung, IBM and many others patenting inventions based around graphene – a new material that can be used to make foldable, interactive digital newspapers like the one Tom Cruise reads in the subway in *Minority Report*, among other things. Another development in this direction is interaction via a tiny projector on, say, a watch or a pair of glasses that enables dynamic engagement with an environment.

Invocation – Next-Level Voice Activation

To invoke is to call upon something or someone to carry out a particular action. It has a spiritual meaning, as in calling upon a deity or spirit in prayer, a legal meaning, as in calling upon an authority or precedent to support a case or procedure, and a computing one, as in calling upon a computer code to do something for you.

Dr Chris Chesher coined the brilliant term 'invocational media' to describe the special nature of online media, where computer instructions and data – which are named in special and careful ways – are called into action or invoked by the user. Chesher says, 'invocation, which has an ancient heritage, mixes command and memory to produce decisions'.[1]

Although Chesher's employment of the term is broad and extends beyond simply using our voices, as in the Aladdin's Cave invocation 'Open sesame', the literal use of our voice with the web so far has been fairly limited, and we will see some exciting developments in the decade ahead. Many of us will have some experience and glimpse of the future potential with Apple's speech recognition personal assistant Siri – a built-in feature available to iPhone users since 2011 that provides hands free control of the smartphone, dictation and voice-activated access to simple information services like the weather and directions. There's also a built-in backstory to Siri's personality – try asking her 'Who are your parents?' and she says 'It's just you and me'; whether she is married and she answers 'Do you start many of your conversations this way?' and how many children she has, she replies 'None, the last time I checked.'

Significant advances have been made in technology that detects where in a room sounds are coming from, so players of console video games can now be easily distinguished by their voices and locations in the room. This has future potential in classroom and conference environments with many people interacting in the same session, where the speakers can automatically be distinguished from each other.[2]

As with metavision, there have been significant research developments around extra information that can be determined from a speaker's voice alone. Machine-learning researchers at NICTA, including Fang Chen, have worked out a way to detect stress in people's voices. Their patented techniques are finding application in a range of industries including in call centres, emergency services and air traffic control.

These two developments, coupled with another long-sought-after advance – real-time, simultaneous language translation – could provide the keys to a very important new platform for global communication between speakers of different languages. Imagine a smartphone that let you speak with people from anywhere in the world as if they were speaking your language, and to them you appeared as though you were speaking their language – now that's a smartphone I'd want! With the power of Online Gravity, it won't be long before it's within our reach.[3]

Telekinesis – the Ultimate Remote Control

Telekinesis, or psychokinesis, as any science-fiction fan will know, is the ability to move things at a distance using your mind, often involving levitation of people and objects. Stephen King's *Carrie*, Melissa Mathison's *E.T.*, and the Wachowskis' Neo in the *Matrix* all share this ability.

Scientists such as Todd Coleman at the University of California, San Diego, are working on temporary 'tattoos', which are computer circuits that attach non-invasively to your skin and give you 'telekinesis', or the ability to move things at a distance such as prosthetic arms and personal drones. It's not exactly telekinesis yet, but it does offer a glimpse into the potential thought-controlled user experience of the future as well as hope for people who are partially or fully paralysed to have greater freedom and autonomy in their lives in future.[4]

In the same vein, and already on the market, Emotiv is an advanced technology company that sells a kind of joystick for the brain. Emotiv's EPOC headset enables the wearer to control games and other things online from the small electrical signals we emit around the scalp when we're thinking thoughts and feeling emotions.

HEALTHCARE SHERLOCK

Another 'superpower' enabled by Online Gravity is the access we now have to health information and online self-diagnosis tools. There is a funny cartoon about an online-era patient who visits his doctor for a check-up and dumps a fat collection of printouts on the doctor's desk with a thud. He then announces with delight, 'Now tell me what *you* know.'

One key trend I suspect we will see from this is the emergence of a new type of health-care professional: the Healthcare Sherlock. Over time, a personal Healthcare Sherlock, equipped with access to the right information and a new set of advanced tools and data-science skills, but not necessarily with a medical degree as we know it now, could provide a low-cost, high-quality health-management service to many people around the world online.

Aladdin's Cave of Health Information

Today, you and I have the same access to most of the source medical reference materials that doctors do, via huge, federated, free data collections such as PubMed – a massive, searchable online index of America's premier medical and medical science reference collections. It was launched by Vice President Al Gore in 1997. The database contains more than 21 million records from over 5000 selected publications covering medicine, nursing, pharmacy, dentistry, veterinary medicine and health care. It has been hugely popular and is now the world's most visited medical information web service.[5]

While online hubs like PubMed offer access to the latest detailed medical research there are also numerous simple, consumer-oriented online health-information services run by government departments, such as the National Institutes of Health in the United States (health.nih.gov), the National Health Service portal in the United Kingdom (nhs.uk), and the Victorian Government's Better Health Channel in Australia (betterhealth.vic.gov.au), as well as commercial health-information services such as WebMD (webmd.com).

Online Gravity is also contributing to a growing number of new and very interesting practical sources of information that are born from people's shared experiences of specific health conditions, health services and treatments. In the area of home remedies, for example, the effectiveness of various natural treatments for common ailments is self-reported and aggregated on the excellent web service mentioned earlier in this book, Earth Clinic. (If you recall, it cured my plantar wart.)

One area where I understand this has already paid huge dividends is in drug interactions, for people taking more than one type of medicine in combination. Sometimes, there can be negative (or positive) interactions between the two medicines, and the industry cannot test them all, as the possible number of combinations is almost infinite. So new online platforms such as PatientsLikeMe are invaluable in collecting field data and organising it in a way that can provide a viable new source of reported health data.

But Isn't This My Doctor's Job?

Having direct access to the world's medical literature and data is one thing, but it becomes another thing altogether without the medical knowledge and experience to be able to understand it. Which brings us back to the traditional role of the doctor. It is worth reflecting on this with a view to better understanding how this role is likely to evolve in the coming decade.

When you visit your local or family doctor, you receive the benefit of their knowledge, wisdom and expert advice, but often they also offer:

- *Context.* Good general practitioners listen to their patients well. Some suggest this is their primary and most important role. They use what you tell them to set your health concerns within a larger context, including your personal medical history, family medical history and the health of the community.
- *Physical examination.* Physicians do an on-the-spot physical examination and perform a range of checks and measurements, such as taking your blood pressure, listening to your breathing and taking blood samples.
- *Diagnosis or referral.* Doctors take all of the previous two things into account and make an assessment of your health or a diagnosis of your illness. In some cases, they will refer you to a specialist doctor or to a clinic for testing to shed more light on your condition.

- *Treatment.* They will recommend a course of action to improve your health. This may involve a call for more bed rest, a call for more exercise or a visit to the pharmacy. They'll also give you a sense of what to expect from this treatment and what to do if the results differ.

Now let's unpack each of these to see where they are headed in the age of Online Gravity – and how a Healthcare Sherlock could offer a version of them plus an advanced diagnostic capability:

- *Perfecting context.* It is now possible to securely store your personal medical history, including a growing volume of data from test results, online. Many governments are helping to advance this process. Records such as these could also optionally include your family health history and demographic information about where you live and what you do for a job, to provide a rich source of context.
- *Self-service physicals.* We have learnt how to put petrol in our own cars, scan our own groceries and check ourselves in at the airport. There are now robotic dairy farms where the cows decide when to milk themselves! The range of technologies to measure your body, from internet-connected bathroom scales and digital pedometers to heart-rate monitors on your iPad, is growing daily.

  Breakthroughs in technology related to measuring your body is a very interesting space. In addition to blood-pressure and heart-rate monitoring, new types of biometric-data devices will emerge to provide Healthcare Sherlocks with better clues, such as measurements of your gait (how you walk), your skin resistance (stress measurement) and the chemistry of your saliva.
- *Machine-aided diagnostics.* Diagnostics is where the Healthcare Sherlock could come into his or her own. There's always a delay in research literature informing day-to-day practice. In health science and medicine, this was recognised as a major issue in

the United Kingdom, with specialist doctors behind current best practice in research literature by three to five years.

In 1993, an independent, non-profit, non-government organisation called the Cochrane Collaboration was founded to systematically review and collate all randomised controlled-trial data into one source, to provide up-to-date best-practice advice for practitioners and policymakers. It leverages a network of over 13,000 volunteer reviewers, and the 'Cochrane Reviews' they produce have been a huge global success, demonstrating the demand for practitioner-ready information in this space.

In the future, advanced online-learning systems such as the one labelled Watson – after IBM's founder, not Sherlock's partner – have the potential to perform a Cochrane-like review service automatically, directly summarising the latest scientific literature and then using this to provide an accurate and completely up-to-date diagnosis.

- *More informed referrals.* As more and more physicians and specialists also have a presence online, establishing a market-place for open referrals becomes increasingly practical. This could have many benefits and also help traditional physicians to make better referrals, which are currently largely limited to their peer network.

  Many global platforms for online auctions, outsourcing and accommodation, such as eBay, Freelancer.com and Airbnb, are continuing to develop online tools to record and encourage transparency in the performance and reliability of its users. While fully open customer reviews may not always make sense in the field of medicine, because, by its nature, it sometimes has negative outcomes for its 'customers' (including death), some movement in this direction is inevitable.

- *Tailored treatment.* Around half of all visits to your local doctor result in a prescription and one in ten in a referral.[6] So some kind of mechanism for online prescriptions would make sense as a companion piece to the Healthcare Sherlock role. This could have significant benefits too. If not urgent, it could be bought and fulfilled from an online pharmacist stocking a huge range of products like Amazon. Personalised medicines and supplements are possible using this model too. You could, for example, have a multivitamin created specifically for your needs.

Trust and Health

Trust is a vital ingredient with any health practitioner, and that involves maintaining the utmost patient confidentiality, as outlined in the pledge or promise to their future patients often taken by doctors since Ancient Greece known as the Hippocratic oath:

> What I may see or hear in the course of the treatment or even outside of the treatment in regard to the life of men, which on no account one must spread abroad, I will keep to myself, holding such things shameful to be spoken about.

And this is also enshrined in law in many jurisdictions under the term 'patient–physician privilege'. A Healthcare Sherlock would need to offer similar protections.

The option of an anonymous consultation service online could provide a good way of encouraging people to seek confidential professional help where they might find it difficult to confront a doctor in person.

In addition to privacy, patient trust reflects confidence in the training and methods of the practitioner. There are a few ways I imagine that Healthcare Sherlocks of the future could go about fostering this trust. One is through providing a platform that encourages reputation building, like Airbnb. A more likely outcome, I suspect, is the emergence of branded online health enterprises that share in the well-earned reputations of their traditional parent companies, such as the Mayo Clinic or the Royal

Flying Doctor Service. Existing national reputations for excellence in differing health fields, such as Swiss pharmaceuticals, Thai dental tourism and the general longevity and overall good health of people from Japan, Sweden and New Zealand may also play a part in winning the trust of this emerging global market.

THE FUTURE OF ONLINE LEARNING

The third 'superpower' bestowed by Online Gravity, and growing day-by-day, is our access to self-directed learning. There has been an explosion in this area in recent years, largely due to the wide-spread rollout of high-speed internet connections that support video. We saw earlier how online educational resources like Khan Academy and Apple's iTunes University provide remarkable, free online resources for self-directed learners of any age. Other examples include the emergence of a whole new category of online courses: the massive open online course, or MOOC – that are connected to formal colleges or universities.

MOOCs are designed for unlimited participation and open access via the web. In addition to traditional course materials such as videos of lectures, problem sets and course readings, MOOCs offer ways to interact and collaborate with other students, tutors and professors via blogs, forums and chat spaces.

MOOCs began in the mid-2000s but have only really become mainstream since 2012 – the 'Year of the MOOC', according to *The New York Times*. Indeed, many of today's leading services were launched in 2012, including Coursera, Udacity and edX. Today, there are a myriad of MOOC providers, and these are lining up for an Online Gravity showdown. Some, such as edX and Coursera are aligned as platforms for traditional universities to deliver their courses, while others, such as Udemy, Udacity and OpenLearning are positioned for online vocational education from any provider.

The intense competition around MOOCs, and the responses and approaches of different colleges and universities to these, is illustrative of a broader quest for brand differentiation among tertiary-education providers in an increasingly competitive education sector.

Traditionally, most colleges and universities enjoyed a relative monopoly on students and faculty from their region. They served the educational and research needs of the state, county or city in which they were based. And a lot of the competition for attracting the best and brightest students and faculty was with neighbouring institutions. Not many people travelled across their country to study, and fewer still travelled abroad.

Now, over four million students pack their bags each year to leave their home country and study at a university or college overseas. Since 1975, the number of students enrolled in overseas higher education programs has grown 400 per cent, with most of that growth occurring since the emergence of the web in 1990.[7]

Is Online Gravity accelerating the globalisation of education?

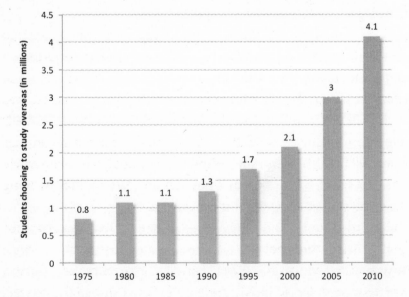

The emergence of the web from around 1990 coincides with the explosive growth of students choosing to study overseas.
Data Source: OECD & UNESCO Institute for Statistics, 2012.

Today, the web and online academic publishing are making educational institutions, their students and faculty much more visible and connected.

Facebook's birth and growth on campus illustrates how students from one campus – initially Harvard – can and do connect with others via the web. The world's social-media gravity giant is a result of college students connecting via the web.

Increasingly, students, governments and funding bodies are looking to the web for more information about research leadership too. To support this powerful trend, free web-based tools have emerged, such as Google Scholar and Microsoft Academic Search, that allow anyone to freely search and connect with the works of millions of academics and researchers from around the world. Further services that are providing academics with new venues for online collaboration, such as ResearchGate and Academia.edu, are also emerging.

Caruso-Effect Applied to Academic Talent

One consequence of the increasing global competition between universities to attract the best students, funding from government and partnerships with industry is what I think of as a 'Caruso effect' in the marketplace for academic talent. Enrico Caruso was an Italian opera singer and the first to make significant inroads into recording. He made 290 commercially released recordings from 1902 to 1920, and they were hugely popular in his day. He was, in a sense, the world's first pop star and was credited as being the greatest opera singer of his generation.

Recorded music and the gramophone provided a platform for global distribution not just of music but also of talent. It demonstrated to the world a global basis for excellence, and Caruso was rewarded for it handsomely too. For a one-night concert in Cuba, he was said to have been paid $10,000 in 1920, which equates to around $120,000 in today's money.

Online Gravity is fuelling this kind of blockbuster economy in higher education. Dr Steven Weinberg, for example, is a Caruso of physics. No ordinary professor, he is a Nobel laureate and is considered by many to be the top theoretical physicist alive today. Dr Weinberg is also the bestselling author of *The First Three Minutes: A Modern View of the Origin of the Universe*. And he, too, is well rewarded for his efforts. He was hired by the University of Texas at Austin for his role as Josey Regental Chair in Science in 1982 on an annual salary of $535,969.

RENAISSANCE 2.0: THE NEW SCIENCE OF DATA IN THE ERA OF ONLINE GRAVITY

Globalised academia, computer software, networked computers and robotics are ushering in a new type of Renaissance – most likely one that will be more potent and powerful than the one 500 years ago.

In the last Renaissance, a lot of the work was theoretical – Leonardo da Vinci's inventions were paper-based thought experiments. Even in the twentieth century, Einstein worked in the theoretical realm, and the world had to wait a considerable time to be able to validate many of his theories through difficult and elaborate experiments.

Today, a new generation of science is emerging – one involving massive amounts of data, huge computational power and a global army of networked scientists. A prime example of this is the Higgs boson experiment – the hunt for the so-called 'God particle' involving a huge particle accelerator that cost $4.75 billion to construct deep under the European Alps. The number of pages listing the names and universities of the 3000 authors of the 'Higgs Boson Paper' outnumbered the pages outlining the experimental results.

Huge amounts of money, data and sheer computational might resulted in a vindication of the theoretical conjecture since the

1960s about the existence of this particle. Perhaps appropriately, this experiment was conducted at the birthplace of the web, at CERN, in Switzerland.

And this is not a one-off case. In 2001, an influential research paper published in the world's top scientific journal, *Nature*, about unscrambling the codes in the human genome had a staggering 2900 authors.[8]

Some suggest we are entering a new age of data-intensive science. A book of essays guided by the vision of the late Dr Jim Gray at Microsoft Research, *The Fourth Paradigm*, takes this view.[9] Gray's idea is that we are entering a new fourth age of science, which we have arrived at in the following way:

1. A thousand years ago, we had an age of *experimentation*, involving direct observation and description.
2. Within the last few hundred years, we had an age of *theory*, resulting in such breakthroughs as Newton's laws of gravity, Kepler's laws of planetary motion and Maxwell's equations.
3. Within the last few decades, we entered an age of *simulation*, using computers to emulate dynamic and complex situations that theory was unable to.
4. Today, we are entering an age of *data science*, characterised by analysis of masses of machine-generated or simulation data using a series of statistical and computer-based techniques to automatically look for patterns, connections and unexpected observations.

The potential to accelerate science and make profound new discoveries using these techniques is huge. And there are many areas of science where this could result in major breakthroughs. One of these is in the quest for the 'periodic table of ecology', which is noted as a major unsolved scientific riddle of our time.

The periodic table in chemistry, which lists and organises all the known elements, has enabled our chemical understanding to progress substantially over the past 300 years. But, as has been noted by many, including the former head of the University of Oxford, Sir Richard Southwood, there is no such structural map for ecology – or at least so far.

Could you have a 'periodic table' that describes, for example, how different trees evolve and interact with one another in a forest? Which factors, such as leaf size and tree height, are the keys to success or failure?

Many distinguished researchers in ecology, such as Professor Mark Westoby and postdoctoral research fellow Dr Daniel Falster at Macquarie University, believe that such an underlying structure may exist; it simply may not have been revealed yet. One research project that Westoby and Falster are leading is called 'Big Data Knowledge Discovery'. It explores the adoption of big data technologies used for high-speed online financial market trading to move towards a closer understanding of the periodic table of ecology.

Forests and jungles, it turns out, share many of the features of stock markets. They each are complex systems that have a number of actors (trees or traders) that compete for resources (light, nutrients and water, or talent, capital and information) using a variety of different strategies (grow tall and spread as much seed as possible, or grow enterprise value and distribute maximal dividends). Some thrive (bountiful fruits, record leaf mass, or record profits) and others die and become recycled (dead plants and leaves, or bankrupt companies). One can see that, should a solution to either the market or forest problem be found, there may be valuable lessons or applications in the other domain.

This book is an attempt to do this for our increasingly online world – to provide some scaffolding to enable us all to better understand the forces that lead to certain outcomes and not others online.

I hope that, like the pioneering work of the scientists of the eighteenth and nineteenth centuries who developed the early versions of the periodic table for chemistry, this book has added to your understanding of the way things work online, and that you can apply this in practical ways in your professional and personal life.

KEY POINTS

In the future, we can look forward to the following technological advances and more:

- *Metavision*. Visual overlays that give us extra information about the products, people and environment around us.
- *Invocation*. Next-generation voice activation and recognition, which has the power to have computers at our beck and call to do advanced things like simultaneously translate our speech into the language of the person we're talking to, and vice versa.
- *Telekinesis*. The ability to instruct digital devices remotely, even through thoughts alone.
- *The Healthcare Sherlock*. A new type of data analyst who can use the health information freely available on the web to support or replace the role of our doctor.
- *MOOCs*. These massive open online courses are already here, and they're going to get bigger and better.
- *Data science*. A new type of science involving massive number crunching, huge computational power and a global army of scientists, with the potential to deliver staggering results.

ACKNOWLEDGEMENTS

Many people helped me with this book. It's the result of the sustained kindness and goodwill of the talented people at Simon & Schuster Australia. I'd especially like to thank Roberta Ivers for her amazing support as managing editor, for her expert guidance all along and for believing in this book from day one. Thanks to Larissa Edwards for her vision to make waves with this book and for reminding me of the power of fine arts. Thanks to Anabel Pandiella, Carol Warwick, Elissa Baillie for their enthusiasm, insights and generous support in marketing and PR for this project. And to Lou Johnson for assembling and inspiring such a stellar team. Thanks too to Dan Ruffino for bringing his considerable experience in global digital publishing to this project. Special thanks and major kudos to Kevin O'Brien, whose editorial work on the project was nothing short of spectacular.

I'd like to acknowledge: W. Brian Arthur, without whose inspirational work on increasing returns this book would not exist; Tim Wu, whose beautiful book *The Master Switch* gave me great historical perspectives; and Ross Taylor, whose guidance and excellent book about the formation of our solar system, *Destiny or*

Chance Revisited: Planets and their Place in the Cosmos, was also both inspiring and instructive. Thanks to Hal Vogel, the author of the authoritative *Entertainment Industry Economics*, whose work has been a long-time inspiration for me. To Professor Kimberly Clausing, whose informed views on taxation in an era of increasing globalisation will no doubt be more and more sought after. And Professor Barry Marshall, for his generous insights into the world of elite medical science.

Thanks to Chris Milne for introducing me to Clayton Christensen, Charles Russell for his enthusiasm, interest and engagement, Igor Jazbec for his unparalleled insights into the computer-networking world, Kieran Sharp for his good counsel, patience and expert guidance on actors cum dentists, and Daniel Falster for introducing me to the fascinating world of evolutionary ecology.

I'm grateful to Pia Waugh for her tech leadership chutzpah and together with Julie Grimson introducing me to the wonderful Sir Tim Berners-Lee without whom none of us would enjoy the wonderful web we do today.

Also thanks to Steve Hare for good conversations on the beach some years ago that became the germ of the idea for this book and to Charis Palmer and Kylar Loussikian from the Conversation whose early interest proved invaluable. Thanks too to Morri Pagnucco, Professor of Computer Science at University of New South Wales, for his excellent support.

Thomas Barlow, thank you for his excellent and kind recommendations and ideas – now I've finished, I look forward to reading his latest book!

Ross Dawson, thank you for your excellent thoughts on media and the future, and, most importantly, for introducing me to Improv.

I'm grateful to many fellow authors and researchers whose work has expanded our understanding of a diverse range of subjects that has contributed to this book especially Adam Alter, Andreas M. Antonopoulos, Alain de Botton, Rachel Botsman, Remco Bloemen, Chris Chesher, David Court, Stephen J. Dubner, Richard Florida, Thomas Friedman, Malcolm Gladwell, Nicholas Gruen, David Hallerman, Walter Isaacson, Arif Jinh, Jaron Lanier, Steven D. Levitt, Michael Lewis, Jean-Baptiste Michel, Thomas Piketty and Eric Ries.

Thanks to founders and executives of many leading online companies who have given their time, thoughts and support to this project, including: Leni Mayo, co-founder, Influx; Matt Barrie, CEO and founder of Freelancer.com; Matt Cooper, vice president of oDesk; Michael Roberts, CEO and founder of SpyFu; Luke Metcalfe, CEO and founder of NationMaster; Gary Brewer, CEO and founder of BuiltWith; Owen Kerr, founder and director of Pepperstone; Mike Knapp and Joel Pinkham at Shoes of Prey; Jamie Mackintosh at Hitwise; Simon Dewulf, CEO and founder of Aulive; Christian Bartens, CEO and founder of Datalicious; Christian Faes, co-founder of LendInvest; and Simon Baker, executive chairman at ListGlobally, former CEO of REA Group.

Thanks to Judith Curr and her team at Simon & Schuster in New York, especially Leslie Meredith, the US editor on this project, and Donna Loffredo, associate editor. Thanks, too, to the team at Simon and Schuster UK, especially Ian Chapman, Suzanne Baboneau and Iain MacGregor. Your support for this project has been wonderful.

Special thanks to Catherine Drayton, who provided wise and expert counsel, and her team at Inkwell and esteemed colleague Richard Pine gave me great ongoing support and advice for which I am deeply grateful.

Thanks to Liz Jakubowski for planting the seed for this book many years ago, and also Colin Griffith for his support and encouragement. Mike Briers, Chris Mendes, Satish Nair, Rasika

Amarasiri and all my colleagues and friends at SIRCA – I really appreciated your support.

And a special thanks to Jude McGee, who gave me the encouragement and expert advice I needed to pursue this project in the first place.

Lastly, I'd like to pay special tribute to my beautiful family: Rennie for the wonderful bookmarks and interest; Checker for his up-to-date insights into the frontiers of video gaming and good humour at my bad jokes; and Nicky for her practical wisdom and magic.

Paul X. McCarthy

NOTES AND
SELECT BIBLIOGRAPHY

NOTES
Why Does Online Gravity Happen?

1. Arthur, W. Brian, 'Competing Technologies, Increasing Returns, and Lock-In by Historical Events', *The Economic Journal*, 1989, pp. 116–31.
2. Arthur, W. Brian, 'Positive Feedbacks in the Economy', *Scientific American*, 262.2, 1990, pp. 92–9.
3. Andreessen, Marc, 'Why Software is Eating the World', *The Wall Street Journal*, 20 August 2011.

What Are the Features of Online Gravity?

1. Vogel, Harold L., *Entertainment industry economics: A guide for financial analysis*, Cambridge University Press, 2010.
2. De Vany, Arthur, *Hollywood Economics: How Extreme Uncertainty Shapes the Film Industry*, Routledge, London and New York, 2004.
3. US Bureau of Labor Statistics, 'Occupational Employment and Wages, May 2013', US Bureau of Labor Statistics | Division of Occupational Employment Statistics, http://www.bls.gov/oes/current/oes272011.htm.
4. Pomerantz, Dorothy, 'Robert Downey Jr. Tops Forbes' List of Hollywood's Highest-Paid Actors', *Forbes*, 16 July 2013, www.forbes.com.
5. Merz, Joachim, 'The Distribution of Income of Self-employed, Entrepreneurs and Professions as Revealed from Micro Income Tax Statistics in Germany', Springer, Berlin, Heidelberg, 2000.
6. Source: Brighter.com, July 2014.
7. Elberse, Anita. *Blockbusters: hit-making, risk-taking, and the big business of entertainment*, Macmillan, 2013.
8. Ryan, Bryce and Gross, Neal, 'The Diffusion of Hybrid Seed Corn in Two Iowa Communities', *Rural Sociology*, 8.1, 1943, pp. 15–24.
9. Rogers, Everett M., *Diffusion of Innovations*, The Free Press: Simon & Schuster, New York, 1995.

10. Bass, Frank, 'A New Product Growth Model for Consumer Durables', *Management Science*, 15 (5), 1969, pp. 215–27.
11. Fischer, Claude S., *America Calling: A Social History of the Telephone to 1940*, University of California Press, Oakland, 1992.
12. Womack, Brian, 'Google Gets Record 75,000 Job Applications in a Week', Bloomberg, 4 February 2011, www.bloomberg.com.
13. Wu, Timothy, *The Master Switch: The Rise and Fall of Digital Empires*, Vintage, New York, 2010, p. 279.
14. Evans, David S., 'Some Empirical Aspects of Multi-Sided Platform Industries', *Review of Network Economics*, 2.3, 2003, pp. 194–201.
15. Lee, Robin S., 'Vertical Integration and Exclusivity in Platform and Two-Sided Markets', *American Economic Review 2013*, 103(7): 2960–3000.
16. Olson, Parmy, 'The Rags-to-Riches Tale of How Jan Koum Built WhatsApp into Facebook's New $19 Billion Baby', *Forbes*, 19 February 2014, www.forbes.com.
17. University of Georgia, 'Industry Fact Sheets: Mechanical Automobile Repair (NAICS 8111)', Applied Research Division, December 2001, www.georgiasbdc.org/pdfs/automotive.pdf.
18. Orcutt, Mike, 'One Way of Thinking about WhatsApp's Staggering Price', *MIT Technology Review*, 25 February 2014, www.technology review.com.

How Does Online Gravity Function?

1. Also commonly referred to as preferential attachment.
2. Data from Banjo, Shelly, 'Apple Jumps to Second Place in Online Retail', *The Wall Street Journal* , 6 May 2014, http://online.wsj.com.
3. And while Apple is also a gravity giant in its own right, its online-retail business is just a satellite of Amazon here. It is in mobile internet devices where it dominates. There, Apple is king, and the overwhelming majority of its sales are from just two products: the iPhone and the iPad.
4. Data from 'Global General Purpose Cards by Dollar Volume in $ Billions', Nilson Report, March 2014.
5. Relative market share approximated from the percentages of global PageViews in Alexa.

The Life Stages of Online Gravity

1. Wu, Timothy, *The Master Switch: The Rise and Fall of Digital Empires*, Vintage, New York, 2010, p. 6.

2. Evans, David S., 'Some Empirical Aspects of Multi-Sided Platform Industries', *Review of Network Economics*, 2.3, 2003, p. 201.
3. US National Science Foundation, 'On the Origins of Google', www.nsf.gov.
4. Roberts, Karen B., 'Tech Pioneers', UDaily, University of Delaware, www.udel.edu.

Counterexamples and Exceptions
1. Tesla website, 2014, www.teslamotors.com.
2. Data from Google Finance, market capitalisation, 2014.
3. Cortizo, José Carlos, 'The State of eCommerce in 2014: Is There any Room for New eCommerce Models?', BrainSINS, 28 January 2014, www.brainsins.com.
4. Nike Company Statement, 'Nike Redefines "Just Do It" with New Campaign', 21 August 2013, http://nikeinc.com/news.
5. Cunliffe, Peter, 'Tesco Lifted by Surge in Online Sales over Christmas', *Daily Express*, 10 January 2014, www.express.co.uk.

Law 1: Online Gravity Is Naturally Global
1. Ou, Carol Xiaojuan and Davison, Robert M., 'Technical Opinion Why eBay Lost to Taobao in China: The Glocal Advantage', *Communications of the ACM*, 52.1, 2009, pp. 145–8.
2. Drucker, Jesse, 'Google 2.4% Rate Shows How $60 Billion is Lost to Tax Loopholes', 21 October 2010, Bloomberg, www.bloomberg.com.

Law 2: Online Gravity Loves Big Winners
1. Morgan Stanley, *The Technology IPO Yearbook: 9th Edition*, 2003.
2. Graham, Paul, 'Black Swan Farming', September 2012, http://paulgraham.com/swan.html.
3. Data from *Forbes*, 'The World's Billionaires', 2014, www.forbes.com/billionaires.
4. Acs, Zoltan J., and Pamela Mueller, 'Employment effects of business dynamics: Mice, Gazelles and Elephants', *Small Business Economics* 30.1, 2008, 85–100.

Law 3: Online Gravity Applies to Intangible Goods
1. Halaburda, Hanna and Oberholzer-Gee, Felix, 'The Limits of Scale', *Harvard Business Review*, April 2014.
2. Jefferson, Thomas, 'Letter to Isaac McPherson', The Founders' Constitution Volume 3, Article 1, Section 8, Clause 8, Document 12,

The University of Chicago Press, http://press-pubs.uchicago.edu/founders/documents/a1_8_8s12.html, 13 Aug 1813.

3. Siracusa, John, 'Code Hard or Go Home', April 12, 2013. http://hypercritical.co/2013/04/12/code-hard-or-go-home

4. Shirky, Clay, 'Larry Sanger, Citizendium, and the Problem of Expertise', 18 September 2006, Corante, Many 2 Many, http://many.corante.com.

5. Data from Aulive, 2014.

6. Antonopoulos, Andreas, 'Why Bitcoin Terrifies Big Banks', television interview, *Breaking the Set*, YouTube, www.youtube.com.

7. The World Bank, 'Migration and Remittances', 2014, http://econ.worldbank.org.

8. Davis, Kevin and Jenkinson, Martin, 'Remittances: Their Role, Trends and Australian Opportunities', Australian Centre for Financial Studies and Western Union, www.westernunion.com.au.

9. McEvoy, Neil and Birch, David G.W., 'DIY Cash', *Wired*, 2 May 1996.

10. Evans, Judith, 'China Funds: Web Coup by Yu'e Bao Spurs Rivals into Action', *Financial Times*, 15 June 2014, www.ft.com.

11. Anshe Chung Studios, 'Anshe Chung Becomes First Virtual World Millionaire', media release, 26 November 2006, www.anshechung.com.

Law 4: Online Gravity Accelerates Everything

1. Manyika, James, Bughin, Jacques, Lund, Susan et al., 'Global Flows in a Digital Age', McKinsey Global Institute, April 2014, www.mckinsey.com.

2. Eisenmann, Thomas, Parker, Geoffrey and Van Alstyne, Marshall, 'Platform Envelopment', *Strategic Management Journal*, 32.12, 2011, pp. 1270–85.

3. Manyika, James, Bughin, Jacques, Lund, Susan et al., 'Global Flows in a Digital Age', McKinsey Global Institute, April 2014, www.mckinsey.com.

4. Jinha, Arif, 'Article 50 Million: An Estimate of the Number of Scholarly Articles in Existence', Ottawa, 2010. http://www.ruor.uottawa.ca/handle/10393/19577

5. Ibid.

6. Intel's longstanding and widely acclaimed CEO Andy Grove has been quoted as saying a similar thing about its approach to management.

7. Lichstein, Henry, 'Telephone Hackers Active', MIT Student Newspaper 'The Tech', Vol. 83, No. 24, 20 November 1963, http://tech.mit.edu.

8. Poulsen, Kevin, 'How a Math Genius Hacked OkCupid to Find True Love', *Wired*, 21 January 2014, www.wired.com.

9. Barrie, Matt, 'How to Get Hypergrowth', *Business Review Weekly*, 1 November 2012, www.brw.com.au.

10. Needleman, Sarah E. and Safdar, Khadeeja, '"Growth Hacking" Helps Startups Boost their Users', *The Wall Street Journal*, 28 May 2014, http://online.wsj.com.

11. Ries, Eric, *The Lean Startup*, Crown, New York, 2011.

12. Halligan, Brian, and Dharmesh Shah, *Inbound Marketing, Revised and Updated: Attract, Engage, and Delight Customers Online*, John Wiley & Sons, 2014.

13. Fernandez, Phil, *Revenue Disruption: Game-changing Sales and Marketing Strategies to Accelerate Growth*, John Wiley & Sons, 2012.

Law 5: Online Gravity is Revealed Through Data

1. Stukeley, William, *Memoirs of Sir Isaac Newton's Life*, 1752, at the Newton Project, University of Sussex, United Kingdom. http://www.newtonproject.sussex.ac.uk/view/texts/normalized/OTHE00001

2. Computers have a hierarchy of processes starting with the most simple like the light switch examples that are hardwired in that enable them to interpret these simple strings as characters and numbers. Many of these most basic operations are hardwired into the computers' electronics inside integrated circuits or microprocessor chips made by Intel, AMD and others – which means they can run really fast. They also have an operating system such as Windows, or Mac OS or Android or iOS for mobile devices that provide services to software programs such as Microsoft Word to store and retrieve data on the hard disc, or send information across the network. It's an elaborate but orderly hierarchy of command like that of an Edwardian manor house. The user (you) requests something – say to save a file; the software then commands the operating system which in turn calls the microprocessor(s) which in turn activate the electrons!

3. All three of these excellent applications are developed by Columbia University.

4. This collection was created by the University of Chicago's Center for Research in Securities Prices (CRSP).

5. Merton Miller was key to developing portfolio theory and Myron Scholes was the co-inventor of the Black–Scholes model – the pioneering approach to pricing derivatives. Both won Nobel Prizes, along with fellow University of Chicago scholar Ronald Coase, 1991; Gary Becker, 1992; Robert Fogel, 1993; and Eugene Fama, 2013.

6. *The Economist*, 'The Last Kodak Moment?', 14 January 2012, www. economist.com.

7. Source: *Alexa Top 500 Websites*, December 2014: http://www.alexa. com/topsite.

8. Isaac, Mike, 'Topping 5 Million Android Downloads, Instagram Shows No Signs of Slowing', 4 October 2012, *Wired*, www.wired.com.

Law 6: Online Gravity is Networked not Tribal

1. Source: Google Books Ngram Viewer.

2. 'Of men, nappies and beer', 1999, *Business Asia*, vol. 31, no. 20, p. 12.

3. Plummer, Joseph T., 'The concept and application of life style segmentation', *The Journal of Marketing* (1974): 33–37.

4. Marshall, Professor Barry J., quoted on the website of the Office of the Nobel Laureates in Western Australia, Government of Western Australia Department of the Premier and Cabinet Office of Science, www.helicobacter.com.

5. Author interview with Professor Barry J. Marshall, 2 April 2014.

Law 7: Online Gravity Loves Renaissance Talent

1. Guest, David, 'The Hunt is on for the Renaissance Man of Computing', *The Independent*, London, 17 September 1991.

2. Olding, Rachel, 'Straddle, not Struggle, as Slashies Prove Ultimate Multi-Taskers', *The Sydney Morning Herald*, 23 April 2011, www. smh.com.au.

3. You can see this by looking at the count of Wikipedia edits by hour by language. While the edit rate of say the German and Japanese editions of Wikipedia does slow down between 11 pm and 4 am in those countries, contributions are still coming in at 20–40% the daytime rate. The English language edition has more constant contributions as there are contributors in many timezones from

the UK, to US to Australia and India. See: http://www.wikichecker.
com/editrate/

4. Norby, Vibhu, 'How Many Founders Do Successful Tech Companies
Have?', Philosophically, 17 November 2012, http://philosophically.
com.

5. A few were also adopted: Steve Jobs (Apple); Larry Ellison (Oracle);
and Jeff Bezos (Amazon), who was adopted by his stepfather after
his mother remarried.

Work and Money in the Online Age

1. Berners-Lee, Sir Tim, 18th International World Wide Web Conference, Madrid, 2009.

2. Clarke, Arthur C., *Profiles of the Future*, Victor Gollancz, 1982
(1962).

3. Bolles, Richard N., *What Color Is Your Parachute? 2014: A Practical Manual for Job-Hunters and Career-Changers*, Ten Speed Press,
New York, 2013, p. 22.

4. 'Economic Report of the President', February 2012, The White
House, www.whitehouse.gov.

5. Nicholson, David, 'Freelancer.com's Matt Barrie on How to Monetise
5 Billion People', *Forbes*, 4 February 2014, www.forbes.com.

6. Cited by Harold Jarche in Amplify talk (https://amplifybusiness.
com), 12 May 2014, Sydney. https://twitter.com/paulxmccarthy/
status/465678886886322176

7. *The Economist*, 'My Big Fat Career', 10 September 2011, www.
economist.com.

8. Russell, Bertrand, *In Praise of Idleness*, George Allen & Unwin,
London, 1986, p. 16.

9. Jones, Barry, *A Thinking Reed*, Allen and Unwin, Sydney, 2007,
p. 324.

10. Hesiod, *The Homeric Hymns and Homerica with an English Translation by Hugh G. Evelyn-White. Works and Days.* Cambridge,
MA., Harvard University Press; London, William Heinemann Ltd.
1914. Accessed online via Perseus Digital Library, Tufts University
http://www.perseus.tufts.edu/hopper/text?doc=Perseus:abo:tlg,
0020,002:108'

11. Francis, David R., 'Why High Earners Work Longer Hours',
National Bureau of Economic Research, July 2014, www.nber.org.

12. Source: BuiltWith, July 2014, http://trends.builtwith.com.

13. Top 20 Markets Total US$19.5 Trillion. Author's calculation using outstanding National Residential Mortgage Balance Data from the European Mortgage Federation (2012), http://www.hypo.org/Content/default.asp?PageID=414 and combined with United States and Key Asian Markets reported on in EMF 2013 p22: http://www.hypo.org/PortalDev/Objects/6/Files/HYPOSTAT_2013.pdf. World GDP "World". CIA World Factbook. 30 December 2014: https://www.cia.gov/library/publications/the-world-factbook/geos/xx.html

14. Gruen, Nicholas, 'Central Banking for All: A Modest Case for Radical Reform', Nesta, 28 April 2014, www.nesta.org.uk.

15. There are 1663 Exchange Traded Funds in the United States listed on NYSE and NASDAQ, Source Reuters and Seeking Alpha, December 2014: http://seekingalpha.com/etf_hub

Strategies for Small Business Owners and Company Executives

1. Steinberg, Daniel H., 'Web 2.0 Podcast: A Conversation with Jeff Bezos', 20 December 2006, O'Reilly, www.oreillynet.com.

2. Gates, Bill, 'How I Work: Bill Gates', CNN Money, 7 April 2006, http://money.cnn.com.

3. A word of warning on the do-it-yourself approach – it works fine if there are no objections to your application though it is more of a challenge if you need to respond. Here is where using a Patent Attorney or services like LegalZoom can offer help.

4. From the LegalZoom prospectus lodged with the US Securities and Exchange Commission (www.sec.gov) when the company was planning to list in 2012. They later decided not to IPO and instead raise money privately.

5. Isaacson, Walter, *Steve Jobs*, Simon & Schuster, New York, 2013, p. 567.

6. Op cit, p. 569.

7. Gross profit gives a better indication of the relative profitability of an industry as it's simply the total sales minus the product costs. So it doesn't include operational expenses e.g. head office, real estate, capital equipment, etc.

8. Denning, Steve, 'Clayton Christensen And The Innovators' Smackdown', *Forbes* magazine, 5th April 2012, http://www.forbes.com/

sites/stevedenning/2012/04/05/clayton-christensen-and-the-innovators-smackdown/

9. Google spent $9.7bn on R&D in year-to-date September 2014 according to company reports: https://www.google.com/finance?q=NASDAQ:GOOG&fstype=ii

10. Pesce, Mark, The Next Billion Seconds: What happens after we're all connected?, Self published online, From 10 January through 20 December 2012, http://nextbillionseconds.com/sample-page-2/hypereconomics/

11. Data source: NetMarketShare, October 2014, www.netmarketshare.com.

12. A bundling or envelopment strategy as an alternative to revolutionary functionality in platform markets – which many Online Gravity markets are – was proposed by Professor Thomas Eisenmann at Harvard Business School, Professor Marshall Van Alstyne at MIT and Professor Geoffrey Parker at Tulane University.

13. Planes, Alex, 'The IPO that Inflated the Dot-Com Bubble', The Motley Fool, 9 August 2013, www.fool.com.

14. Borland, John, 'Victor: Software Empire Pays High Price', CNET News, 15 April 2003, www.cnet.com/news.

15. Sink, Eric, 'Memoirs from the Browser Wars', personal blog, 15 April 2003, www.ericsink.com.

16. Author's correspondence with Igor Jazbec, January 2014.

17. Jessica Livingston, in her book of interviews with tech founders, Founders at Work (2007), recalls in the interview with Apple co-founder Steve Wozniak, '. . . Apple went public in 1980 in the largest IPO since Ford in 1956, creating more instant millionaires (about 300) than any company up to that point'.

18. Gallagher, Dan, 'Apple CEO Jobs says Cash Means Security and Flexibility', MarketWatch, 25 February 2010, www.marketwatch.com.

19. Terdiman, Daniel, http://www.forbes.com/sites/randalllane/2013/09/09/john-sculley-just-gave-his-most-detailed-account-ever-of-how-steve-jobs-got-fired-from-apple/

Society: A Tale of Two Cities
1. Botsman, Rachel, 'The Sharing Economy Lacks a Shared Definition', Collaborative Consumption, 22 November 2013, www.collaborativeconsumption.com.

2. Tanz, Jason, 'How Airbnb and Lyft Finally Got Americans to Trust Each Other', *Wired*, April 2014, http://www.wired.com/2014/04/trust-in-the-share-economy/

3. Roose, Kevin, 'The Sharing Economy isn't About Trust, it's About Desperation', *New York* magazine, 24 April 2014, http://nymag.com.

4. Griffith, Saul, 'Built to Last', Interview with Good Magazine, 14 January 2010, http://magazine.good.is/articles/built-to-last

5. Friedman, Thomas L., *The World is Flat: A Brief History of the Twenty-First Century*, Release 3.0, Macmillan, 2006, p. x.

6. Pink, Daniel, 'Why the World is Flat', *Wired*, Issue 13.05, May 2005, http://archive.wired.com/wired/archive/13.05/friedman.html

7. Ghemawat, Pankaj, 'Why the World isn't Flat', *Foreign Policy*, no. 159, March/April 2007, pp. 54–60.

8. Florida, Richard, 'The World is Spiky', *The Atlantic*, October 2005, www.theatlantic.com.

9. Gruen, Nicholas, 'Open for Business: How Open Data Can Help Achieve the G20 Growth Target', Lateral Economics, Omidyar Network, June 2014, www.omidyar.com.

10. G20 Australia 2014, 'Policy Note: Lifting G20 GDP by More than 2 Per Cent above the Trajectory Implied by Current Policies over the Coming 5 Years', June 2014, www.g20.org.

11. McArdle, Megan, 'Piketty's *Capital*: An Economist's Inequality Ideas are all the Rage', Bloomberg Businessweek, 29 May 2014, www.businessweek.com.

12. Hagel, John, Seely Brown, John, et al., 'Success or Struggle: ROA as a True Measure of Business Performance', Deloitte University Press, 30 October 2013, www.dupress.com.

13. Ocean Tomo, 'Ocean Tomo's Annual Study of Intangible Asset Market Value – 2010', 4 April 2011, www.oceantomo.com.

14. Zillow, 2014 Annual Report, http://files.shareholder.com/downloads/ABEA-6AA1JU/3338284852x0xS1193125-14-56800/1334814/filing.pdf.

15. Amazon, 2013 Annual Report, http://phx.corporate-ir.net/External.File?item=UGFyZW50SUQ9MjI4Njc1fENoaWxkSUQ9LTF8VHlwZT0z&t=1.

16. Spawforth, Tony, *Versailles: A Biography of a Palace*, St. Martin's Griffin, New York, 2008, p. 41.

17. Prices and wages in various French towns (not Paris), 1450–1789, Global Price and Income History Group, http://gpih.ucdavis.edu/files/France_1450-1789_non-Paris.xls.

18. Elliott, Matthew, and Rotherham, Lee, *The Bumper Book of Government Waste: The Scandal of the Squandered Billions from Lord Irvine's Wallpaper to EU Saunas*, Harriman House Limited, Petersfield, UK, 2006, p. 8.

19. Summers, Lawrence, 'Thomas Piketty is Right about the Past and Wrong about the Future', *The Atlantic*, 16 May 2014, www.theatlantic.com.

Superpowers and Renaissance 2.0

1. Chesher, Christopher Bradford, 'Computers as Invocational Media', PhD, Macquarie University, 2001.

2. Professor Farzad Safaei from the University of Wollongong is a pioneer in this space, having created the spatial audio technologies underlying Dolby Axon voice chat and surround sound for Gamers.

3. Microsoft Research is working on this and have demonstrated early versions running on Skype called Skype Translator.

4. Peckham, Matt, 'Finally, Tattoos that Let You Control Objects with Your Mind', 22 February 2013, *Time*, http://techland.time.com.

5. According to Alexa, www.alexa.com.

6. Webb, Sarah, and Lloyd, Margaret, 'Prescribing and Referral in General Practice: A Study of Patients' Expectations and Doctors' Actions', *British Journal of General Practice*, 44.381, 1994, pp. 165–9.

7. Source: OECD & UNESCO Institute for Statistics, Box C4.1, Education at a Glance, 2012, via Mary M. Kritz, Department of Development Sociology, Cornell University, United Nations website, www.un.org/esa/population/meetings/EGM_Migration-Trends/KritzPresentationFinal.pdf.

8. Lander, Eric S., et al., 'Initial Sequencing and Analysis of the Human Genome', *Nature*, 409.6822, 2001, pp. 860–921.

9. Hey, Tony, Tansley, Stewart, and Tolle, Kristin Michele (eds), *The Fourth Paradigm: Data-Intensive Scientific Discovery*, Microsoft Research, Redmond, Washington, 2009. http://research.microsoft.com/en-us/collaboration/fourthparadigm/4th_paradigm_book_complete_lr.pdf

SELECT BIBLIOGRAPHY

Anderson, Chris, *The Long Tail: Why the Future of Business is Selling Less of More*, Hyperion, New York, 2006.

Arthur, W. Brian, *The Nature of Technology*, Simon and Schuster Inc, New York, 2009.

Bolles, Richard N., *What Color is Your Parachute? 2014: A Practical Manual for Job-Hunters and Career-Changers*, Ten Speed Press, New York, 2013.

Botsman, Rachel, and Rogers, Roo, *What's Mine is Yours: The Rise of Collaborative Consumption*, HarperCollins, New York, 2010.

Christensen, Clayton, *The Innovator's Dilemma,* HarperCollins, New York, 2003.

Ferriss, Tim, *The 4-Hour Workweek*, Crown, New York, 2007.

Friedman, Thomas L., *The World is Flat: A Brief History of The Twenty-First Century*, Release 3.0, Macmillan, 2006.

Gansky, Lisa, *The Mesh: Why the Future of Business is Sharing*, Portfolio, New York, 2012.

Gladwell, Malcolm, *Blink*, Little, Brown, New York, 2005.

Gladwell, Malcolm, *Tipping Point*, Little, Brown, New York, 2000.

Isaacson, Walter, *Steve Jobs*, Simon and Schuster, New York, 2013.

Jones, Barry, *Sleepers, Wake! Technology and the Future of Work*, Oxford University Press, 1982.

Lewis, Michael, *Flash Boys: A Wall Street Revolt*, W. W. Norton and Company, New York, 2014.

Levitt, Steven D., and Dubner, Stephen J., *Freakonomics*, William Morrow, New York, 2005.

Piketty, Thomas, *Capital in the Twenty-First Century*, Arthur Goldhammer/Harvard College, Massachusetts, 2014.

Ries, Eric, *The Lean Startup*, Crown, New York, 2011.

Taleb, Nicholas, *The Black Swan*, Random House, New York, 2007.

Weinberg, Steven, *The First Three Minutes: A Modern View of the Origin of the Universe*, BasicBooks, New York, 1997.

Wu, Timothy, *The Master Switch: The Rise and Fall of Digital Empires*, Vintage, New York, 2010.

INDEX